Academic Writing and Dyslexia

Fully revised and expanded, this book presents a unique visual approach to academic writing and composition tailored to the needs of students with dyslexia in Higher Education. It will help you to successfully structure and articulate your ideas, get to grips with critical reading, thinking and writing and fulfil your full academic potential.

The 'writing process' (e.g. genre and style, critical thinking and reading, writing, sentence construction, and proofreading and editing) is de-mystified and translated into innovative, meaningful visual representations in the form of templates, images, icons and prompts designed to meet the visual and 'big picture' learning styles and strengths of your dyslexia. Underpinned by extensive research, this book will help you to present your thoughts and evaluate and critique competing arguments in a compelling way. It is written to help you bridge the gap between your existing coping strategies and the increased demands and rigours of academic writing at university.

This second edition features enhanced visual techniques for reading online, expanded material to cover scientific writing, literature reviews, reflective writing and academic style, and detailed explanations of how dyslexia affects writing, how to reduce pressure on your working memory and how to get your creativity and ideas onto the page in order to excel. This book serves as an invaluable resource for dyslexic students, academics, dyslexia specialists, learning developers and writing tutors throughout the Higher Education sector.

Adrian J. Wallbank is a Lecturer in Educational Development at Oxford Brookes University, UK, and is a Senior Fellow of the Higher Education Academy.

Academic Writing and Dyslexia

A Visual Guide to Writing at University

Second Edition

Adrian J. Wallbank

Routledge
Taylor & Francis Group

LONDON AND NEW YORK

Cover design: Lisa Dynan

Second edition published 2023
by Routledge
4 Park Square, Milton Park, Abingdon, Oxon, OX14 4RN

and by Routledge
605 Third Avenue, New York, NY 10158

Routledge is an imprint of the Taylor & Francis Group, an informa business

© 2023 Adrian J. Wallbank

First edition published by Routledge 2018

British Library Cataloguing-in-Publication Data
A catalogue record for this book is available from the British Library

ISBN: 978-1-032-04007-3 (hbk)
ISBN: 978-1-032-04006-6 (pbk)
ISBN: 978-1-003-19018-9 (ebk)

DOI: 10.4324/9781003190189

Typeset in Bembo
by codeMantra

For Layla Wallbank

Contents

Preface

Sometime in the mid-1990s, filming was taking place for an ITV News report on the teaching strategies used at Maple Hayes School and Research Centre (where I was a pupil). During a break in filming, I vividly remember a reporter quizzing one of the students about why using a visual system of icons to learn how to spell was effective. The reporter repeated the same comments and suspicions that many of us had heard before and which have plagued the reputation of its inventor and school's Principal, Dr E. Neville Brown. 'I don't get it,' the reporter quipped, 'I don't understand how words can have visual meanings!' 'You wouldn't,' the student replied rather cheekily, 'you're not dyslexic!'

Despite this student's rather brazen dismissal of the reporter's questions, this memory has stayed with me ever since and I feel is central to understanding the rationale behind this book. Individuals with dyslexia are predominantly right-brain, visual thinkers – words are often secondary considerations. People with dyslexia think holistically and visually. This is why it is necessary to visualise the patterns and underlying meanings of writing to understand its content and structure. This is a different way of doing things to left-brain thinkers, hence why the reporter mentioned above just didn't 'get it'. So while this book may be of considerable use to those who do not have dyslexia, the aim here is to tap into your dyslexic visual strengths and add additional coping/compensatory strategies to the ones that have brought you this far.

If you have dyslexia and are reading this, you've undoubtedly done an excellent job of adjusting to, if not excelling within, a system that simply does not suit your right-brain learning preferences and visual strengths. The next step, however, is a big one. 'Stepping up' from school/college to university, irrespective of your dyslexia, is a challenge, but is one that I guarantee you will succeed in, providing you adjust and learn new, more sophisticated coping strategies. However, this next step has also been complicated recently by the global Covid-19 pandemic and the acceleration of online learning. Since the first edition of this book, reading and searching online has become the standard (and sometimes only) way of accessing material, and assessment methods are becoming more varied. Furthermore, more students than ever are taking 'STEM' subjects in response to concerns about employability. This second edition is expanded and updated to cater for all of these developments. New material, strategies and tips have been added to help you navigate online reading and searching for information, and new sections have been developed to help you consider how to structure and write scientific essays, laboratory reports and literature reviews. Meanwhile, in response to feedback from the first edition, sections have been added on reflective writing (a genre of assessment that is becoming increasingly popular as markers try to diversify their assessment methods and help individuals develop and reflect upon their skills for employment), and a new chapter has been developed on academic writing style. Academic language is not like everyday talk or the informality of a social media or blog post, but needs to have clarity at its heart. This can be tricky, so you'll find new material and guidance on how to give your writing the correct 'tone', polish and style.

Finally, lots of students with dyslexia often think their unique ways of thinking are either a problem, or something that other people don't encounter. It can be incredibly beneficial to be reassured that how you process ideas is precisely because of your dyslexia. You're not alone, and these unique ways of thinking can be turned into a strength. To help with this, you'll not only find new and expanded tips relating to the 'dyslexic experience' of studying and writing, but the first chapter provides a simplified, visual overview of how the dyslexic brain works, what it's good at/bad at, and why. With the help of a few academic studies and our old friend Albert Einstein, this can give you a powerful sense of how and why your thoughts come out in certain ways (or struggle to go in at all), and will help you understand how you can maximise your strengths to overcome your weaknesses. If Einstein could do it by figuring out how his brain worked, so can you.

Your dyslexia will never go away; all we can do is find ever more inventive ways of working with or around it. You need better aids to help you succeed, and this is what this book aims to provide. But remember, you also have an edge – individuals with dyslexia usually have high intelligence and a unique ability to discern patterns and connections and think holistically. It has brought you and sustained you thus far, so with the guidance provided in this book, why not see where else it can take you?

This book is dedicated to individuals with dyslexia everywhere, with faith in the fact that success is obtainable, can be achieved, and is ours for the taking...

Dr Adrian J. Wallbank
Oxford Brookes University, October 2021

Acknowledgements

As a pupil at Maple Hayes School and Research Centre in the mid-1990s, I was introduced to the concept of learning how to spell using visual icons through the pioneering work of Dr E. Neville Brown. I arrived at Maple Hayes as an underachieving pupil with dyslexia who had been placed in the lowest possible band at high school and told that although I'd 'never amount to much', one day I'd 'at least make someone a good husband'. Brown, along with his staff, formed the basis of my transformation into a successful academic, lecturer and researcher, and their influences lie behind much of this book. More recently, I have accrued numerous debts during the course of writing the second edition of this textbook. I owe a great deal to my students, both at Warwick and Royal Holloway. Their difficulties and triumphs have frustrated and inspired me in equal measure, and without having read hundreds, if not thousands, of their essays, I'd not have been able to formulate my ideas. But again, my greatest debt is to my wife, Mona Khatibshahidi, who is responsible for battling with the vagaries of technology and the murky depths of graphic design in order to painstakingly construct all of the visual elements of this book. This nearly killed both of us at times, not least because she has consistently challenged my thinking and my predilection for making 'piles' everywhere in ways that only married couples will know about, and I'm sure she'll be heartily glad to see the back of this project. To her patience and design skills, I owe more than words can say.

1 Understanding Dyslexia and 'Stepping up' from School/College to University

'Whenever people talk about dyslexia, it's important to know that some of the smartest people in the world, major owners of companies, are dyslexic. We just see things differently, so that's an advantage. I just learn a different way; there's nothing bad about it'.

(Charlotte McKinney: American model and actress)

The potential to excel

In the Foreword to the third edition of Ronald D. Davis's famous book *The Gift of Dyslexia* (2010, p.xi), Linda Silverman highlights the 'essential gifts of dyslexics', these being:

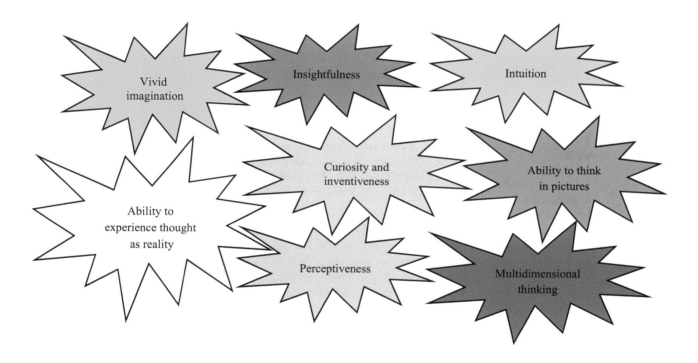

Unfortunately, the current pre-university education system (in the UK at least), with its focus on passing exams, on hitting 'Assessment Objectives' and 'Learning Outcomes' rather than critical thinking, creativity and curiosity, is often ill-suited to the learning styles and 'gifts' of people with dyslexia. Does this sound familiar? This is precisely what Albert Einstein, himself dyslexic, probably had in mind when he stated that 'it is a miracle that curiosity survives formal education…Education is what remains after one has forgotten everything…learned in school' (TheDyslexiaProject, 2017). As a consequence, you may well have had a considerable struggle to make it to university in the first place and feel as though your experience of education so far has been stifling or even traumatic rather than enlightening. Fortunately, studying at university is rather different and gives you much more intellectual and creative space to spread your wings. Indeed, as

DOI: 10.4324/9781003190189-1

Silverman points out, in today's world, student success (both within and beyond university) depends upon the

> ability to see the big picture, to predict trends, to read customers, to think outside the box, to see patterns, to inspire collaboration among peers, to empathise, to synthesise information from a variety of sources, and to perceive possibilities from different perspectives. These are the natural talents of dyslexics (p.xi).

While these words are undoubtedly inspiring and hopeful, and undoubtedly relevant in a world witnessing increasingly complex and sometimes contradictory agendas, let us not get ahead of ourselves. School may have been challenging, but a new battle awaits you in the form of the higher intellectual demands associated with advanced study. ALL students, not just those with dyslexia, face new challenges when 'stepping up' from A levels, Access, BTECs or the International Baccalaureate to an undergraduate course. Indeed, you will need to 'step up' again as you transition from your first year to second year, from second year to third year, from third year to masters, and from masters to doctorate. This may seem obvious, but in contrast to students without dyslexia, this natural process of 'stepping up' also means that you need to develop increasingly sophisticated coping, learning and writing strategies so as to meet the higher demands placed on you as a result of your dyslexia. Unfortunately, nobody can wave a magic wand and make your dyslexia disappear. As such, what is required is the development and expansion of the coping strategies that have brought you this far to help you meet the new, advanced challenges you are likely to encounter. Remaining static or relying on the coping strategies you have already developed are unlikely to work. Your dyslexia doesn't mean that you cannot compete with your peers, or that the increasingly sophisticated coping strategies you need to develop mean that your progress will be slower or hindered. Rather, the coping strategies proposed in this book harness and tap into your gifts as a visual, 'big picture' and multidimensional thinker. By adopting them, you will not only cope at university, but will thrive and excel to your full potential.

Understanding and harnessing your dyslexia

Nobody really understands what causes dyslexia or how the dyslexic brain/thought processes work. As you are probably all too aware, dyslexia affects concentration, short-term memory, reading speed/focus, spelling, time management, organisation, and the ability to structure and sequence ideas – especially in writing. Yet, equally, as we have seen, many people with dyslexia are highly creative, can make links that other people can't, and can be incredibly successful (think Albert Einstein, Richard Branson, Stephen Spielberg, Leonardo da Vinci, Agatha Christie and possibly Winston Churchill). How is this possible? And how does having dyslexia affect your ability to study and write effectively at university?

Dyslexia mainly affects how the working memory receives and processes information. The brain's right hemisphere (known for its role in visual processing and holistic thinking) is bigger and more active than non-dyslexic brains. In non-dyslexic brains, however, the left hemisphere/language-processing operations are more active and developed. With dyslexia, because the working memory is weaker and the brain is wired differently, when receiving or presenting information through language, mental activities are more difficult and you can quickly become overwhelmed – a scenario called 'cognitive overload'. This can leave you feeling exhausted. Cognitive overload can happen with anyone of course, but if you have dyslexia, this happens much sooner because of how inefficiently and ineffectively the working memory processes language. The best way of thinking about these processes is to visualise them as follows:

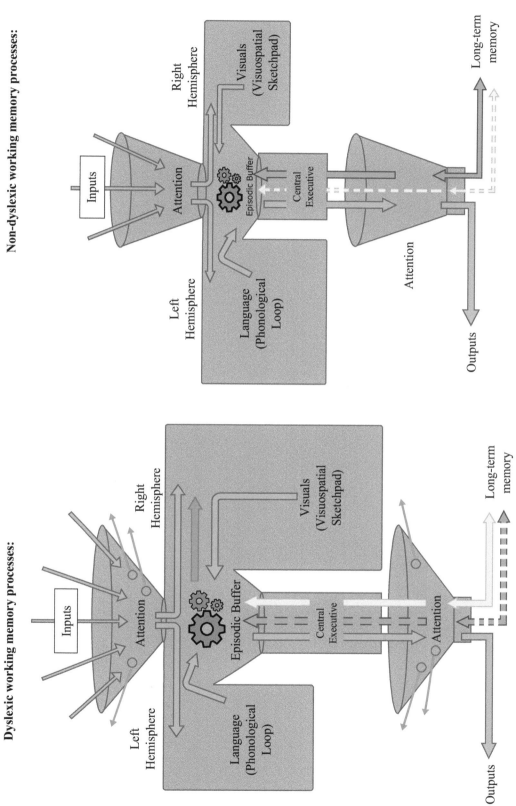

Non-dyslexic working memory processes:

Dyslexic working memory processes:

The key differences can be summarised and explained as follows:

Dyslexic working memory	Non-dyslexic working memory
Wide, 'big picture' search and input capabilities, but inputs have to negotiate relatively short/limited attention span so less information gets through into the working memory. In addition, some information is lost/'leaks' out before it even gets processed.	Less global, 'big picture' search capabilities but longer attention span, and so more information gets through into the working memory.
Weaker, smaller language-processing ability, stronger visual, right–hemisphere, holistic processing ability. Inputs are more effective when visual.	Stronger, larger language-processing ability, weaker right–hemisphere, visual/holistic processing ability. Inputs more effective when language based.
The episodic buffer, which brings together and puts into order the inputs from the visual and language functions, has to route language over to the visual side for processing (as indicated by the red arrow) because of a) the brain's preference for the visual and b) the language side is impaired/not as strong. This takes additional mental effort and time, and as a result there's an increased likelihood of information being lost. Research has suggested that learning to do things automatically takes considerably longer than individuals without dyslexia, so working memory has to work pretty hard (Nicolson and Fawcett, 1990, 2008).	Episodic buffer combines inputs from the visual and language functions to make sense of the world and impose order.
The central executive (the boss of the whole system) processes the ideas and decides what to do with them, but this takes longer because of the increased length of neurological pathways.	The central executive processes the ideas and decides what to do with them (relatively quickly).
Outputs are generated to go either into the world (e.g. speech, action or writing) or into the long-term memory, but weaker attention span means less outputs are achieved and some information is 'lost'.	Outputs are generated to go either into the world (e.g. speech, action or writing) or into the long-term memory. Stronger, longer attention span means that more outputs are achieved and more ideas are memorised.
According to something called 'Fuzzy Trace Theory' (Reyna and Brainerd, 1995), memories are encoded through two parallel memory traces are created – one literal or verbatim, and one based on 'gist' (i.e. incomplete, or 'fuzzy' traces often based on clues, situational or cultural context and non-literal representations). Gist memory traces are stronger in individuals with dyslexia (Obidziński and Nieznański, 2017). Memories are created through gist, fragments and contexts rather than being literal representations. Some verbatim memory traces are formed, but these are not as strong as in individuals without dyslexia.	Memories are encoded through both gist and verbatim traces, but literal, verbatim traces are stronger.
Material from the long-term memory goes to the episodic buffer for processing before being converted to outputs, but the process is impaired owing to weaker attention span and longer neurological pathways. However, because more memories are created through gist (rather than being literal), and because of the longer neurological pathways, clues and intuition enable patterns to be formed and original ideas to be generated.	Material from the long-term memory goes to the episodic buffer for processing before being converted to outputs. Memories are more literal and less based on clues and context.

As you can see here, the more the information being received or communicated is based in language, the more restrictions there are and the more mental effort is required to find workarounds (as indicated by the red arrow) or compensatory strategies (Helland and Morken, 2015, p.20). Unlike the non-dyslexic brain, most information has to be decoded via the visual, right hemisphere because the left, language-based phonological loop is impaired. Any information that does get to the left, language-based side of the system has to be routed back towards the visuospatial sketchpad to be decoded (thus taking up yet more valuable energy and again increasing the likelihood of forgetting information). Indeed, brain imaging (Waldie et al., 2013) has actually shown 'over activation' of the right hemisphere as a result of this, which can again lead to tiredness.

The episodic buffer also works differently in the case of individuals with dyslexia. Whilst it handles visual inputs extremely well (better than in the case of the non-dyslexic brain), unfortunately, it acts as a further hurdle to communicating ideas in a coherent, structured manner. In the case of the language-based messages and inputs it receives, instead of combining them and putting them into a cohesive and logical order, further issues arise, especially when writing. In effect, language-based inputs have to undergo the following increasingly problematic, restrictive hurdles in the episodic buffer:

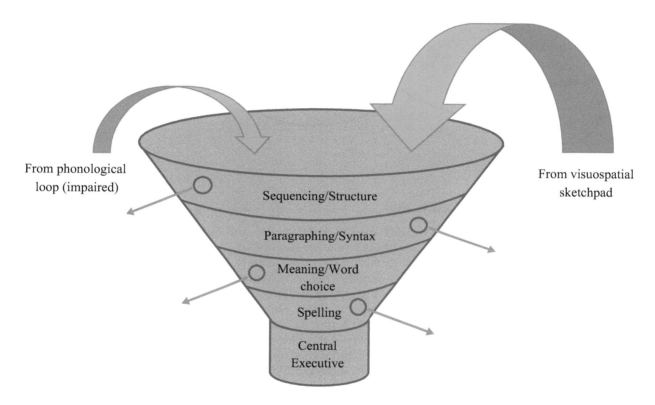

With each hurdle/restriction, not only does information get blocked (think of it like a traffic jam or the internet with limited bandwidth), but the risk of ideas being 'lost' increases. To make matters worse, the attention span controlling all of the above activities is not only weaker, but captures/transmits less information in the first place. Indeed, it's believed that a high percentage of people with dyslexia also have Attention Deficit Hyperactivity Disorder (ADHD), which makes it harder to concentrate and thus dedicate effort to these processes.

Reading and writing entails the working memory handling various tasks simultaneously (decoding words/images, putting together sequences to piece together meaning, blending visual/language-based inputs, maintaining concentration, processing inputs, combining them with both 'gist' and literal inputs from the memory, and turning them into various outputs). Given that in individuals with dyslexia the whole operation is impaired (and full of leaks), cognitive overload quickly occurs. Put another way, your brain is like a computer with limited RAM – the more demands you place on it (browsers, applications etc.), the slower it gets. However, whilst you may have limited RAM, the bigger, more developed visual side of the system can compensate. But that's not the only thing. As already mentioned, in the dyslexic brain, neurological signals have to travel much greater distances. Although this perhaps slows down some activities, it is suggested that greater connections with other neurological signals and pieces of information can be made because of the greater distances travelled. This, especially when combined with the episodic buffer's greater input from the visuospatial sketchpad, inputs from 'gist' memory, and its talent for making sense of visual materials, is why individuals with dyslexia often excel at seeing the 'big picture' and making connections.

THE DYSLEXIC EXPERIENCE:

Have you ever noticed that when you're reading, you can't remember what you read a few pages previously, but you have a good idea what's going to happen on the next page / in a few pages? This is due to cognitive overload. Because of all the processes taking place, for the sake of self-preservation you have started reading on auto-pilot. In other words, you're reading the words, but you're not taking in their meaning (to conserve mental energy). Owing to the space this has freed up, you've started thinking creatively about the content. From the brief clues you pick up, you're able to make / see connections and anticipate what's likely to be said next (but can't remember what's just been said). In fact, when you get there, you're likely to feel frustrated with having to go through the sequence of reading everything to get to the main points. In other words, for people with dyslexia, sequences are not only difficult, but boring / too slow. We make the connections quicker than the sequence can lay them out. If they could be presented in an image rather than as a chapter, we'd be much better off!

Dyslexia, creativity and studying

So where does creativity and the so-called 'gift' of dyslexia come in? Again, it's not clear, but it's thought that all parts of the working memory contribute to the creation of 'aha' moments. One theory, as just mentioned, is that because neurological pathways within the dyslexic brain are further apart, there's more opportunities for seemingly unconnected ideas to merge – hence why people with dyslexia excel at 'big picture' thinking but also, crucially, need the context/'big picture' in order to more easily make sense of inputs (verbal, reading, sensory etc.). Furthermore, drawing on Fuzzy Trace Theory, whilst non-dyslexic individuals remember things literally, people with dyslexia remember better via clues and 'big picture' context. By remembering via the 'big picture' and clues/gist, the brain is able to piece clues together in new ways and come up with new ideas. So while working memory may be weaker, the ability to piece together 'global' information and ideas is actually stronger (Todd et al., 2012). This is why Eide and Eide (2011) have suggested that individuals with dyslexia excel at seeing 'relationships of likeness and togetherness; connections between perspectives and fields of knowledge; and big-picture or global connections that create heightened abilities in detecting gist, context and relevance' (p.105) – all skills that should enable you to excel at university if you play to your strengths.

Whilst processing speeds associated with language-based inputs may be slower in people with dyslexia, the ability to make connections (especially via visual inputs) is actually faster – one of the so-called 'paradoxes' of dyslexia (Shaywitz, 1996). Indeed, it has been shown that individuals with dyslexia score more highly than people without when it comes to non-verbal memory, non-verbal reason and creativity (Everatt and Denston, 2020, p.104). It's thought that it is the visuospatial sketchpad and the right hemisphere's holistic processing strengths that contribute to creativity (Jaswal, 2015, p.223), and that overall, if you take language out of the equation, individuals with dyslexia can perform as well as, if not better than, people without dyslexia (Everatt and Denston, 2020, p.103). Albert Einstein made precisely this claim when he suggested that in his 'mechanism of thought', 'signs' and 'images' being 'voluntarily reproduced or combined', coupled with 'combinatory' or 'vague play' in the absence of the urge for 'logical construction', was 'the essential feature in productive thought – before there is any connection with…words or other kinds of signs that can be communicated to others'. In essence, he claimed that 'words or…language…do not seem to play any role in my mechanism of thought' (Einstein, 1995, p.25). As such, people with dyslexia can often excel when we minimise the role of language, and the 'combinatory' or 'vague play' resulting from less focused, weaker attention spans actually helps to create more eureka moments.

In terms of writing and studying at university, then, owing to the dyslexic brain's preference for visual material, the more the information can be received or transmitted visually, the better. Indeed, it has been proven that reading techniques and compensatory strategies that exploit right-brain visual networks not only help improve the activation of that part of the brain, but they result in better reading skills. Conversely, traditional techniques that persevere with improving reading and writing skills via left-brained, language-based systems can actually make matters worse (Waldie et al., 2017). <u>This is where the visual templates, icons, prompts and structures contained within this book come in.</u> By aligning the principles of academic writing to meaningful visuals, it can help you make sense of writing essays by a) harnessing your visual/'big picture' strengths, and b) making the passage of information in and out of your working memory easier by harnessing the strengths of the right hemisphere of your brain.

Getting started – understanding the differences between writing at school/college and university

Studying and writing at university is very different from what you have probably encountered at school or college. Some of the key differences are as follows:

A level/Access/BTEC	University
Taught, coached and mentored.	Emphasis is on independent learning.
Prescriptive (coursework titles are often chosen by the teacher or exam board, or if the student chooses it you are coached to create a title which allows you to focus on meeting the exam boards' very precise criteria).	Student increasingly autonomous and independent, minimal coaching/guidance.
Focused on fulfilling the exam boards' very explicit criteria ('Assessment Objectives' – these are set in the UK by OFQUAL).	Focused on articulating an argument which is engaged critically and creatively with the question.
Limited engagement with secondary reading.	Extensive, critical and evaluative engagement with secondary materials and theories.
Focused on exhibiting or achieving a specific aim or demonstrating a specific acquisition of knowledge rather than exhibiting wide-ranging, critically perceptive knowledge of the discipline.	Critical evaluation, analysis and creativity/independent thinking.

If you have studied for A levels, an Access or BTEC qualification, you'll probably have already seen how these priorities are mapped onto the assessment criteria. Exam boards have to adhere to 'Assessment Objectives', and these are designed to provide teachers and examiners with a framework for assessing work in a fair, transparent and rigorous manner. These aims are entirely understandable, but this often leads to students being taught how to 'jump through hoops' rather than gaining an in-depth knowledge of the subject. Indeed, as a former teacher of A level English, I probably spent 80% of my time teaching my students how to meet the 'Assessment Objectives' rather than teaching them about English! This results in rather formulaic, precise writing which is obsessed with hitting targets rather than exploring ideas creatively or in depth. Let's look at the following exemplar A level literature essay which seeks to compare Shakespeare's *Hamlet* with William Blake's *Songs of Innocence and Experience* to see how this happens:

Exemplar paragraph:	Assessment objectives:
One of the main themes around which the play pivots is Hamlet's despair and alleged madness. In <u>Act Three Scene One</u> we find him uttering **the** now famous and thought-provoking <u>line</u> 'To be, or not to be- that is the question'; which initiates a bout of <u>philosophical questioning</u> concerning life and death. The <u>definitive determiner</u> 'the' emphasises the level of despair that Hamlet feels as it is 'the question'; no other question matters. **Moreover**, 'is', the <u>third person singular</u> of 'be', reinforces the <u>definitive determiner</u> by preventing any possibility of <u>modal questioning</u> such as 'might be the question'. Hamlet's questions thus stand in sharp contrast to the rather more emotive, rhetorical questions **Blake poses in relation to poverty, abuse and religion (such as** 'Is that trembling cry a song?' in 'Holy **Thursday' and in respect of child abuse,** 'are such things done on Albion's shore?' **in 'A Little Boy Lost'),** although they clearly engage the reader in a similar form of self-examination as that encouraged by Hamlet and are perhaps intended to make the reader question not their life, but their conscience in relation to the ongoing suffering of children caught up in the exploitation of early industrial society.	AO1: Articulate informed, personal and creative responses to literary texts, using associated concepts and terminology, and coherent, accurate written expression (Note – terminology is underlined) AO2: Analyse ways in which meanings are shaped in literary texts AO3: Demonstrate understanding of the significance and influence of the contexts in which literary texts are written and received AO4: Explore connections across literary texts

As you can probably see by the sheer number of colours used here (and even these are not enough), an awful lot of thought went into this extract to make it fit the assessment criteria. The fact that there is only limited analysis/evaluation and that comparing Shakespeare's *Hamlet* with Blake is a very odd decision indeed is irrelevant. The main thing that matters is the student hitting the Assessment Objectives, which, in this case, they have done superbly.

Access assignments are similar. Access courses are marked as a pass, merit or distinction in accordance with the following criteria:

1) Understanding of the subject (e.g. student demonstrates an excellent grasp of the relevant knowledge base)

2) Application of knowledge (e.g. student makes use of relevant ideas, facts, theories, perspectives, models, concepts)

3) Application of skills (e.g. student consistently selects/applies appropriate skills, techniques, methods)

4) Use of information

5) Communication and presentation

6) Autonomy/Independence

7) Quality

The assessment criteria for BTECs are very similar, but more usefully differentiate the grade boundaries using key words such as 'explain' (pass), 'analyse' (merit) or 'evaluate'/'justify' (distinction), which more closely align with university-level marking criteria. But again, the emphasis here is upon testing the acquisition, application and use of knowledge (often in an almost box-ticking manner) rather than wide-ranging analysis, independent thinking, critical analysis, evaluation and argumentation. These are assessed, but, like in A levels, they are not the primary focus. Indeed, at A level, analysis and evaluation often only accounts for around 28% of the overall mark (English), and for science subjects, this is often lower. A much higher weighting is often allocated for demonstrating and applying knowledge (AO1 and AO2), which often constitutes as much as 70–80% of the total mark (Biology and Physics).

In addition to the 'Assessment Objectives', the assessment criteria and assignment briefs you'll have encountered thus far often dictate the sequence of ideas within the essay and, along with the tutor's guidance, this schema coaches students towards responding in a set way. For example, take the following Access assignment for psychology:

Assignment title: Outline and evaluate the causes, effects and treatment of stress (1500 words)

No	Assessment criteria: the learner can	Achieved?	
		First submission	Second submission
1	Define the term stress and describe potential sources of stress (internal or external stressors) and their biological effects.		
2	Explain and evaluate some of the effects of chronic stress on the body and behaviour.		
3	Evaluate three different treatments/therapies for stress.		

(Openawards, 2016)

Notice here that the student is practically told what to write in their essay, and in what sequence. In fact, one could even match up the 3 aspects of the assessment criteria to the word count and simply allocate 500 words to each criterion. It is no surprise, therefore, that this incredibly formulaic, assessment-driven way of teaching results in extremely formulaic, assessment-driven essays. Indeed, note that two submissions are allowed – a situation that usually leads to the tutor 'coaching' their students towards fulfilling assessment criteria rather than giving them the intellectual space and freedom to explore their own ideas. This level of intervention, coaching and prescriptiveness simply doesn't happen at university. Take a look at the following extract from a typical university mark scheme. As you will see, it is rather less prescriptive and considerably vaguer:

Category	1st	2:2
Relevance:	Demonstrates an accurate grasp of the issues raised by the question or brief, and engages with them fully.	Demonstrates partial recognition of the issues, and the material presented may lose focus in places.
Argument:	Elucidates a sustained, coherent, original and persuasive argument.	Argument may not be fully sustained or relevant, may be over-general or oversimplified.
Knowledge:	Demonstrates excellent skills in marshalling appropriate evidence; engages critically and creatively with a range of materials.	Received ideas may be repeated or described rather than critically interrogated.

(Royal Holloway, University of London, 2017)

The vagueness within these descriptors may appear unsettling at first, and many students react with frustration or even panic as they simply cannot see what is expected of them. This is understandable given that you are moving from an educational setting where you are coached and guided, to one where independence and autonomy are more highly valued. <u>If you try to follow the templates for hitting 'Assessment Objectives' that you used successfully at school or college, you simply won't achieve good marks, no matter how hard you try, as the goals are completely different.</u> Let's examine at this passage from an undergraduate law essay to see how different it is from the A level literature exemplar:

Exemplar undergraduate paragraph	Descriptor from mark scheme
Assignment title: Despite many changes to law and policy relating to domestic violence, criminal justice responses still fail to provide adequate protection for those at risk. Discuss.	
Although CPS reports suggest that 'highest volumes ever' of domestic violence referrals were charged last year, totalling over 70,000 (CPS 2014b), there are numerous significant counterarguments pointing out inadequacies in the legal framework and its ambiguous definitions. Despite repeated, valid attempts to create a definition of domestic violence which encompasses a wide array of actions (Smith, 1999 and Jones, 2001), the notion of domestic violence as meaning physical beating, and nothing less, remains the 'dominant view' (Stark, 2007, p.84). As Stark (2007) has testified, victims are reluctant to acknowledge their situation absent of physical violence (Stark, 2007, p.111). Furthermore, no specific 'domestic violence' offence exists, with instances being artificially categorised as regular offences instead. Indeed, they are mostly classified as merely 'common assault' (Hester, 2006, p.85), which does not accurately reflect the severity of domestic violence. **State liability for failing to prevent domestic violence,** though welcome, is set to a very high threshold (Osman v UK), and as such may not be robust enough to have much effect domestically save in exceptional circumstances (Burton, 2010, p.134) and domestic case law interpreting the obligation has only watered down this obligation further (Burton, 2010, p.292).	Demonstrates an accurate grasp of the issues raised by the question or brief, and engages with them fully (notice how nearly all the words, sentences and ideas are specifically engaged with the assignment task). Elucidates a sustained, coherent, original and persuasive argument. Demonstrates excellent skills in marshalling appropriate evidence; engages critically and creatively with a range of materials.

As you can see, there is a considerable amount of primary and secondary source use here, but that doesn't dominate what is said. The student drives an argument, with critical analysis and evaluation, through the entire passage and uses the sources to either support their points or as a means of initiating critical engagement with the fact that the criminal justice system, even in its very definitions of what constitutes domestic violence, is flawed (and as a result, is failing those at risk). The passage is concise, focused and uses evidence in a sophisticated and thorough manner. Notice also that the student is not attempting to tick boxes and meet assessment criteria (simply because they are not specific enough for you to do this), but focuses on insightful argumentation, evaluation and answering the question. They are not setting out to merely exhibit knowledge in an attempt to acquire marks, but he/she is using that knowledge as the background to the analysis and argument.

In summary

In making the transition from school/college to university, then, you need to adopt new approaches and techniques in your writing and engage in much more critical thinking. This involves:

- Moving on from 'Assessment Objectives' and 'jumping through hoops' towards a more independent, less structured approach.

- Writing independently (little teacher guidance or coaching).

- Deciphering assessment questions, tasks and marking criteria which is often quite vague (to give you more creative space and independence).

- Making an argument.

- Critical thinking, analysis and evaluation rather than simply displaying knowledge.

- Incorporating and engaging with secondary reading and theoretical perspectives.

- Weighing up the evidence (as is often indicated by key activity words in the assignment title) in order to make an argument amid considerable complexity, uncertainty and competing views/evidence:

Discuss
Evaluate
Assess
Consider
How far is x true?
To what extent is x true

- Higher-level thinking – as can be depicted on Bloom's famous taxonomy of educational objectives:

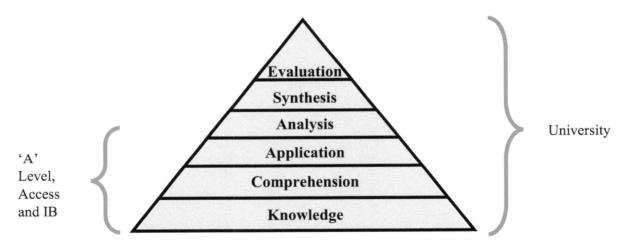

These skills apply to all university students, but making this transition will necessitate using your dyslexia and ability to engage in 'big picture' thinking, synthesis, perceptiveness and making connections, and making these traits work for you rather than against you. This is precisely where this book comes in. This book presents a 'process orientated', step-by-step approach to academic writing and composition specifically tailored to the needs of students with dyslexia in Higher Education. The writing 'process' (e.g. understanding the genre and style, reading, critical thinking, writing and proofreading/editing) is explored and demonstrated in detail, but the content is translated into meaningful visual representations in the form of templates, frameworks, images, icons and prompts. The purpose of this is to help you harness your innate visual learning preferences and strengths and thus help you present your thoughts in a structured, sequenced and ordered manner. As the dyslexic poet, playwright and author Benjamin Zephaniah has commented, how we read and write is 'unnatural...If you look at a pictorial language like Chinese, you can see the word for a woman because the character looks like a woman. The word for a house looks like a house. It is a strange step to go from that to a squiggle that represents a sound' (2016, p.223). The visuals presented in this book are thus intended to make writing more 'natural' to students with dyslexia whilst also acting as a system of prompts to enable you to write independently. However, they are also intended to be used as a sophisticated 'coping strategy' to support you in bridging the gap between your existing 'coping' or 'compensatory' strategies and the heightened demands and rigours of academic writing in Higher Education settings. This is undoubtedly a different way of doing things and will thus require perseverance in order to master it fully, but surely this is what has brought you to this point in the first place! Embrace the challenge! Embrace the greater freedom and autonomy associated with studying and writing at university. You are now largely free of the constrictions of 'Assessment Objectives', so take full advantage. University marking criteria give you more space to play to your strengths, so keep fighting – there is no reason to let your dyslexia hold you back. Remember, many of the world's most famous artists, thinkers, writers, philosophers and scientists have dyslexia – keep an eye out for some of their inspiring quotes as you proceed through the book.

Bibliography

Davis, Ronald D., (2010) *The Gift of Dyslexia*. 3rd edn. London: Souvenir Press.

Eide, Brock L., and Eide, Fernette F., (2011) *The Dyslexic Advantage: Unlocking the Hidden Potential of the Dyslexic Brain*. London: Hay House.

Einstein, Albert, (1995) *Ideas and Opinions*. New York: Three Rivers Press.

Everatt, John, and Denston, Amanda, (2020) *Dyslexia: Theories, Assessment and Support*. London: Routledge.

Helland, Turid, and Morken, Frøydis, (2015) 'Neurocognitive Development and Predictors of L1 and L2 Literacy Skills in Dyslexia: A Longitudinal Study of Children 5–11 Years Old', *Dyslexia*, 22, pp.3–26.

Jaswal, Snehlata, (2015) 'Creativity and Working Memory', in Manjaly, Jaison A., and Indurkhya, Bipin (eds.) *Cognition, Experience, and Creativity*. New Delhi, India: Orient Blackswan, pp.215–230.

Nicolson, Roderick, I., and Fawcett, Angela J., (1990) 'Automaticity: A New Framework for Dyslexia Research?' *Cognition*, 30, pp.159–182.

_____, (2008) *Dyslexia, Learning and the Brain*. Cambridge, MA: MIT Press.

Obidziński, Michal and Nieznański, Marek, (2017) 'False Memory for Orthographically versus Semantically Similar Words in Adolescents with Dyslexia: A Fuzzy-trace Theory Perspective'. *Ann Dyslexia*, 67(3), pp.318–332.

Openawards, (2016) *Access to HE Psychology Exemplar Assignment*. Available at: http://openawards.org.uk/media/1818/access-to-he-psychology-exemplar-assignment-2016.pdf (Accessed: 30th March 2017).

Reyna, V.F., and Brainerd, C.J., (1995) 'Fuzzy-trace Theory: An Interim Synthesis'. *Learning and Individual Differences*, 7, pp.1–75.

Royal Holloway, (2015) *Complete General Regulations*. Available at: https://www.royalholloway.ac.uk/ecampus/documents/pdf/completegeneralregulationsoctober2015.pdf (Accessed: 30th March, 2017).

Shaywitz, Sally E., (1996) 'Dyslexia', *Scientific American*, 275(5), pp.98–104.

TheDyslexiaProject, (2017) *Famous Dyslexics*. Available at: https://www.thedyslexiaproject.com/famous-dyslexics (Accessed: 30th March 2017).

Todd, P.M., Hills, Thomas T., and Robbins, T.W., (2012) 'Building a Foundation for Cognitive Search', in Todd, P.M., Hills, Thomas T., and Robbins, T.W., (eds.) *Cognitive Search: Evolution, Algorithms, and the Brain*. Strungmann Forum Reports, Vol. 9. Cambridge, MA: MIT Press, pp.1–7.

Waldie, K.E., Haigh, C.E., Badzakova-Trajkov, G., Buckley, J., and Kirk, I.J., (2013) 'Reading the Wrong Way with the Right Hemisphere'. *Brain Sciences*, 3(3), pp.1060–1075.

Waldie, K.E., Wilson, A.J., Roberts, R.P., and Moreau, D., (2017) 'Reading Network in Dyslexia: Similar, yet Different'. *Brain & Language*, 174, pp.29–41.

Zephaniah, Benjamin, (2016) 'We've Got it Going On', in Rooke, Margaret (ed.) *Creative, Successful, Dyslexic: 23 High Achievers Share their Stories*. London & Philadelphia: Jessica Kingsley Publishers, pp.223–231.

2 Reading to Write

'I had to train myself to focus my attention. I became very visual and learned how to create mental images in order to comprehend what I read'.

(Tom Cruise: actor with dyslexia)

At university, you will undertake large amounts of reading, often in a very short space of time. This can be a daunting prospect (even for students without dyslexia). Discussion forums, student blogs and feedback to tutors often highlight academic reading as a major challenge, especially when first making the transition from school or college to university. Indeed, a 2018 survey in the Centre for the Development of Academic Skills at Royal Holloway, University of London, revealed that students ranked academic reading as being their number one challenge during the first year of their degrees. So why is academic reading so challenging? Why is extensive reading so important? What is its function?

Why is academic reading so challenging?

Firstly, academic language and writing styles can be complex – more complex than you will have encountered at school or college. If you have undertaken any secondary reading before, it may well have been textbook or explanatory 'introductions' to the leading theorists or sources. For example, suppose you studied Russian History at A level. In this case, the syllabus requires you to 'explore concepts such as Marxism, communism, Leninism and Stalinism, ideological control and dictatorship' (AQA History 7042 Syllabus, p.53). However, it's unlikely that you'll actually have to read Marx's original *Communist Manifesto* (1848), Lenin's *The State and Revolution* (1917, or scholarly/theoretical works on ideological control. However, as an undergraduate, you will need to read and engage with these sorts of theoretical texts or academic reactions to them by subsequent scholars (maybe even your own lecturers). The writing style of such texts is complex, dense and often challenging, and it can often feel like you're reading in a strange, different language. Stick with them, though – they are challenging for a reason – often because the content itself is meant to challenge you. Scientific writing, meanwhile, despite being precise, is often highly technical and reliant upon numerous acronyms and subject-specialist vocabulary. Again, this can take time to get to grips with, but with practice, it will become second nature.

Secondly, academic reading is supposed to be challenging, and is probably more challenging than ever because of the pace and accessibility of modern life. We live in a world where to 'swipe left' isn't just reserved for a dating app or social media advert, but applies to nearly all our consumption of information. Social media, apps, news websites or nearly anything accessed via a smartphone or tablet are consumed via swiping or scrolling, often at speed. Indeed, how many of us are guilty of sharing something interesting on social media without actually having read it (we were only attracted by the headlines or picture, thought it looked interesting and then scrolled on)? Indeed, this has now led to the term 'clickbait'. Academic reading (aside from skimming and scanning, which we will cover shortly) is very different – it requires focus, effort and hard thinking. This is why the novelist Virginia Woolf recommended slowing down and giving reading proper attention. 'Wait for the dust of reading to settle; for the conflict and questioning to die down,' Woolf suggests. 'Walk, talk, pull the dead petals from a rose, or fall asleep' (Woolf, 2014, p.75). I don't necessarily recommend falling asleep here, but the point is that academic reading is difficult, it raises questions, and it needs time and contemplation. Given that reading speed and comprehension is often challenging for students with dyslexia, it is especially important to develop techniques for finding relevant information quickly and efficiently to give you more time and mental space/energy to devote to comprehension and contemplation. This chapter will show you how to do just that.

DOI: 10.4324/9781003190189-2

The purpose of reading

Reading at university is essential for two primary reasons:

1) To expand your knowledge of the subject and its writing conventions

Never lose sight of the fact that you came to university to learn, and not just to pass exams and gain a degree. You won't need all of your reading for your essay writing or exams – large quantities of it is simply to fill your brain with information, ideas, questions and skills which you hadn't previously encountered, and at a much higher level than that learnt at school or college. But additionally, as Steven Pinker has pointed out, 'good writers are avid readers. They have absorbed a vast inventory of words, idioms, constructions, tropes, and rhetorical tricks, and with them a sensitivity to how they mesh and how they clash. This is the elusive "ear" of a skilled writer' (2014, p.11). Wide reading, then, will help you to write well.

2) To find specific information for use in your academic writing (essays/exams)

Here the purpose is driven entirely by what has been set by your lecturers in the assignment task/essay question. The task of finding and using specific information will primarily be informed by the reading you have done to expand your knowledge, so it is essential you read with both of these purposes in mind, rather than just focusing on reading for essay writing as your only priority. The two main purposes of reading are interrelated and inseparable – reading for knowledge will enrich your essay writing, and reading for specific information will enrich your knowledge. Try to view reading as a holistic process, and don't short-change yourself by only reading in preparation for assignments.

The reason you need to use sources in your writing is to demonstrate the following skills and abilities:

- That you have read around the subject and can conduct independent research.

- That you can select and prioritise appropriate sources and information, filtering out what is/is not needed.

- That you can harness evidence in support of your views /arguments. Throughout this book, evidence is visualised as a fingerprint, because, like a lawyer or police officer, you need to present evidence for your case/argument.

- That you can consider and evaluate arguments/counterarguments and integrate these into your argument.

Evidence can take several forms, but the most common are as follows:

Evidence:	Symbolic representation used in this book:
Data and statistics	
Formulae	$E = MC^2$
Direct quotation from primary or secondary sources	

Summary of something from a primary or secondary source	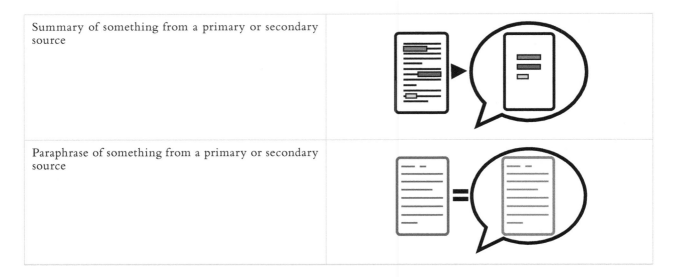
Paraphrase of something from a primary or secondary source	

Without adequate sources and background reading, your essays and assignments are likely to score poor marks. This is because your essays need to show how your ideas enter into an intellectual conversation with, are informed by, or even challenge, the work of others. In other words, academic writing, and university life generally, is largely dialogic:

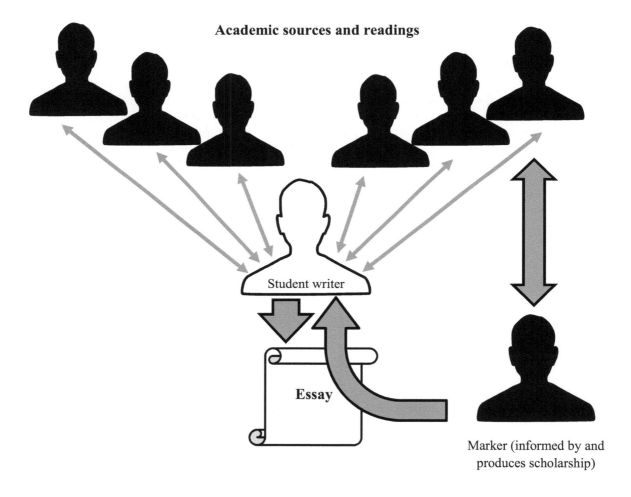

It is essential, therefore, that you spend time reading and enriching your knowledge.

Types of sources

Not all sources are created equally, and some are more suitable than others. Which of these sources do you think might be the most appropriate for an essay about global warming?

1) Global temperature is subject to short-term fluctuations that overlay long-term trends and can temporarily mask them. The relative stability in surface temperature from 2002 to 2009, which has been dubbed the global warming hiatus by the media and some scientists, is consistent with such an episode. 2015 updates to account for differing methods of measuring ocean surface temperature measurements show a positive trend over the recent decade.

2) A recent spate of shark attacks in North Carolina may have been partly caused by global warming, an expert has claimed. The warmer weather not only brings sharks further north, but also entices more people to get into the water. Coupled with other factors such as higher salinity and an increased number of 'bait fish', this has supposedly created a 'perfect storm' of conditions for shark attacks.

3) Model calculations have, for the last decade, suggested that a doubling of CO_2 will lead to increases in globally averaged temperature of 1.5 to 5 degrees (NRC 83)…However, such large predictions suggest that the changes in CO_2 that have occurred over the last 150 years should already have produced warmings of 0.5-2 degrees. Yet the warming effect is logarithmic and increases in CO_2 have become progressively less influential.

The first source looks very useful indeed, gives a good overview of the main issues at stake and is written in an accessible yet authoritative manner. As such, you'd be forgiven for thinking that it is an entirely suitable source to use. However, it is taken from Wikipedia (2017). Many students wrongly use Wikipedia and often either quote from it in their essays or even copy and paste from it and try and pass passages off as their own work (plagiarism). One of the reasons the Wikipedia extract sounds so authoritative is because it is largely a patchwork of ideas, phrases and direct, but sometimes unattributed, quotations from academic sources, most notably Marion Henkel's book *21st Century Homestead: Sustainable Agriculture II* (2015). Wikipedia is undoubtedly a valuable source of information and is a great place to go as a STARTING POINT for your research, particularly for the references at the end of each article. However, none of the material on Wikipedia is subjected to 'peer review' (the process by which material is assessed by experts in the field before publication). This means that its quality and accuracy has not been independently validated and cannot be relied upon. Furthermore, markers often think that using Wikipedia looks 'lazy', as it is clear that the student has not done their own research or read anything that was recommended on their reading lists.

The second source comes from the *Daily Mail* newspaper (O'Callaghan, 2015). Again, this is an unsuitable source. Although the article cites 'an expert', it is merely a news report, and is neither academic nor peer reviewed. Indeed, many newspapers resort to rhetorical strategies and sometimes deliberate misrepresentation of the facts to scare (hence the story about shark attacks), inspire or sway their readers, either politically or ideologically. They are, therefore, overtly biased rather than neutral. As such, they cannot be used as an authority in your reading and writing (except if you were perhaps citing a newspaper or other media production as evidence of bias or as a cultural phenomenon).

The third source is from a journal article by Richard S. Lindzen, which appeared in the *Bulletin of the American Meteorological Society* (1990, p.289). Although perhaps not as entertaining as stories about shark attacks, the source is authoritative (since it is written by an eminent professor) and has been subjected to peer review before publication. Furthermore, notice how the argument is balanced in that the author subjects the 'model calculations' to scrutiny and analysis based on evidence. Not all academic sources are unbiased or even-handed, but there is a noticeable degree of critical analysis within their arguments, unlike the openly biased or inflammatory publications produced by newspapers or other mass-media outlets.

TIPS

Use only peer-reviewed, quality academic sources.

Steer clear of mass-media publications and websites.

Avoid online revision guides (these are aimed at A level or Access students and are thus too basic for undergraduates/postgraduates).

When reading at university, then, use mostly textbooks, monographs, edited collections and journal articles (as recommended by your lecturers). However, even some academic sources are more useful than others, and textbooks in particular need to be read with a different purpose in mind. Let's look at how each can be used and why some might have distinct advantages and drawbacks.

Textbooks

What are they?

- Usually chronological or thematic introductory guides for students.

- Provide a synthesised summary of key events, topics or themes within an easily understood and accessible framework.

- Help students gain a sense of perspective and see the 'big picture'/how everything fits together.

Do you think, then, that textbooks are a suitable source to use in your essays?

You might be surprised to learn that the answer is essentially no! A student textbook is an introduction to the subject, rather than a piece of original, academic research. Although this can make textbooks a handy, easily digestible source of information, they are a little too basic for use in essays. What you need is the 'real deal', the original academic source rather than merely a watered-down version or an introductory summary. By using journal articles and monographs, you will go deeper into the subject, use the original, authoritative sources and impress your marker with your ability to conduct research and engage with complex, higher-level thinking and theory. This will inevitably result in better marks.

TEXTBOOK TIPS

Use the bibliography as your cue to hit the library in search of the monographs and journal articles they recommend or cite.

Many textbooks provide quotes from the key theorists or critics working in the field and thus often highlight what is most important for you to read.

Textbooks are ideal for exam revision and for finding out about the main topics, key debates, who the key theorists are and what they said, and the overall context of the field, topic or discipline. This makes them an ideal starting point for your research and provides a good sense of perspective and the 'big picture', precisely what students with dyslexia find invaluable. Furthermore, as we shall see on p.38, they can help you understand the complexities of monographs and journal articles if you alternate between reading materials (dual assistive reading).

Monographs

What are they?

- Extended investigations/research of 60,000 words or more on a specific topic.

- Written primarily for academics and subject-specific professionals.

- Undergo an extensive 'peer-review' process to ensure academic integrity.

Pros

- Present up-to-date research when first published.

- Have convenient contents pages and indexes to help you find information quickly.

- Are academically robust and show that you have undertaken scholarly research.

Cons

- Obscurity (focus can be too narrow).

- Can be hard to read owing to subject technicalities and length.

- 'Date' rapidly.

- Students with dyslexia can easily become 'lost' whilst reading them as it's difficult to keep sight of the 'big picture'. This is particularly problematic if reading online (i.e. via Google Books or from a publisher's 'open access' portal).

- If borrowed from a library, you can't make notes on them or highlight passages with a pen; you can only use Post-it notes or bookmarks.

- Often unfeasible to print out large sections of the text (this could also breach copyright laws).

Journal articles

What are they?

- Short essays written by academics that investigate a problem/issue or present the results of research.

- Written primarily for academics and subject-specific professionals.

- Undergo an extensive 'peer-review' process to ensure academic integrity.

Pros

- Present up-to-date research.

- Usually have short abstracts providing a summary of the topic – this gives you a useful 'snapshot' of what the article is about and the main findings/argument.

- Are academically robust and show that you have undertaken scholarly research.

- Often accessible online through your university's library catalogue, Google Scholar or the publisher's website.

- Easy to print out, make notes on and carry with you.

Cons

- Obscurity (focus can be too narrow).
- Can be hard to read owing to subject technicalities.
- No index, so it can be harder to scan for specific information.

Edited collections

What are they?

- Short essays written by academics that investigate a problem/issue or present the results of research, but they are collected together by an academic editor around a core theme.
- Written primarily for academics and subject-specific professionals.
- Undergo an extensive 'peer-review' process to ensure academic integrity.

Pros

- Academically robust and show that you have undertaken scholarly research.
- Narrow focus, but grouped around a core, general theme.
- Relatively easy to print out, make notes on and carry with you if you only require one or two chapters.

Cons

- Obscurity (focus can be too narrow).
- Can be hard to read owing to subject technicalities.
- 'Date' rapidly.

All of the above sources can be accessed either in physical form (bought or borrowed from the university's library) or in an electronic format (e-journal, e-book or viewed as a PDF document accessed via your library catalogue, Google Scholar or search engine). Whichever way you access them, ensure they are academic sources. Avoid the temptation to use websites (which are often easier to access as they can be found either through searches or hyperlinks). Unless the website is an authoritative source (e.g. WHO, government website, professional society website), avoid them or use them merely for familiarising yourself with the basics of a topic.

Academic reading and dyslexia

For students with dyslexia, reading can be problematic, disorientating, frustrating, and even demoralising. The following issues are often encountered:

1) Reading slowly and falling behind (the average non-dyslexic student can read approximately 200–250 words per minute as opposed to 90–120).

2) Having difficulty maintaining attention.

3) Losing sight of or completely forgetting what has just been read only a few pages previously.

4) Being unable to see the purpose of the reading.

5) Having difficulty following the argument advanced by the author.

6) Frustration at what has been termed 'the paradox of dyslexia' – namely that you read slowly but your brain works extremely quickly (Shaywitz, 1996). This means that readers with dyslexia can often 'jump' or anticipate what is going to be said on the next page but cannot remember what was said on the previous one. This can have a severe and negative impact on your self-esteem.

One of the biggest differences between a dyslexic and non-dyslexic reader is that people without dyslexia read in a linear, sequential manner, taking one step/sentence/paragraph/section/chapter at a time. People with dyslexia, on the other hand, need to see the 'bigger picture' and make connections based on 'gist' rather than detail. In other words, because the dyslexic brain can think and form connections quickly and from clues, it needs to be at the end of the paragraph or chapter at the same time as being at the beginning, thus getting a picture of the whole meaning in an instant. This is obviously impossible when reading word-by-word, line-by-line, and even chapter-by-chapter. The dyslexic brain, by preferring visual, 'big picture' thinking, is more than capable of seeing and comprehending the whole, but is constrained by the fact that the information is not present on the page in one, complete, entire and instantly comprehensible, preferably visual package. This can prove immensely frustrating and often leads to lapses in concentration and even boredom. But equally, some dyslexia and study skills specialists recommend strategies that make the problem even worse:

 School teachers often get students with dyslexia to read even more slowly, 'sounding out' or pronouncing individual words. This focus on 'vocalisation' divorces words (and particularly clusters of words) from their meaning, leading to decreased comprehension.

 Being taught to slow down runs contrary to natural eye movements. By forcing yourself to read from left to right in a slow, careful and deliberate manner, you force the eyes out of their natural tendency to wander all over the page. Studies with high-speed cameras have proven that during reading the eyes can wander up to 18 times per minute (Toikka, 2008, p.4). Why not capitalise upon this tendency rather than forcing yourself to read more slowly and deliberately? By slowing down, you place greater visual stress upon your eyes, something which individuals with dyslexia often suffer from anyway.

 Students with dyslexia are often told to use a pencil, ruler, finger or even a card to point to or exclude sections of text to help them maintain focus on the sentences and words they are reading, while blocking out what surrounds the words/sentences in question. This again slows the reader down and again runs counter to 1) the tendency of the eyes to wander and our ability to use 'peripheral' vision (which is capable of viewing between 5–7 words at a time) and 2) the preference readers with dyslexia have for making connections via 'gist'/clues. In other words, such techniques prevent you from seeing the 'big picture' of the sentence or paragraph and making connections between ideas, especially if sentences or paragraphs straddle lines or pages.

Dyslexia and reading online/electronically

 Since the Covid-19 pandemic, reading materials that you might have accessed in hard copy in your university library have now moved almost entirely online. You can access these via your Moodle/Blackboard pages as PDFs or find them yourself via library catalogues or searches on Google Scholar. However, reading on a screen versus reading a hard copy of a book or journal article is VERY different. With a physical copy of a text, you undergo a fairly simple, logical, sequential process of reading from left to right. You see two pages simultaneously, without multiple distractions in the form of hyperlinks, adverts, 'clickbait' or even reminders to install updates! On-screen reading, however, involves not only reading from left to right, but scrolling up and down and clicking, and more distractions are present. As such, reading online is 'nonlinear' because you are encouraged to jump from source to source, or article to article, via the use of hyperlinks (Carter, 2014). One advantage of this is that it encourages skimming and scanning (which we shall discuss shortly), but deep, concentrated reading is more difficult because of the greater number of distractions – not good if you have dyslexia. Indeed, on the back of research conducted by Hooper and Herath (2014), it has been suggested that 'concentration, comprehension, absorption and recall rates' when reading online are all worse, and thus Google, if not the internet itself, 'makes us stupid' (p.9). This is probably a rather unfair assessment! Certainly, reading online can be more superficial, but provided you exploit its benefits as a research tool, it's

actually a really effective way of learning. Indeed, providing you keep focused and avoid drowning in hyperlinks, skimming and scanning across information suit the ability of students with dyslexia to read quickly and decipher the 'big picture'. Undoubtedly, more discipline is required to stay focused. For this reason, it's better to print the material out or copy and paste the text into a separate document (e.g. Word, OneNote) if possible when you find useful information. This helps minimise distractions and enables you to engage in more focused, deep reading.

TIPS AND NOTES OF CAUTION FOR ONLINE READING

 Ensure your device is up to date and has installed updates before you start reading (or schedule them for a time when you are not studying). This will help minimise unwanted distractions and interruptions.

 Experiment with your Internet Service Provider's 'Homework' settings. Yes, this is designed for parents to block children from gaming and social media during certain times, but if you suffer from a lack of self-discipline, you can set times for yourself to help keep you on track. There are also many settings available now that restrict screen time (to help you have breaks) and avoid online distractions. Again, whilst they're mainly designed for use by parents, they're good to set up yourself to help keep you on track!

 As we'll discuss in the next chapter, reading online requires much greater discipline in terms of critical thinking. You'll need to work doubly hard when reading online to ensure that your reading is **authentic, authoritative and academic.**

 If you copy and paste text into separate documents to read without distractions, ensure you copy and paste the source or webpage. Then, if you use the material in your essays, you can reference it properly. Too much copying and pasting without remembering where everything came from can lead to 'patching' – a scenario where your essay is a casserole of words, sentences and even passages that are not your own, which can lead you to accusations of plagiarism.

Note of caution regarding immersive reading/learning tools

The difficulties people with dyslexia have with reading have spawned an e-learning/assistive technology industry. Some apps, learning tools and assistive technologies are undoubtedly helpful, but they slow you down too much. For example, the immersive reader tool in OneNote usefully allows you to decode words and phrases by combining highlighting and voice readout (thereby exploiting two senses). Meanwhile, the comprehension tool can highlight verbs and bracket subordinate clauses, thus allowing information to be broken down into smaller units. Similarly, scanning pens can be great for helping you to understand difficult words and allow you to scan words, paragraphs and even pages, hear them read aloud, hear/read dictionary definitions and even transfer text to your computer. This can all be incredibly helpful if you have limited reading abilities. However, these strategies and interventions are too slow and do not allow you to grasp the 'big picture' and make connections. In effect, whilst helpful in certain circumstances, in equal measure, these techniques constrain your dyslexic strengths. So, in summary, use assistive technologies if you find them helpful (and if you need coloured backgrounds, OneNote provides an array that can help you read on the screen), but they are more useful for detailed reading and basics rather than reading long academic texts, finding information quickly and making use of your dyslexic strengths in 'big picture' thinking.

Reading techniques: skimming and scanning

Given your dyslexia and the challenges outlined above, what is needed is a reading strategy which allows you to grasp the 'big picture' quickly while avoiding long, unproductive, frustrating and even demoralising reading sessions. A form of speed reading is the answer. Indeed, 'speed reading' is an activity in which people with dyslexia can excel. One prominent advocate of speed reading, George Stancliffe, claims that individuals with dyslexia are usually 'gifted' when it comes to rapid reading, primarily because the right hemisphere of the brain is precisely where such rapid, holistic reading occurs (2003). The issue of time/speed here is crucial, and is something which, rather than causing anxiety, can be turned into a strength. The reading process needs to be quick to tap into your brain's ability to form ideas rapidly from clues/'gist' while also minimising the risk of 'zoning out', reading on 'autopilot', and thus not understanding what is being read.

One of the most effective ways of speed reading is to practise the skills and processes associated with skimming and scanning (some aspects of which are referred to as the SQ3R approach). In what follows, we will go through these skills in detail but relate the processes involved to visual icons, which can act as quick references to/explanations of the activity being undertaken. Use these as 'big picture' prompts to keep focused on the different stages involved. Detailed, close, analytical reading and critical thinking will be covered in the next chapter.

Skimming

As the name and the icon on the left suggest, skimming is a very superficial, fast activity which requires little depth. For this reason, we can visualise it as akin to flicking through the pages of a book. It is a great technique to acquire a sense of the 'big picture', overall structure and content of the text quickly. Lecturers will sometimes recommend that you read an entire book or article. Thus, it might seem as though there is little point in skimming, or that it is too superficial. Not so. Skimming gives you a good sense of the entire text, so it is a vital preparatory exercise for students with dyslexia to do so that when the text is read in-depth, the various elements you read can be seen within the context of the whole. In the case of extended reading lists or 'recommended reading', it is very tempting to think that you should read the texts from cover to cover. Indeed, sometimes it can feel like cheating not to do so. However, as a student, you are looking to find RELEVANT information QUICKLY, so skimming is an effective way of doing this, and it can be a valuable technique for very quickly assessing whether it's going to be worth reading the text at all or, if so, which parts might be read or excluded. So, what sort of things are you looking for when you skim read a book or article? In order of importance, you should pay particular attention to the following:

1) Title and subtitle

Occasionally, titles can be a little cryptic or abstract, but generally, the title and subtitle can give you valuable clues as to whether the book or article is worth reading. Imagine you are researching the benefits of Higher Education on society in the UK for an assignment. A search in a library catalogue might offer the following results. Let's decipher and evaluate the potential usefulness of each in turn:

> This author has used the question type main heading to pose a cryptic, contentious and thought provoking topic. There are some potentially very interesting ideas here but the article's relevance is not immediately clear.

1) Adrianna Kezar, 'Obtaining Integrity? Reviewing and Examining the Charter between Higher Education and Society', *The Review of Higher Education*, 27:4 (2004), pp.429-459.

> The emphasis upon the word 'review' again indicates an approach which is underpinned by critical analysis, but the emphasis on 'higher education' narrows the focus and makes it immediately relevant.

> The subheading clarifies the problem and narrows the focus down to the supposed 'charter' between higher education and society. This looks immediately of interest, even if it raises more questions than it solves. The verbs 'reviewing' and 'examining' also seem useful because we may be able to gain some useful critical analysis in the light of current developments (as of 2004).

The main heading immediately identifies a political position, namely that the author is arguing 'for' the university and everything which such establishments and their underlying principles stand for or represent. The fact that this author is arguing 'for' universities also hints at the possibility of an underlying problem or threat which needs to be countered. Although interesting, the main heading doesn't seem of immediate relevance to our purposes.

2) Thomas Docherty, *For the University: Democracy and the Future of the Institution* (London: Bloomsbury Academic, 2011).

The text is a monograph produced by a reputable publisher and as such it is clearly an authoritative and suitable source. Of the three texts under consideration it is the most up to date, which makes it even more useful for our assignment.

The subheading seems far more relevant as it immediately identifies the issue of democracy and the future of universities, although at this stage it is not clear whether democracy refers to societal democracy or democracy within the institution itself.

The main title indicates three distinct, but possibly interrelated or competing aspects of the topic, all three of which are relevant to the assignment task.

3) Ronald Barnett, 'Knowledge, Higher Education, and Society: A Postmodern Problem', *Oxford Review of Education*, 19:1 (1993), pp.33-46.

The subtitle narrows the focus to the issue of postmodernism and the fact that the aforementioned issues are a 'problem' of some sort. There could be tensions between the three aspects of education mentioned in the main title, which makes it seem not only relevant, but may present revealing and useful ideas about the drawbacks of considering higher education in respect of 'benefits'. There is no mention of the UK, which, along with the 'big' issues identified in the main title, indicates that the book is more theoretical or conceptual rather than focused on a specific context (although we may find a specific chapter on the UK in the contents page or in the index, so it might be worth digging deeper).

The title of the journal identifies it as credible, reputable and peer-reviewed academic source and thus a suitable article to use. The word 'review' appears to indicate a possible emphasis upon critical approaches to education studies. The article is clearly somewhat dated, and this limits its applicability to today's situation (especially if we are seeking data), although the indications of a philosophical approach may mean that it has ongoing relevance

They always say you should 'never judge a book by its cover', but as you can see here, you can get an awful lot of information from titles. They can give you a good indication of how relevant they are to your task, so always pay attention to them.

2) **Abstract or synopsis**

As we saw above, some titles contain keywords or statements which are of immediate relevance to the topic under consideration, whereas others are more cryptic or ambiguous. To clarify whether these texts are likely to be useful, the next step is to look at the abstract or synopsis. Journal articles have abstracts (located at the beginning of the article or as part of a 'preview' online), and monographs have a synopsis (usually either on the back cover or inside the front cover). In both cases, they consist of one or two short paragraphs which outline what the text is about. They usually identify:

1 The subject matter.

2 The research problem or context and why it matters.

3 The argument.

4 Methods or approach.

5 Key results or findings.

6 The implications of the research.

So, digging a little deeper, let's see if Roland Barnett's abstract can help us decide how useful his article may be for our assignment:

In modern society, knowledge, higher education and society act upon each other as separate forces. Two contemporary analytical frameworks help to illuminate this triangle of forces, but the stories they tell seem opposed to each other. Critical theory points up the skewed character of rationality in modern society: on this view, the changing definitions of knowledge in higher education can be said to be a shift in the direction of instrumental reason, with other (hermeneutic and critical) forms or reason being down-played. Postmodernism, on the other hand, argues not for any such one-dimensionality but underscores a heterogeneity of thought forms. Higher education can be viewed in this way, too: the university is a social institution which celebrates differentiation of forms of thought. Can the circle be squared? Can these differences between critical theory and postmodernism – as interpretations of higher education – be reconciled? This paper argues that they can be.

The subject matter and the 'problem' seem relevant but only from a strictly theoretical perspective. Questions about the interrelationships between society, knowledge and higher education are clarified through the fact that they are a 'triangle of forces'. This may be very relevant to our assignment.

Although the background to the two opposed theoretical approaches is illuminating, it may not be of relevance to our assignment, especially if we want to focus upon 'benefits' rather than getting into detail about theory.

Clear identification of an argument, namely that the 'triangle of forces' can be reconciled within the modern university, thereby having a positive impact on society.

What is also important about abstracts and synopses is that they often contain keywords (as underlined above). Keep an eye out for these to see whether they match what you are looking for. If the abstract/synopsis looks of interest and is relevant to what you are looking for, then read further. If it does not, reject it in favour of more immediately useful material.

3) Contents page/chapter titles

Chapter titles can also sometimes be cryptic, but the contents page should be your next port of call when skimming a text. Look for keywords or phrases which are relevant in the titles and reject any chapters which do not appear to be immediately relevant. Again, time is of the essence here – don't waste time reading chapters that might be interesting but ultimately irrelevant. Don't waste time reading them because you feel not doing so will be cheating (especially if the text has appeared on a mandatory reading list). For example, in the case of Docherty's monograph, we can see that only around half of the book is of direct relevance to our purposes, even though the rest of the book may be very interesting indeed:

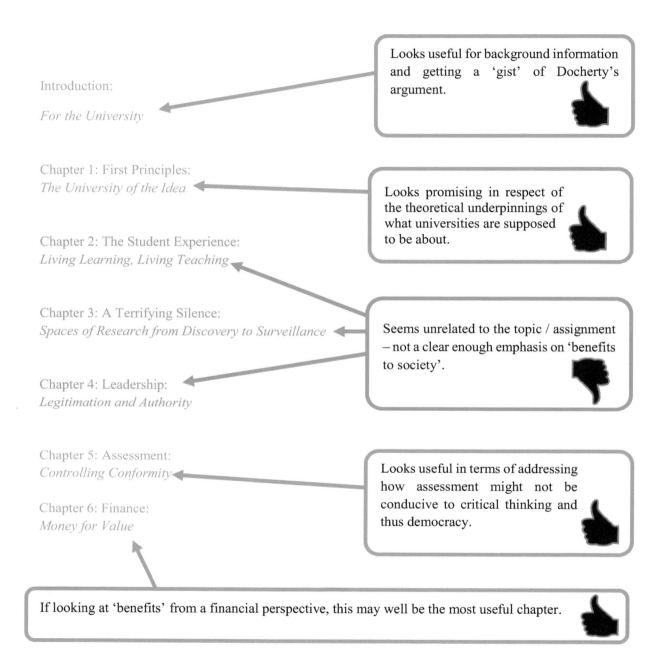

Introduction:

For the University

> Looks useful for background information and getting a 'gist' of Docherty's argument.

Chapter 1: First Principles:
The University of the Idea

> Looks promising in respect of the theoretical underpinnings of what universities are supposed to be about.

Chapter 2: The Student Experience:
Living Learning, Living Teaching

Chapter 3: A Terrifying Silence:
Spaces of Research from Discovery to Surveillance

> Seems unrelated to the topic / assignment – not a clear enough emphasis on 'benefits to society'.

Chapter 4: Leadership:
Legitimation and Authority

Chapter 5: Assessment:
Controlling Conformity

Chapter 6: Finance:
Money for Value

> Looks useful in terms of addressing how assessment might not be conducive to critical thinking and thus democracy.

> If looking at 'benefits' from a financial perspective, this may well be the most useful chapter.

4) Index

The index is probably the most overlooked resource at your disposal. If you have access to a good index, finding the information you want can be very quick and efficient. Some books have two indexes, one for key names, critics, authors or theorists and one for topics. Simply find the keyword or name you want and then look up the page number and find the issue/individual under consideration by scanning (more on scanning below). Let's have a look at snapshots from Docherty's topic index (pp.196–197) to see if there is anything that might relate specifically to our assignment:

The issues surrounding imagination and how they relate to autonomy and democracy appear to be very interesting for discussions of the place of higher education in relation to society and freedom, whilst equally, the commodification of knowledge and its transfer have direct applicability to the issue of 'benefits' (or otherwise).

Again, the issue of knowledge in respect of freedom and autonomy comes up, but perhaps more immediately relevant to the discussion about the 'benefits' of higher education are in relation to social mobility, so these pages definitely need consulting.

TIPS

 The index can help you narrow down which aspects of the chapter identified in the contents page are relevant, so use them in conjunction with each other.

 Not all indexes are as good as the one above and not all have subdivisions under each term. This is why you can't necessarily rely upon them and why you need all of the other skimming skills.

5) Subheadings

Skim through the text and look for subheadings (just like the ones used here!), which can be invaluable in helping you to navigate the chapters and sections and can help you decide which are worth reading. In particular, look out for keywords (e.g. multiculturalism, profiteering or European Convention on Human Rights), key names (e.g. Shakespeare, Einstein or Obama) and key verbs (e.g. analysis, processing or applying). These will give you an excellent indication of what the section is about, and like titles, an immediate impression of its usefulness and relevance.

6) Imagery

'A picture is worth a thousand words' may well be a popular English idiom, but visual material really is an essential part of grasping meaning from a text quickly when scanning – especially given that individuals with dyslexia have particular strengths in visualising ideas. Skim the text for diagrams, photographs, maps, graphs, pie charts, icons, bullet points or any other visual indicators of meaning. Humanities subjects tend to have less visual material, but the sciences and social sciences use them frequently (depending on the subject). Obviously, some visuals may be quite technical, but generally, any visual material, especially if a brief written explanation or key accompanies it, can help you quickly understand what the subject is about or what the key findings may be.

7) Introductions

Introductions can be a useful place to focus upon when skimming. Even if the text you are reading has an abstract, the introduction can still be an excellent place to start as it can provide valuable, immediate information about the study and its implications. Introductions are useful because they usually give the reader the following information:

- What the book/study/chapter is about.

- Why it's important.

- Some background to 'set the scene' and give the study a context.

- The purpose of the study.

- An argument.

In other words, the introduction gives us a sense of the 'big picture' and additional context over and above that provided by the abstract or synopsis. For this reason, it is an invaluable tool in the task of assessing the usefulness and relevance of the text, and it can provide a snapshot of what we need to know about the subject and why it's important. At that point, we can make an informed decision as to whether to continue reading or not.

8) Conclusions

Conclusions can also be a valuable source of immediate information, especially in journal articles or essays in edited collections. They can sometimes be a little disorientating as obviously, you only have a limited idea of what the author has said throughout the rest of the text, but they can be an effective way of quickly finding out the following information:

- Whether the author's argument/thesis/research hypothesis has been proven or disproven (or was perhaps unsuccessful).

- The key, headline results.

- Why the study matters – how it has changed our understanding of the subject and its impact in relation to the world or the discipline.

- What further questions need answering or what further research needs undertaking.

In many respects, then, a good conclusion can again give us a snapshot of the 'big picture' (both of the research and its implications). This will provide you with a sense (in addition to that gleaned from the abstract, synopsis, introduction, imagery and subheadings) of whether it is relevant and useful and thus worth reading in more depth.

9) Assisted online navigation

If you're reading online, skimming can be greatly assisted by some journal websites which very usefully offer help with article navigation and key information BEFORE you decide to download the PDF version. In some very good/helpful cases, you can jump to the sections of information you want using the navigation panes and keyword links. Often, keywords and theorists/references can be hyperlinked. This can be useful for skimming because they are coloured blue, but they also allow skimming by clicking on them to quickly find further information that may/may not be relevant. In some, even the main 'highlights' of the article are pulled out and bullet-pointed (perhaps even with keywords hyperlinked to the relevant sections in the article). This will save you even having to read the abstract. Here's one such example with further suggested reading and links and with various options to download or do further, advanced searches:

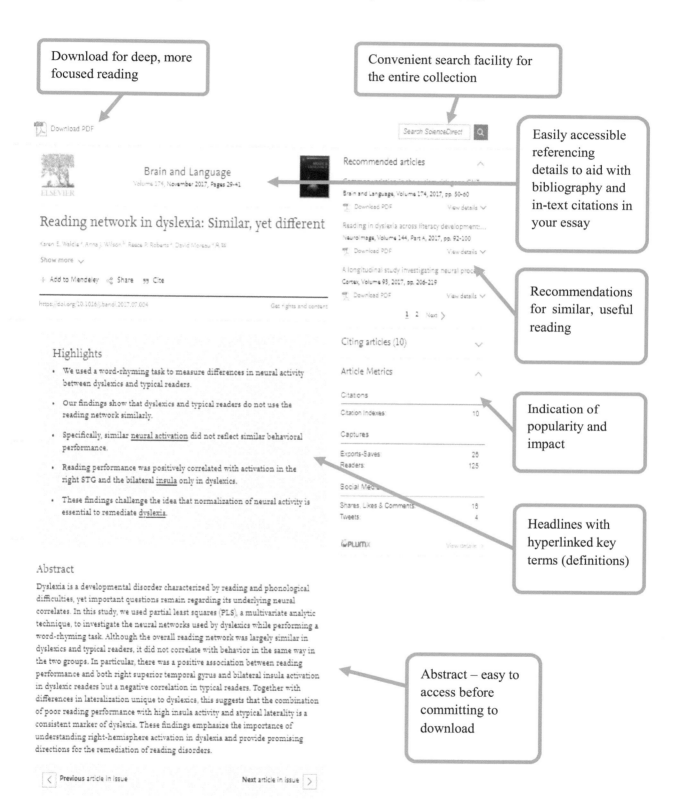

TIP

 When downloading recommended articles, ensure that you keep track of the links you have followed (see point 11 below).

10) Topic sentences

A topic sentence is the first sentence you will come across when you read a new paragraph. You can find them by looking for indentations or spaces between the paragraphs. The significance of topic sentences for skimming is that:

a) They are very easy to find.

b) They should contain two core ingredients that will tell you an awful lot about the paragraph's content.

We will look more closely at how to write topic sentences in Chapter 5, but the key thing to remember is that all good topic sentences should contain:

1) A clear identification of the topic.

2) An indication of an argument or provable opinion.

These two ingredients should give you an obvious and immediate idea of whether the paragraph will be useful or relevant. So, let's look at some examples. Imagine you need to write an essay about post-war British cinema and culture. Based on a cursory skim of the title, contents page and introduction, a book entitled *British Culture of the Postwar: An Introduction to Literature and Society 1945–1999* by Alistair Davies and Alan Sinfield (2000) appears to be relevant, particularly the chapter 'A Cinema in Between: Post-war British Cinema', pp.110–123. Let's look at some topic sentences from this chapter to evaluate their usefulness and relevance:

Paragraph	Topic sentence	Core themes	Relevance	Topic sentence reflects paragraph content
1	'Had matters taken a different course, Brighton and Hove (where some of the earliest British film-makers were based) rather than Hollywood might now be the centre of world cinema'.	Background to the initial creativeness of British cinema, why it declined, and why Hollywood was so successful.	👍	Yes
2	'Despite quotas, tariffs, tax advantages and subsidies to domestic producers, European national cinemas have been unable to reverse the domination of Hollywood'.	Background to the rise of Hollywood and falling cinema attendance.	👍	Yes, mostly
3	'Until the 1950s, cinema-going had been for most British families their favourite form of entertainment, but with the advent of the television (Independent Television began to broadcast in 1955) they preferred to stay at home or to spend their disposable income on new consumer goods and on other leisure pursuits'.	Figures on falling cinema attendance and more recent rise in multiplexes as an outlet for Hollywood films.	👍	Yes
4	'Nothing provides a more striking illustration of these issues than the British situation in the late 1940s'.	In-depth discussion of the British market, government subsidies, import duties on American films, pressures from the American government and the appeal of American glamour absent from post-war Britain owing to austerity.	👍	Yes

As you can see here, the topic sentences give a largely accurate summary of what is within the paragraph. As such, during skimming you can quickly narrow down which paragraphs are of relevance, which are perhaps of limited use, and which are not worth reading. All the above paragraphs look entirely relevant to our topic and provide both good background information as well as specific time periods, trends and influences.

A note of caution

Textbooks, collected essays and introductory monographs such as the one above are usually written with a student audience in mind and are thus fairly accessible. Topic sentences in some journal articles and monographs, on the other hand, are occasionally less clear. This can be owing to the obscurity and complexity of the issues discussed, because the writing itself is of dubious quality (even though the research may be groundbreaking!) or because the writer wrongly presumes that only specialists will read the work. Let's look at a slightly less student-friendly text to see how the topic sentences differ. Imagine you are researching the issue of freedom of speech in readiness for an essay on freedom and democracy in the UK. A book entitled *Extreme Speech and Democracy*, edited by Ivan Hare and James Weinstein (2009), looks useful, particularly the chapter 'Freedom of Speech in a Globalised World' by Dieter Grimm, pp.11–22. Let's have a look at the first six topic sentences to see well they reflect the content of the paragraph:

Paragraph	Topic sentence	Core themes	Topic sentence reflects paragraph content
1	'There is no democracy without public discourse and no public discourse without freedom of speech, freedom of the media, and freedom of information'.	Mutual links between freedom of speech and democracy.	👍
2	'Most socialist constitutions contained a right to free speech'.	Link between socialism and freedom of speech with examples. Specific case of Australia introduced.	Partly 👎
3	'The High Court reasoned that the Constitution declares Australia to be a democracy, and that there is no way to be a democracy without a recognition of freedom of speech'.	Specific example of the Australian legal framework guaranteeing freedom of speech and the mutual importance of democracy and freedom of speech.	👍
4	'This is of some importance because it shows that freedom of speech does not derive its raison d'être from democracy'.	Free speech a necessary element for individuality, yet it is not an absolute right since it can harm others.	Topic sentence and content misaligned and unclear. 👎
5	'Even a country whose constitution reads 'Congress shall make no law…abridging the freedom of speech', as does the First Amendment to the United States Constitution, recognises that not all speech is protected'.	Not all speech is protected, and there is a difference in the purpose for which free speech is protected and its limitations – examples of Chinese vs. Canadian and South African Constitutions.	Topic sentence seems to indicate a focus on US, but this is not really what the paragraph is about. 👎

As you can see, not all topic sentences, especially in academic monographs and journal articles, are accurate in mapping out what the rest of the paragraph will discuss. As such, whilst topic sentences are an extremely valuable tool in helping you skim for information, do not necessarily rely upon them. You may need to dig deeper to find the information you need.

11) Hyperlinks

If you're reading online, hyperlinks can be phenomenally useful as signposts to relevant or additional material. They can even support understanding of complex issues if they link to explanations or definitions (as we saw above), or if hovering over the hyperlink allows a box to appear with supplementary information or the complete reference. This can enable easy, instant comprehension. In academic materials, there tend not to be many hyperlinks (or they may just allow the reference to appear). However, when reading or searching purely to research or gather ideas, hyperlinks can be everywhere and in almost every line. This can be very useful as way of quickly skimming for information and can allow you to quickly delve into other pieces of information and link pieces of information together (thus allowing you to exploit your 'big picture' thinking, 'gist' and speed-reading strengths). However, you could end up in a scenario where you have clicked on so many hyperlinks that the following somewhat disorientating issues arise:

• The original article and focus have disappeared (often when you follow a link, the browser goes to the new article without you still seeing the original). Try to open new articles in new tabs so that you can flick between them. HOWEVER…

• You can end up having so many tabs open that it's difficult to backtrack to the original focus/article.

• Trying to 'tidy' your browser by closing tabs can lead you to overcompensating and deleting the most important / original tabs. Consequently, your search has to start again (using the browser's 'history' can help, but it all takes time and is a distraction).

Avoid drowning in a vortex of hyperlinks by focusing on your priorities. If you don't, your concentration/ability to focus and keep on track will get more and more difficult, and ultimately, you'll experience cognitive overload:

Hyperlink vortex:

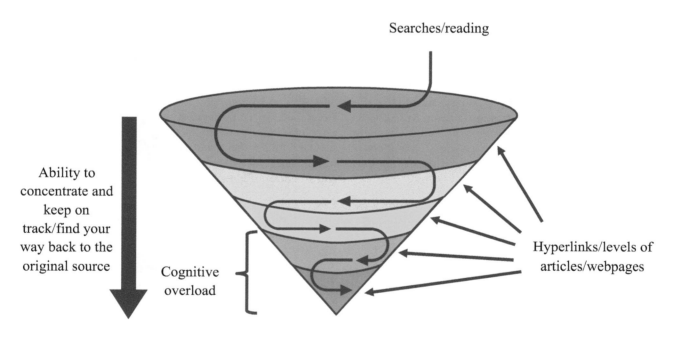

The following three tests should help keep you on track:

1) Is the hyperlinked source/article strictly relevant? If yes, follow it; if not, avoid.

2) Does it add detail to the original focus, or does it tempt you off onto a tangent?

3) Does it ultimately get you to an academic source or piece of verifiable data/evidence? If yes, follow it. If not, avoid.

When and if a new link is opened, skim for relevant detail by looking for subheadings, imagery, introductions, conclusions, topic sentences, and only then look at other hyperlinks. Don't open further hyperlinks until you have subjected them to the three tests above, and CLOSE the new tab/link to get back to where you started before continuing.

It can be helpful to remember that the internet is literally a worldwide 'web'. But it's crucial to keep in mind the structure of the web – YOUR web of searching and reading. This is crucial because once you start following the hyperlinks, the web structure can't be seen and you can get lost in a maze of 'clickbait' material that is out there which is designed to tempt you away from your goal. Make sure you keep in mind how you can backtrack to 'base' or your original starting point/article/link:

World Wide Web of Hyperlinks:

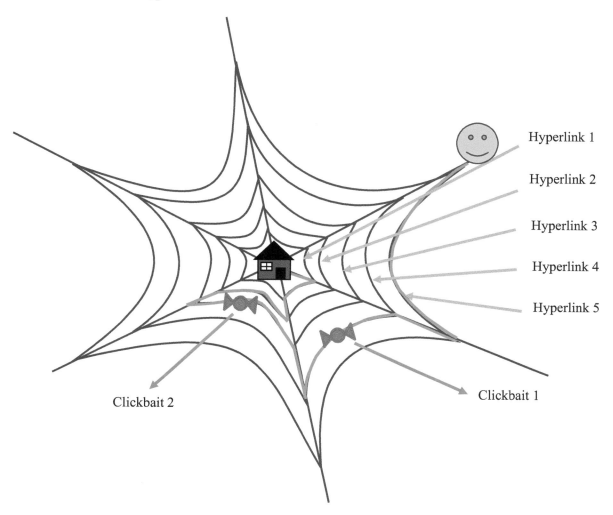

TIPS

 Copy and paste useful links into a references and sources document so you can keep track of where you got the information from, and so you can get back to that information quickly.

 Avoid 'clickbait' – they are designed to tempt and distract you with seemingly interesting or attractive information. However, like sweets (as indicated above), they might look nice and give quick, easily digested information, but they may not necessarily be good for you!

 ALWAYS get yourself to the **authentic, authoritative and academic** information and sources as soon as possible – that's your goal at all times when following hyperlinks.

12) Skimming to make and find connections

Given that skimming is about finding relevant information quickly, it may be that either:

a) The source you are looking at turns out not to be useful, or

b) The source is not useful but contains links to sources which might be useful (and which in turn will require skimming to see if they are useful or not).

You can skim to find connections in the following ways:

1) Look at the further reading/references section (usually at the end of the book next to the index, or at the end of each chapter, like in this book). Skim down the references for keywords related to your topic and then search for that source using your library catalogue or Google Scholar.

2) If you skim the text and find some relevant information, it may be that it is covered in more depth in another source. Such sources should be referenced, so skim for them in the references section (this will be either in a references/works cited section at the end of the book/chapter, and/or will appear as footnotes or endnotes, depending on the publisher/discipline).

3) Skim all the search results in your Google Scholar or library catalogue searches. This can be a useful way of making connections as often the results are ranked according to relevance.

Another more recent tool you can use to skim and make connections between sources is the web resource www.connectedpapers.com. This platform allows you to make meaningful graphs that enable you to visualise connections between sources by date, number of citations and connections. Each graph depicts the sources as 'nodes' which are based on the similarity of articles/subjects, so it's very easy to find additional sources. Indeed, the size of each 'node' corresponds with how popular/influential they are based on citations (the number of times other academics have referenced them and used their research). This can give you an instant idea of their 'impact' on the academic world. The colour of the 'nodes' also indicates the age of the paper, so it's not only possible to see in an instant connections between papers, but also their popularity and how recent they are. This will enable you to find up-to-date papers (in the past, students often had to use merely what articles their university library had in stock, and this often meant that sources were considerably out of date!). The platform even enables you to preview the abstracts so that you can quickly skim them and ascertain the usefulness and relevance of the source. Given that the platform and the graphs are visual (and depict the connections visually and in a meaningful way), it is especially useful for students with dyslexia.

Let's take the source above, *Extreme Speech and Democracy*, edited by Ivan Hare and James Weinstein (2009), as an example. Here's how the related sources look (with a seemingly popular text by Waldron [2012] highlighted and previewed for the purposes of illustration):

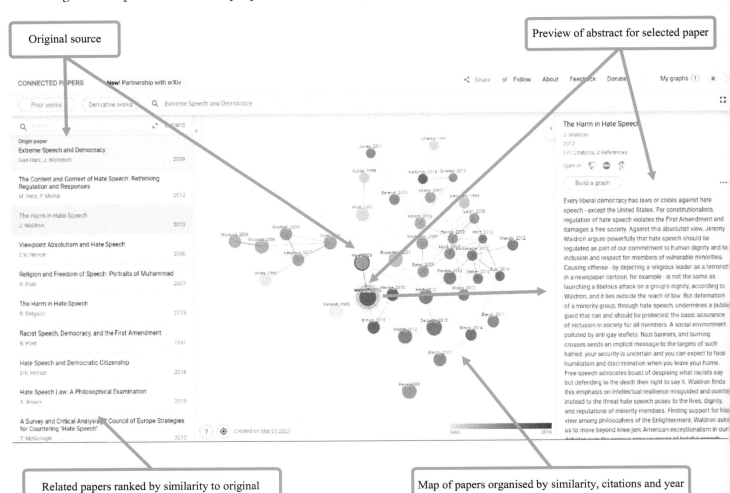

TIP

As with the use and perils of hyperlinks, always keep a record of what you have searched for/skimmed so you don't get lost in a 'vortex' of links and connections.

Skimming in practice: time and making annotations

You should aim to skim as fast as you can (as a guide, a journal article of 5000 words should be skimmed in a maximum of eight minutes). If you start labouring the process, you will end up going too deep and will lose sight of the 'bigger picture' and overall impression of the text. The key thing to remember is that at the skimming stage you are ONLY assessing the RELEVANCE of the text in relation to your PRIORITIES. In other words, if a quick skim of the text/hyperlinks/webpages/PDFs does not reveal material to be immediately applicable to your assignment or gaining specific information/knowledge, you need to move on to another text that does. This will help you avoid wasting valuable time that could be more usefully deployed reading something more productive.

During skimming you should start to annotate the text using a highlighter pen or Post-it notes (highlighting and notes are also available in software such as OneNote) to draw your attention back to the relevant sections and paragraphs. By doing so you can easily return to them later, either to scan for specific information, or to close read in order to understand and analyse the author's ideas, argument or theory.

TIP

One method for enhancing comprehension, seeing its importance in relation to the 'big picture' and revising the material (perhaps in readiness for an exam or just for recalling important points), is to make a note at the side of the paragraph which reduces/summarises what the paragraph is about in just one or two words. This is essentially a clue or indicator of 'gist'. It will jog your memory when you return to it later and helps you identify and visualise the 'big picture' and any connections, especially if you are using the scroll/text-mapping technique outlined below.

Creating a scroll

If you can print out the material (individual chapters and journal articles are only really suitable for this) or download the document into OneNote, one method of skimming in order to see the 'big picture' is to produce a scroll. This is also known as 'text-mapping' and was devised by R. David Middlebrook (2015). A scroll is an effective way of skimming backwards and forwards across a text so as to get an immediate, overall impression, especially when you have marked up the text with your own very brief notes. The way to produce a scroll is to:

1) Print the article/chapter out on single-sided paper.

2) Make notes on the text/highlight the main paragraphs, ideas or sections of relevance. These notes can often be one-word descriptions such as 'introduction', 'background', 'data', 'theory' or 'benefits of consumerism'. You can add to these brief evaluations such as 'useful', 'not useful', 'maybe useful', depending on what works best for you.

3) Lay the papers out in order and Sellotape them together.

The complete scroll or 'text-map' might look something like this:

  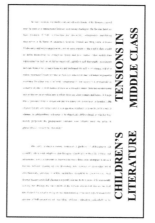 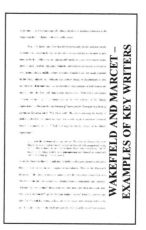

Printing out allows you to skim both up and down, and left to right, but if you prefer to 'scroll' using your computer or device, you can also download the PDF articles into OneNote and do the same thing:

As you can see, one glance can quickly reveal the 'big picture' of the article/chapter, and this makes it easy to quickly find the information you want whilst setting it within the context of the overall argument. For more details about 'text-mapping' see www.textmapping.org/.

TIP

If you prefer looking at things from top to bottom rather than left to right, simply Sellotape the short edges of the papers instead of the long edges or use OneNote. Orientate the scroll in whatever way works best for you.

Once you have briefly skimmed the material and have ascertained that it is indeed worth reading in further depth, the next technique to use is scanning.

Scanning

Like skimming, the process of scanning a text is quick but delves into the material at a deeper level. Here you are aiming to find specific pieces of information as quickly as possible. This information is usually something you already know about (and you are looking for references to it through keywords, dates, names, data or hyperlinks). For instance, you might want to know if the author discusses a specific idea or theory, whether they refer to a specific Act of Parliament or legislation, or maybe you are looking for key phrases such as 'credit crunch', 'climate change' or 'zone of proximal development'. A vital aid in this process is the use of a good index (possibly accompanied by the contents page). As we saw earlier, in many cases you can simply look up the keyword, author, theory or even phrase in the index, and it will list all the pages on which those terms or pieces of information occur.
This means that you can simply scan specific pages rather than entire chapters or sections, thus saving you both time and effort. Not all indexes are good (and in some cases, such as in a journal article, there might not even be one), but they can be a vital tool to use when scanning. If you are reading the

article/source as a PDF document (usually a journal article), you can search for what you are looking for using the 'search' function. This will enable you to do the work of an index, but with much less effort.

TIP

 If there are lots of references to what you are looking for and they occur within a few pages of each other (e.g. 'materialism', pp. 89, 91–92, 95–97), then it's probably worth just reading the entire section rather than looking up each individual reference.

Once you have arrived at the page referenced in the index, scan up and down looking for the keyword, term, date, fact or piece of information that you need. Once found, you have several options which can be summarised like this:

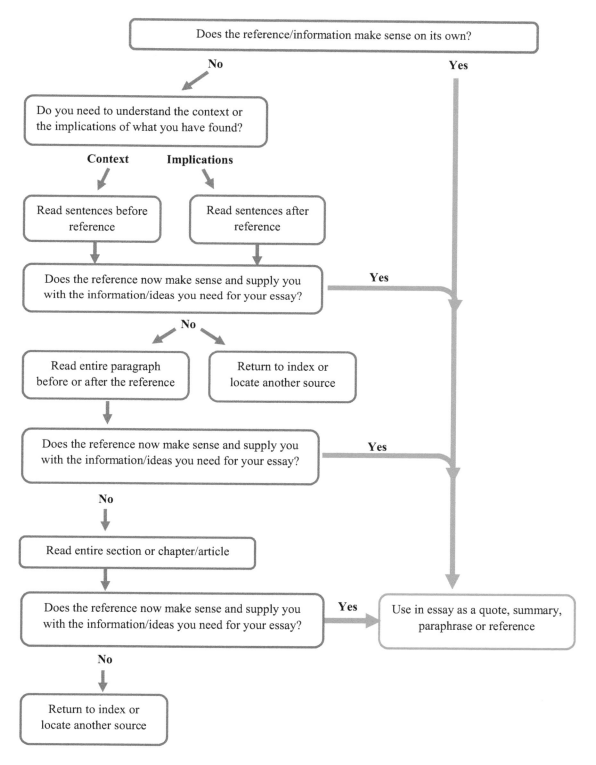

On occasions when the index or word search function is unhelpful or unavailable, you might need to scan larger sections of text (possibly with the help of the contents page). To avoid larger sections of text becoming confusing (perhaps even with words jumping around), you should use coloured overlays if you find them helpful (your dyslexia diagnosis should be able to advise on which colours are best for you).

TIPS

The key thing to remember is to keep scanning rather than getting bogged down in detail. When reading electronically, scrolling up and down is a very useful tactic that is not so easily done with physical texts.

One way of keeping the scanning going is to use your finger to trace the sentences. However, unlike what you may have been taught at school, DO NOT ALLOW YOUR FINGER TO STOP MOVING. Do not slow down – keep scanning/scrolling the pages, keep the momentum and do not start reading sentences. At this point, you are merely looking for key words, facts or phrases and nothing more.

Scanning for the 'gist': identifying key sites of meaning in sentences and clauses

Another aspect of scanning is to quickly look through paragraphs and sentences, to understand the 'gist' of what is going on. To do this, you need to be looking for and identifying key sites of meaning (this will again help you identify the 'big picture' rather than identifying, reading and decoding every word). Once you have identified the key ideas in each paragraph (via the topic sentence or by using the index), you can start looking for specific pieces of information. Begin by identifying individual sentences/clauses and where they begin and end. You should be able to spot them quite easily. The human eye uses what's known as peripheral vision to see items on either side of the main focus. Thus we can see anywhere between 5 to 7 words at any one time. Use this ability to get a sense of the various clusters of sentences quickly. Identifying the key sites of meaning within individual sentences (particularly main clauses) entails scanning for three elements: the topic, the action (usually in the form of a key verb or verb phrase) and specific detail (often in the form of keywords/dates/names). As we shall see in Chapter 6, subordinate clauses largely supply additional or clarifying information and can thus be glossed over at this stage. These elements, as the icon above indicates, are like jigsaw pieces. Separately, they give an indication of the meaning, but see them together (even if they are not actually slotted together) and you can immediately get a 'gist' of the overall picture and how it all fits together. Identifying these aspects will allow you to piece together the meaning and see how it all fits into the 'big picture' of the paragraph and then the chapter/article/section as a whole. Let's take the following sentence by way of illustration:

Despite its popularity, social media has become an insidious, negative and highly addictive means of disseminating 'fake news'.

Here we have what's known as a complex sentence (complex as it involves the dependent/subordinate clause 'despite its popularity'), but there are only really three elements, three pieces of the jigsaw, which are of immediate interest. 'Social media' indicates the topic, 'disseminating' is the verb phrase or action part of the sentence, and 'fake news' denotes the primary object and detail of the sentence – its key purpose and argument. In other words, the sentence follows the standard subject, verb, object (SVO) sequence, which is considered to be the cornerstone of written and spoken sentences in English, and is even thought to be the most inherently 'obvious' to human psychology (Diamond, 2002, p.143). So, irrespective of what type of sentence we are looking at (simple, compound, complex or compound-complex – all of which we will examine in Chapter 6), the main clauses are a means of communicating a 'big picture' – action – detail sequence of ideas. As such, the topic, verb (action) and detail elements of sentence structures form the sites of the keywords and meaning. Indeed, if we strip away all the words in black in the sample sentences above and below (particularly in the subordinate clauses), you can still get a good 'gist' of what the sentence is about, including its key argument, just by scanning for, identifying and reading three key components. Let's have a look at some typical sentences you may encounter in your reading to see how these elements can be identified:

•   'The culture industry as a whole has moulded men as a type unfailingly reproduced in every product' (Adorno and Horkheimer, 1999, p.35).

- 'The unconscious – that is to say, the 'repressed' – offers no resistance whatever to the efforts of the treatment' (Freud, 2015, p.13).

In the case of compound sentences (two independent clauses), you can normally gloss over the second clause (even though it contains its own topic, verb and detail), as the first clause usually lays out the foundations and the second provides additional detail (as is often indicated by conjunctions – words such as 'and', 'that', 'but', 'so', 'as', 'or' – all of which indicate an additional level of detail or clarification). When scanning, you are only looking for the 'gist', so don't worry too much about what comes after the comma – you can read this once you have identified whether it is worth looking at in further detail. For example:

- 'The importance of the role of the bioinformatician as a major player in modern biology cannot be overstated, and it will only grow with the advent of next-generation sequencers and sequencing pipelines' (Janitz, 2008, p.9).

- 'Like most humanities scholars, musicologists are prone to build interpretations on very small data sets or even on single instances, and the less the evidence that has survived from the past, the stronger this tendency will be' (Clarke and Cook, 2004, p.4).

Some reading guides recommend scanning for verbs and nouns to increase reading speed and comprehension, most notably Howard Stephen Berg's *Super Reading Secrets* (1992). But you need to be able to find these elements in the first place. Where do nouns and verbs usually occur? How do you find them? As we shall see in Chapter 6, this is not an easy task for individuals with dyslexia since grammar rules are often too abstract to be easily understood. What is more, on their own grammatical principles do not allow you to *see* how the individual elements fit into the 'bigger picture' of the sentence. The word 'see' here is used very deliberately, because an understanding of grammar, even if you are lucky enough to have grasped it, does not allow us to visualise the 'big picture' of the sentence and thus the units/key sites of meaning. Again, as we shall see in Chapter 6, this is where it is beneficial to conceive of the basic structure of sentences, and main clauses in particular, as like a Christmas Cracker:

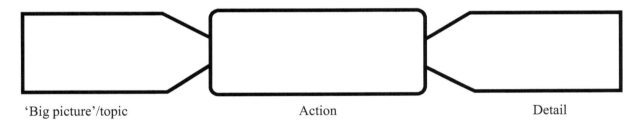

'Big picture'/topic   Action   Detail

When reading, then, visualise each sentence as a Christmas Cracker and look for the 'big picture' – action – detail sequence. Focus on these three elements as a means of locating the most valuable information (usually nouns and verbs) quickly. Once you have done that, you are ready to make the next step and critically evaluate the material, which is the focus of the next chapter.

Maintaining focus and concentration

Many students feel that they need to spend long periods reading without taking regular breaks. However, studies have suggested that concentration declines markedly after 10–15 minutes, whilst recent research has rather controversially suggested that human beings have an attention span which barely rivals that of a goldfish (Wilson and Korn, 2007, Gausby, 2015). Another study has found that attention spans wax and wane during lectures, with attention lapses occurring most notably after 4.5–5.5 minutes, 7– 9 minutes and 9–10 minutes (Bunce, Flens, and Neiles, 2010). People with dyslexia, of course, fair even worse, and it's a well-known fact that short attention spans are a tell-tale symptom of dyslexia. If you try to concentrate for long periods, you will end up exhausted and overtired (yet another characteristic of dyslexia). It is best to have short, intense bursts of activity rather than persevering and ending up frustrated that either you have not fully understood everything, or that your mind has wandered off-course. Try the following techniques to maintain and improve your concentration:

1) Never read for longer than five minutes before having a quick one-minute break to 're-set' your mind. If necessary, do this at the end of every paragraph (this will also help if you suffer from visual stress as it will give your eyes a rest).

2) Try to summarise (in one or two words) each paragraph before your break so that when you go back to it, the note will jog your memory of what you have just read.

3) After each break, take a few seconds to re-read the one- or two-word summaries you have written at the side of the preceding paragraphs so as to re-orientate yourself back into the 'big picture'. This also reinforces what you have learnt.

4) When reading online, minimise distractions (copy and paste the text into a Word/OneNote document or download the PDF version). This is because adverts and moving images can be very distracting and cause cognitive overload and visual stress (both an issue for individuals with dyslexia). Webpages frequently interrupt and unsettle your concentration via things like: 1) notifications to accept cookies, 2) adverts (especially for things you recently searched or shopped for and are unrelated to your study), 3) fly-in boxes asking for you to sign up to a newsletter, 4) feedback or chat boxes, or 5) notifications from other things you have open (e.g. email, social media, the computer needs to restart/update, a website has been blocked, virus protection updates etc.). Get the relevant information into a Word/OneNote or PDF as soon as possible to eliminate as many distractions/temptations as possible.

Using your difficulties in maintaining focus to your advantage: some advanced techniques

Dual reading

Individuals with dyslexia often have a short-term and/or limited working memory, which means that if you read a text for too long, you will lose focus, read on 'autopilot' (you are reading the words but you're actually just daydreaming) or give up entirely. And because individuals with dyslexia need quick, immediate, preferably visual gratification, they often get bored by persevering with one reading at a time. One way around this is to alternate between two chapters/books articles/ websites. Read a paragraph, summarise it, have a break, and then flip to another text you are working on. This might sound confusing (and perhaps it is to someone without dyslexia), but individuals with dyslexia, as Eide and Eide have suggested, often excel at multidimensional or 'multiframework approaches' that 'engage their ability to see interconnections' (2011, p.174), so why not give it a go? It allows you to pursue multiple interests at once, 'resets' your concentration, and it helps you sustain focus whilst also covering a lot of ground. Providing you keep in mind the 'web' of hyperlinks/webpages and avoid the perilous hyperlink vortex, reading across several webpages/hyperlinks or sources can also have the same effect.

Dual assistive reading

This is a very similar technique to that outlined above, but instead of alternating between two different academic texts, the aim here is to alternate between a textbook/study guide/introductory website and an academic text. This is a variation of a strategy that Eide and Eide accurately term 'pre-equipping', whereby students read sections of the textbook/study guide or introductory website to get an accessible, student-friendly overview or 'big picture' of the subject (2011, p.177). Here, however, you alternate these readings with more in-depth academic texts on the same topic. This will allow you to flip between 'big picture' introductions and technical/scholarly detail so that you can situate the latter into its context more easily. Importantly, this technique also allows you to associate new information with what you already know from the textbook/study guide/introductory website. This has an important effect on reinforcing, consolidating and scaffolding learning. Again, try reading a paragraph or two, summarise it, and then flip texts/sources/webpages – don't get bogged down in reading too much from either text without flipping, or your attention will wane.

'Big picture' speed reading at university – bringing it all together

While reading to understand and reading to write remain central to why you should read at university, these purposes are governed mainly by other issues and pressures, most notably:

1) Time (not only in terms of deadlines but also the need to read quickly).

2) Relevance (how relevant is what you are reading to the purposes outlined above?).

3) Priorities (what needs to be read first or most urgently to address the purposes above).

One way of bringing these competing, yet also complementary, aspects of university reading into an easily grasped process is to visualise the task of reading at university as like an old-fashioned egg timer – the shape of which indicates the depth of the reading and how it relates specifically to the pressures of time and the relevance of the material. Let's return to and examine the two purposes of reading outlined at the beginning of this chapter to see how the skills that you need to be learning and practising can be brought together as a process and mapped onto a 'big picture', visual template:

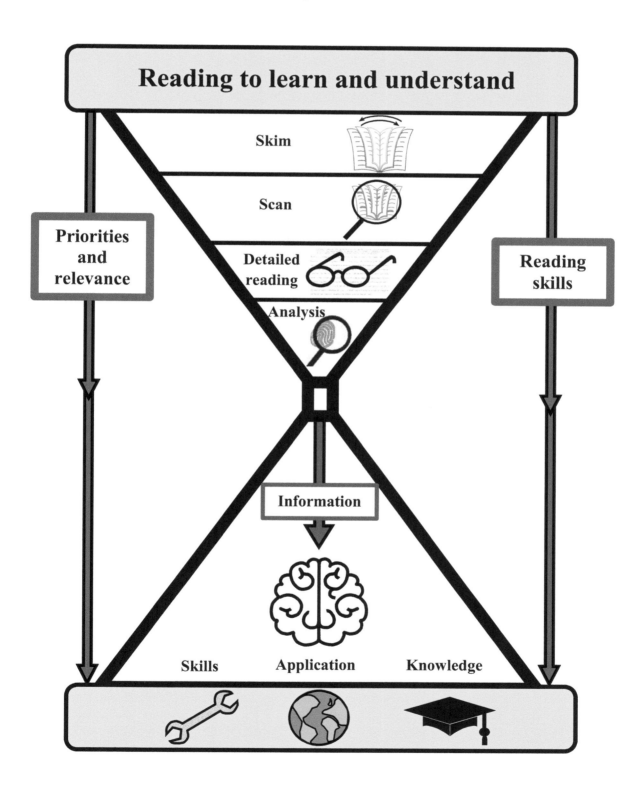

As you can see by the shape of the upper half of the egg timer, the focus gets more specific but also more skilled and time-consuming as you work through the processes of skimming and scanning. Where the information is relevant to your priorities, it leads to understanding and knowledge. This understanding and knowledge can then be applied in a wide range of contexts within your discipline and your life/employment, hence why the second half of the timer broadens back out into the 'bigger picture' and its application to the world. In the case of reading for essay writing meanwhile, the egg timer can be subdivided into preparation and application.

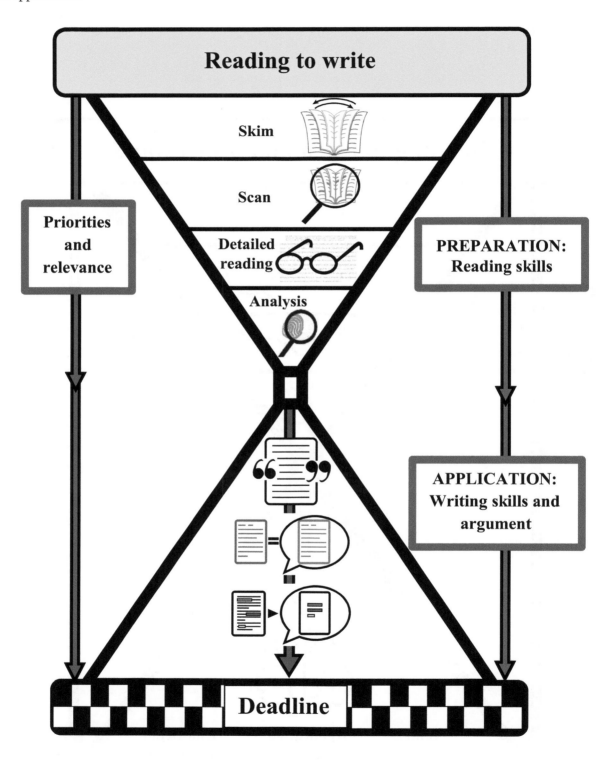

The process here is similar to reading to learn and understand (because without this you cannot use the source effectively in your writing), but then the second half shows how you can apply what you have learnt in your writing. Quotation (see p.102) is specific and detailed, so it appears at the top, narrow or focused point of the triangle. Meanwhile, paraphrasing and summarising (see pp.102–105) get progressively less specific and more general in terms of the way they capture the original author's ideas and how you use them in your essays (we will look quotation, paraphrasing, summarising and their visual icons in Chapter 5). However, governing both reading frameworks is the overarching issues of time, relevance, priorities and application. Time is possibly the most crucial factor here (hence why the reading process is depicted as an egg timer), as even students without dyslexia tend to get bogged down reading detail rather than skimming and scanning. Don't waste time – set yourself short time limits to read articles and chapters to avoid reading detail – you can go back to this later once you have a sense of the relevance of the material and the 'big picture'.

TIP

Keep referring to the two diagrams above to remind yourself to stay on track with your reading. Skim and scan quickly and keep to your priorities. If what you are reading doesn't look relevant, either move on to a section that does or look at the next item on your reading list.

Summary

In the next chapter, we will consider how to subject the information you have found to scrutiny and critical analysis, but for now, practise and keep in mind the following key points – they may well save you an awful lot of time, energy and frustration:

* Read effectively, efficiently and strategically rather than trying to read everything.

* Read abstracts and contents pages first to check suitability and relevance before reading anything else – don't waste time.

* Skim and scan texts before reading in depth.

* Make use of indexes or searches to search for key terms, ideas or authors.

* Read in small doses, with plenty of breaks to 'reset' your concentration (quality is often better than quantity).

* Use online articles and guides for introductory or more accessible information (dual assistive reading), but always reference, quote or summarise academic, peer-reviewed sources to maintain academic credibility and integrity.

* Use textbooks which are laid out in a way which suits you – use them mainly as introductory guides or for revision.

* If reading online, ensure you don't get bogged down in hyperlinks – always have a 'web' map of your route through the material and how to get back safely to base without becoming overwhelmed.

* Always exercise critical thinking (see the next chapter) when researching and reading online and focus on finding **authentic, authoritative and academic** information and sources.

* Read widely as a means of familiarising yourself with the academic community and the writing conventions/styles of the subject you are studying.

* Read to learn and expand your knowledge – not just to write essays.

Bibliography

Adorno, Theodor, and Horkheimer, Max, (1999) 'The Culture Industry: Enlightenment as Mass Deception', in During, Simon (ed.) *The Cultural Studies Reader*. London: Routledge, pp.31–41.

AQA 'AS and A-Level History: AS (7041) A-Level (7042)'. Version 1.4 3rd July, 2019. Available at: https://filestore.aqa.org.uk/resources/history/specifications/AQA-7041-7042-SP-2015.PDF (Accessed: 5th July, 2021).

Barnett, Ronald, (1993) 'Knowledge, Higher Education, and Society: A Postmodern Problem', *Oxford Review of Education*, 19(1), pp.33–46.

Berg, Stephen Howard, (1992) *Super Reading Secrets*. New York: Warner Books, Inc.

Bunce, Diane M., Flens, Elizabeth A., and Neiles, Kelly Y., (2010) 'How Long Can Students Pay Attention in Class? A Study of Student Attention Decline Using Clickers', *Journal of Chemical Education*, 87(12), pp.1438–1443.

Carter, Christine Evans, (2014) *Mindscapes: Critical Reading Skills and Strategies*. 2nd ed. Wadsworth: Cengage.

Clarke, Eric, and Cook, Nicholas, (2004) *Empirical Musicology: Aims, Methods, Prospects*. Oxford: Oxford University Press.

Davies, Alistair, and Sinfield, Alan, (2000) *British Culture of the Postwar: An Introduction to Literature and Society 1945–1999*. Oxford: Routledge.

Diamond, Jared, (2002) *The Rise and Fall of the Third Chimpanzee: How Our Animal Heritage Affects the Way We Live*. London: Vintage.

Docherty, Thomas, (2011) *For the University: Democracy and the Future of the Institution*. London: Bloomsbury Academic.

Eide, Brock L., and Eide, Fernette, F., (2011) *The Dyslexic Advantage: Unlocking the Hidden Potential of the Dyslexic Brain*. London: Hay House.

Freud, Sigmund, (2015) *Beyond the Pleasure Principle*. New York: Dover Publications, Inc.

Gausby, Alyson, (2015) 'Attention Spans', 'Consumer Insights'. Microsoft Canada.

Grimm, Dieter, (2009) 'Freedom of Speech in a Globalised World', in Hare, Ivan, and Weinstein, James, (eds.) *Extreme Speech and Democracy*. Oxford: Oxford University Press, pp.11–22.

Hooper, Val, and Herath, Channa, (2014) 'Is Google Making Us Stupid? The Impact of the Internet on Reading Behaviour'. In *BLED 2014 Proceedings*. 1. Available at: http://aisel.aisnet.org/bled2014/1 (Accessed: 2nd July, 2021).

Janitz, Michal, (2008) *Next Generation Genome Sequencing: Towards Personalized Medicine*. Weinheim: Wiley-Blackwell.

Kezar, Adrianna, (2004) 'Obtaining Integrity? Reviewing and Examining the Charter between Higher Education and Society', *The Review of Higher Education*, 27(4), pp.429–459.

Lindzen, Richard S., (1999) 'Some Coolness Concerning Global Warming', *Bulletin of the American Meteorological Society,* 71(3), pp.288–299.

Middlebrook, D., (2015) *Unrolling the Book* [Online]. Available at: http://www.textmapping.org/whyUseScrolls.pdf (Accessed: 7th April, 2022).

O'Callaghan, Jonathan, (2015) 'Is Global Warming Increasing the Risk of Shark Attacks? Higher Temperatures Blamed for Record Number in North Carolina', *Daily Mail*, 2nd July [Online]. Available at: http://www.dailymail.co.uk/sciencetech/article-3147050/Is-global-warming-increasing-risk-shark-attacks-Higher-temperatures-blamed-record-numbers-North-Carolina.html#ixzz4cv4qE5br (Accessed: 30th July, 2017).

Pinker, Steven, (2014) *The Sense of Style: The Thinking Person's Guide to Writing in the 21st Century*. London: Penguin Books.

Shaywitz, Sally, E., (1996) 'Dyslexia', *Scientific American* 275(5) [Online]. Available at: https://www.scientificamerican.com/article/dyslexia/ (Accessed: 30th March, 2017).

Stancliffe, George, (2003) *Speed Reading 4 Kids*. The American Speed Reading Project.

Toikka, Tarmo, (2008) *Effective Screen Reading: Manage E-mail and the Internet More Effectively*. Amherst, MA: HRD Press, Inc.

Wikipedia, (2017) *Global Warming*. Available at: https://en.wikipedia.org/wiki/Global_warming (Accessed: 27th December, 2020).

Wilson, Karen, and Korn, James H., (2007) 'Attention during Lectures: Beyond Ten Minutes', *Teaching of Psychology*, 34, pp.85–89.

Woolf, Virginia, (2014) 'How Should One Read a Book?' In *Virginia Woolf: Essays on the Self*, edited by Joanna Kavenna. London: Notting Hill Editions, pp.64–80.

3 Critical Reading and Thinking for Critical Writing

'We are the visionaries, inventors, and artists. We think differently, see the world differently, and solve problems differently. It is from this difference that the dyslexic brain derives its brilliance'.

(Tiffany Sunday: author and expert on dyslexia and entrepreneurship)

After engaging in quick scanning and skimming to find specific details or pieces of relevant information, the next step is to read in more depth and subject the material to critical analysis. The ability to subject material and ideas to critical analysis will enable you to score higher marks because, rather than simply displaying knowledge, you'll be able to demonstrate skill in evaluation, problem-solving, criticality, reflection, perceptiveness and originality.

What is critical reading and thinking?

Take a look at the following definition of critical thinking:

'Critical thinking is self-guided, self-disciplined thinking which attempts to reason at the highest level of quality in a fair-minded way. People who think critically consistently attempt to live rationally, reasonably, empathically. They are keenly aware of the inherently flawed nature of human thinking when left unchecked...They use the intellectual tools that critical thinking offers – concepts and principles that enable them to analyse, assess, and improve thinking...They realize that no matter how skilled they are as thinkers, they can always improve their reasoning abilities and they will always at times fall prey to mistakes in reasoning, human irrationality, prejudices, biases, distortions, uncritically accepted social rules and taboos, self-interest, and vested interest. They strive to improve the world in whatever ways they can and contribute to a more rational, civilized society. At the same time, they recognize the complexities often inherent in doing so...They strive never to think simplistically about complicated issues and always consider the rights and needs of relevant others... They embody the Socratic principle: The unexamined life is not worth living, because they realize that many unexamined lives together result in an uncritical, unjust, dangerous world' (Elder, 2015).

In essence, then, critical reading and thinking is the ability to subject ideas (written or otherwise) to:

- Analysis
- Criticism
- Evaluation
- Interrogation
- Questioning
- Healthy scepticism

Anything can, and probably should, be critically analysed, so let's see if we can subject the definition above to analysis. Is there anything Linda Elder says above which you find problematic or questionable? Is it biased? Let's go through her statement and subject it to critique:

DOI: 10.4324/9781003190189-3

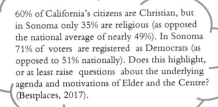

60% of California's citizens are Christian, but in Sonoma only 35% are religious (as opposed the national average of nearly 49%). In Sonoma 71% of voters are registered as Democrats (as opposed to 51% nationally). Does this highlight, or at least raise questions about the underlying agenda and motivations of Elder and the Centre? (Bestplaces, 2017).

Elder is Executive Director of the Centre for Critical Thinking at Sonoma State University in Northern California, which promotes critical thinking and campaigns for its inclusion in US schools, colleges and universities, so this statement is clearly part of that 'campaign' and thus seeks to legitimise and advertise her Centre.

Despite my own trimming, Elder's statement is very repetitive and laboured– it could easily have been shortened without undermining her core argument.

Elder's suggestion that an uncritical majority would lead to an 'unjust, dangerous world' seems rhetorical and almost threatening/scaremonge-ring, and thus needs to be treated with caution and scepticism. The final statement amounts to propaganda rather than a rational, well-reasoned argument and appears to be a final attempt to convince if the preceding arguments have failed.

Elder is clearly biased towards the virtues of critical thinking (which often translates into left-wing ideologies, ideas and politics). She is troublingly judgemental in the way she states that an 'unexamined life is not worth living'.

So, as you can see, almost anything (even critical thinking itself!) can be subjected to interrogation and critique. Indeed, it can be the most fun part of academic study. Human thought and nature is indeed 'inherently flawed' as Elder suggests, especially when left 'unchecked'. The following examples illustrate precisely this problem:

In 1999 NASA 'lost' a $125 million Mars orbiter because one team of designers used metric and another used imperial measurements. The result was that it travelled too close to the surface of Mars and was presumably destroyed.

2013 saw the construction of the 'Walkie-Talkie' skyscraper in Eastcheap, London. The concave shaped building is largely constructed out of glass and thus reflects sunlight onto the street. Temperatures of between 91–117 degrees were observed – enough to melt parts of a Jaguar car and one newspaper reporter even managed to fry an egg in a pan placed on the pavement. The shape has also created a wind-tunnel effect at ground level, leading to complaints of drafts. In 2015 the construction was awarded the Carbuncle Cup for being the worst new building in the UK.

These examples are all the more shocking given that humankind is now equipped with high-tech assistance in the form of computer-aided design, modern machinery, and the lessons learnt from history. As such, they highlight the importance of critical thinking and subjecting everything you encounter to questioning.

TIP

 Before approaching the challenges of academic analysis, one way of approaching and practising critical thinking is to think about scams and satire. How many of you have received phone calls or texts informing you that you're owed compensation owing to an accident in your car or at work (yet you had no such accident and perhaps don't even work or own a car!)? You use your critical thinking skills here automatically to dismiss such claims as a scam. Another way into critical thinking is by looking at satire. There are numerous websites and social media platforms devoted to satire (political, religious and cultural), and they all use critical thinking skills to make fun out of the 'inherently flawed' nature of human thinking. Try watching programmes such as the BBC's *Have I Got News for You* or BritBox's *Spitting Image*, or read satirical magazines such as *Private Eye* to accustom yourself to thinking critically. This is a fun and amusing way of getting started.

Why do critical reading and thinking at university?

Critical thinking is a valuable skill to learn for university study, as you need to be able to subject the ideas, opinions, arguments and sources you come across in your reading to scrutiny. Being able to spot inconsistencies, flaws, drawbacks and shortcomings and being able to critique and evaluate what you read will enable you to fulfil the national standards and frameworks laid out (in the UK at least) by the Quality Assurance Agency for Higher Education (2014). These descriptors are often translated into simplified, discipline-specific mark schemes which you should find in your departmental Student Handbook, but the main aims of university study can be summarised as follows (note the emphasis on critical thinking, which is underlined):

Bachelor's degree	*Master's degree*
A systematic understanding of key aspects of their field of study, including acquisition of coherent and detailed knowledge, at least some of which is at, or informed by, the forefront of defined aspects of a discipline	A systematic understanding of knowledge, and <u>a critical awareness of current problems and/or new insights, much of which is at, or informed by, the forefront of their academic discipline, field of study or area of professional practice</u>
<u>An ability to deploy accurately established techniques of analysis and enquiry within a discipline</u>	A comprehensive understanding of techniques applicable to their own research or advanced scholarship
Conceptual understanding that enables the student: - <u>to devise and sustain arguments, and/or to solve problems, using ideas and techniques, some of which are at the forefront of a discipline</u> - <u>to describe and comment upon particular aspects of current research, or equivalent advanced scholarship, in the discipline</u>	<u>Originality in the application of knowledge, together with a practical understanding of how established techniques of research and enquiry are used to create and interpret knowledge in the discipline</u>
<u>An appreciation of the uncertainty, ambiguity and limits of knowledge</u>	Conceptual understanding that enables the student: - <u>to evaluate critically current research and advanced scholarship in the discipline</u> - <u>to evaluate methodologies and develop critiques of them and, where appropriate, to propose new hypotheses</u>
The ability to manage their own learning, and <u>to make use of scholarly reviews and primary sources (for example, refereed research articles and/or original materials appropriate to the discipline)</u>	<u>Deal with complex issues both systematically and creatively, make sound judgements in the absence of complete data, and communicate their conclusions clearly to specialist and non-specialist audiences</u>
Apply the methods and techniques that they have learned to <u>review, consolidate, extend and apply</u> their knowledge and understanding, and to initiate and carry out projects	Demonstrate self-direction and <u>originality in tackling and solving problems, and act autonomously in planning and implementing tasks at a professional or equivalent level</u>
<u>Critically evaluate arguments, assumptions, abstract concepts and data (that may be incomplete), to make judgements, and to frame appropriate questions to achieve a solution – or identify a range of solutions – to a problem</u>	Continue to advance their knowledge and understanding, and to develop new skills to a high level
Communicate information, ideas, problems and solutions to both specialist and non-specialist audiences	

(QAA, 2014, pp.28–31)

Critical thinking, then, is a vital, integral part of university study. While knowledge is undoubtedly the foundation, critical thinking is the key to unlocking good marks. It will be what most of your lecturers will be looking for when they assess your work.

TIPS

 Any text or idea/argument/methodology will have its strengths and weaknesses – analysing and evaluating them will add marks to your assignment.

 Not recognising flaws or weaknesses in other people's thoughts or writing means you might base your analysis on a flawed argument.

What is the best way to approach and practise critical thinking?

How do you start the process of critical thinking? Where do you begin? Firstly, do not be daunted by it. Individuals with dyslexia often excel at critical thinking and analysis. It is well known that while people with dyslexia struggle with procedural learning, rules, planning and sequencing, once they are let 'off the leash' and into an area where creative thinking is prized, they can excel. Critical thinking is precisely one of those areas. As Eide and Eide (2011) have suggested, individuals with dyslexia have the 'ability to perceive relationships like analogies, metaphors, paradoxes, similarities, differences, implications, gaps and imbalances', often from multi-dimensional and 'big picture' perspectives. This is why people with dyslexia often struggle with multiple-choice tasks, because instead of playing by the rules and choosing the correct answer, they 'excel at in detecting secondary meanings or distant word relationships...finding loopholes, ambiguities, and potential exceptions where none are intended' (pp.5, 95). Critical thinking, then, is an area in which you have the potential to shine. So how do you get started? The following 'critical questions' framework is loosely adapted (and expanded) from M. Neil Browne and Stuart Keeley's *Asking the Right Questions* (2015), which has become an immensely popular student guide to critical thinking. However, given that people with dyslexia like to process ideas and see connections visually, and reference those ideas to the 'big picture', here each question has a quick reference symbol which corresponds to the core critical activity and how this fits in with the overall, 'big picture' aims of critical thinking and reading. The framework is an ideal way of helping you to evaluate and critically analyse what you read, and the icons can be downloaded as bookmarks from the companion website so you can use them to mark specific pages in your texts.

Broadly speaking, critical thinking and reading involves looking at three key areas:

a)   The research background and motivations (the 'big picture')

b)   The authors' methodology and evidence (the 'big picture' in respect of what they actually did)

c)   The argument (the reasoning involved and how the findings are presented)

In what follows, each of these areas will be examined in turn, although in reality you ought to be asking all of these critical questions all the time (not only in your academic reading but in life generally so as to become a more critically aware citizen).

A) The research background and motivations

Critical question 1: what's the issue or problem?

 As you can see by the symbol/prompt on the left, this question entails going back and questioning the original purpose of the research and subjecting it to scrutiny, evaluation and analysis. When undertaking a piece of research (irrespective of the discipline), academics typically start from one of two positions:

1)   Prescriptive: A problem/issue which is known about and the researcher is providing a solution to it, OR

2)   Descriptive: There is a new problem/issue which has previously been unexplored or insufficiently researched.

These two starting points dictate what type of literature researchers produce. The three main subgenres of literature you are likely to encounter are as follows:

1) Theoretical – approach the 'problem'/issue using theories and models instead of practical, 'hands on' research.

2) Research – writes up the results of actual experiments or enquiries involving 'real' situations.

3) Practice – approaches the 'problem'/issue from the perspective of professional experience, evaluation and reflection.

None of this looks particularly contentious, but there are several areas here in need of interrogation. Firstly, is the problem/issue under consideration a credible/worthy problem/issue in the first place? Let's take the example of rising CO_2 levels in the atmosphere. This is clearly a valid problem as it has a direct impact on climate change, thereby endangering both ourselves and the world's ecosystems. On the other hand, let's take Dr Andrew Stapley, a chemical engineer at Loughborough University, who in 2003 researched the question of how to make a perfect cup of tea (apparently, the secret is to add the milk before the tea bag rather than the other way around!). The underlying research question/problem/issue here is definitely dubious and may well reflect Stapley's love of tea rather than a more legitimate research 'problem'. This may seem like a somewhat exaggerated example, but the underlying issue or 'problem' which the research is attempting to address is often worth subjecting to scrutiny. Let's practise this by taking the following example, the topic of which is potentially very relevant to you as a student:

Nzekwe-Excel, Chinyere, (2014) 'Academic Writing Workshops: Impact of Attendance on Performance', *Journal of Academic Writing*, 4:1, pp.12-25.

Abstract

The purpose of this study is to explore if academic writing workshops contribute to students' learning and performance in assessment. Academic writing workshops provide an opportunity to discuss specific learning areas and promote student engagement. The results of an assessed essay for a group of 65 first-year mathematics students at Aston University, UK show that academic writing workshops have an association with students' academic performance. An Independent Samples T-test was conducted to compare the mean performance of the students based on their attendance of academic writing workshops. The analyses reveal that students who attended 2-5 academic writing workshops had a far better performance (mean: 58.60%) in comparison to students who attended 0-1 workshop (mean: 46.37%). In addition, the analyses show a statistically significant difference in the mean performance of students who attended and of students who did not attend an academic writing workshop specifically relating to the assessment.

Can you spot whether this is descriptive or prescriptive? Is the problem/issue underlying this research valid? Is it explicit or unstated?

As you may have noted, the article is clearly prescriptive as the author appears to be advocating academic writing workshops as a way of improving student performance. But what exactly is the problem? Is there a problem or issue needing to be addressed? This brings us to the second consideration you need to focus on when reading – namely, is the underlying problem/issue/motivation even stated? Is it hidden or unclear? In this case, it is somewhat unclear, but we can assume that poor grades or the desire to increase students' grades are the underlying problems. Or maybe it is a lack of student 'engagement'? But are these valid issues? They undoubtedly are, but given that they are somewhat hidden, I would suggest that the issue is more questionable than it would first appear. Could there be an underlying problem or motivation which the author is reluctant to reveal? This would require some research and subject knowledge on your part, so obviously you need to use your reading and notes to help you. Using my knowledge of academic writing and writing centres, I would question the underlying motivation behind this research for several reasons:

1) Academic writing centres throughout the UK tend to experience low student take-up, so a study that can show that the provision is effective could lead to greater enrolments or 'engagement' by students. This means that the underlying motivation behind the study might not actually be improving student achievement.

2) Academic writing centres are under financial pressures and need to legitimise and bolster their existence (otherwise, staff might be made redundant), so again the motivation and underlying problem behind this research might not be all that it seems and may have very little to do with helping students succeed.

3) The study looks at maths students, which are, in my experience, often none too keen on writing essays! Maybe there is a particular problem with student take-up of academic writing courses in this discipline, and the academic writing centre at Aston wants to attract more maths students? Again, this throws into question the assumption that the underlying problem here is student performance.

4) The article appears in a journal dedicated to academic writing, so there is a vested interest here in promoting the benefits of academic writing. This again throws the validity of the underlying problem or issue into some doubt or at least politicises it.

As this example has shown, you need to look carefully at the underlying problem/issue, which is the motivation for the study you are reading. Question it, subject it to scrutiny, and never take things at face value.

TIPS

 Identify whether the writer's position is prescriptive or descriptive. Ask yourself – are these valid positions based on what you know of the subject? Does the writer maintain this stance or change stance? If so, why? If they change stance, maybe the original problem/issue is not as clear-cut as it first seems.

 Pay particular attention to research in which the underlying problem/motivation is obscure or hidden. If the underlying problem/issue is not explicit, it may be because it is problematic.

 Always question the validity of the problem/issue at stake – don't just assume that because it comes from an authoritative journal/monograph or that the author is a famous academic, its underlying motivations are valid or unproblematic.

Critical question 2: what's the motive?

 This question can be easily confused with critical question 1, but it differs in the sense that, as the arrow in the icon indicates, it seeks to examine why the study was conducted in the first place. Key questions to consider here are:

1) What are the motivations behind the research?

2) Why conduct the project in the first place?

3) Why were specific specialists chosen to do the research and not others?

4) Who funded the project and why?

5) And why now? Why was the problem/issue not investigated earlier – are there contextual issues which are relevant?

Let's examine the following article regarding family law advice as a way of illustrating how you can unpack the motivations behind the research:

 Balmer, Nigel, Denvir, Catrina, Miles, Joanna, Patel, Ash, and Smith, Marisol, (2013) 'In Scope but out of Reach? Examining Differences between Publically Funded Telephone and Face-to-face Family Law Advice', *Child and Family Law Quarterly*, 25:3, pp.253-69.

Balmer et al. claim that 'this paper aims to address our lack of understanding about the provision of telephone-based legal advice in the area of legal law and compare its results with face-to-face legal advice' (p.256). Initially, the reasons for undertaking this research appear straightforward, useful and entirely reasonable. There appears to be little to call into question. But let's dig a little deeper:

The main author is a researcher at the Ministry of Justice. He states that ' the opinions in this paper are the author's own, and do not represent the views of the Legal Aid Agency of the Ministry of Justice' , but surely by virtue of the connection there may be bias or at least a vested inte rest?

If we read further, we discover that the government wants a 'digital by default' policy in which traditional modes of access are used only in 'exceptional circumstances'. As such, there is clearly pressure to find evidence that this transit ion is at least not detrimental to service users.

The paper is clearly in favour of telephone provision, so appears to support government policy – a stance which seems questionable and potentially unreliable, especially as the research was funded by the Ministry of Justice.

Suddenly, the motives behind this research seem to be political and economic rather than centring on the 'lack of understanding about the provision of telephone-based legal advice'. This exemplifies why it is often worth investigating and calling into question the motives behind a piece of research.

TIPS FOR FINDING MOTIVES

 Look carefully at the footnotes/endnotes/preface and acknowledgements to see who funded the research, who influenced it and where it was undertaken. Authors can sometimes 'bury' small but potentially problematic details in their footnotes which can sometimes be very illuminating.

 Don't take the authors at face value – do some internet searching to find out who they are, their research interests, who they work for, who funds them and what learned societies or interest groups they belong to.

Critical question 3: what's the context?

 Knowledge, the production of knowledge, and how knowledge is interpreted does not occur in a vacuum. Rather, knowledge is shaped and influenced, as is indicated in the icon, by the context and surroundings within which it is produced, whether this be:

- social

- political

- economic

- religious

- ideological

- cultural

- what is fashionable

- racial

- biological

- or even the priorities set within individual institutions.

For example, although Isaac Newton was a devout (albeit unorthodox) Christian, his ideas (mainly those associated with the idea that things happen because of laws that can be rationally understood) helped foster Enlightenment philosophies which were increasingly challenging received knowledge and authority, especially religion. This resulted in numerous competing publications which sought to minimise any questioning of God's authority and 'design' and thus harmonise Newtonian ideas with Christianity. The most notable of these was William Paley's *Natural Theology* (1802), in which he argued that evidence of God could be found in the very fact that everything in the natural world had a design. This resulted in his famous 'watchmaker analogy', through which he argued that just as observing the rational laws and mechanics of a watch proves the existence of a watchmaker (a designer), the rational laws of nature prove the existence of God. But as we can see, Paley's ideas were not produced purely owing to a desire to seek and promote knowledge and understanding. Rather, his publication was anti-Newtonian/Enlightenment propaganda, and was very much motivated by a religious, if not political, agenda. In turn, Enlightenment philosophers were not only seeking 'truth', but wanted to seek and advocate a truth which legitimised their claims for a fairer, more enlightened, rational society. So nothing, even today, occurs within a vacuum. No matter how seemingly unbiased or abstract the ideas you come across may seem, they are shot through with influences from their content (present, past and even future). As a critical thinker, your job is to investigate or at least consider those influences, whether they manifest themselves in trends, gaps, ambivalence, or even silences. Indeed, what is NOT said is often as important, if not more important, than what is.

TIP

Always check the date and think about when the original research was conducted. Then consider what, if any key background events or pressures may have influenced the research and what the author's stance may have been. Use your subject knowledge to help you.

B) The methodology and evidence

Critical question 4: is the methodology sound?

As depicted in the icon on the left, the methodology is the process the researcher undertook to carry out and produce their findings. This needs subjecting to scrutiny using your subject knowledge. You may be tempted to believe that all academics and experts use valid methodologies because they are experts in their field, but this is not necessarily the case. A good way to start thinking about and exploring methodologies is to first look at popular culture, particularly advertising. Have you ever noticed that television adverts for anti-ageing or anti-wrinkle creams always feature models who are young and free of wrinkles in the first place? Surely a better method would be to take someone who actually has wrinkles and then show them after using the product to demonstrate how effective it really is? The methodology behind the adverts is decidedly questionable. Academic articles and research are unlikely to have such glaring problems, but issues very often exist. A good starting point is to think about the potential problems or inadequacies which may arise from the type of literature which the research has resulted in. As we saw earlier, there are three main types of academic literature produced (which derive from their underlying methodologies). The areas you might want to explore here, according to Wallace and Wray (2011, pp.95–97), are as follows:

Literature type	Typical methodologies	Potential issues
Theoretical	Theories, principles, concepts.	Too theoretical and abstract to be of practical use. Theories might be outdated. 'Real world' might not reflect or be compatible with the theory.
Research	Experiments, literature reviews, qualitative and quantitative data.	Might not have a clear theoretical perspective. Methodology might be flawed or unsuitable. Study might be too focused to apply to general situations and principles. Could be biased or prejudiced owing to funding pressures/bodies, flawed data sampling etc. Literature might not be applicable, transferable or up to date.
Practice	Personal and professional, practice-based reflections and evaluations.	Evidence might be too restricted to apply to general situations. Reflections might not have enough academic rigour and may not be underpinned by adequate theory or methodology. Personal/professional reflections might not be valid enough.

After considering the overarching, 'big picture' of the researcher's approach and methodology, it's time to dig deeper and consider the specifics of what they did. Some key questions to ask when assessing a methodology include:

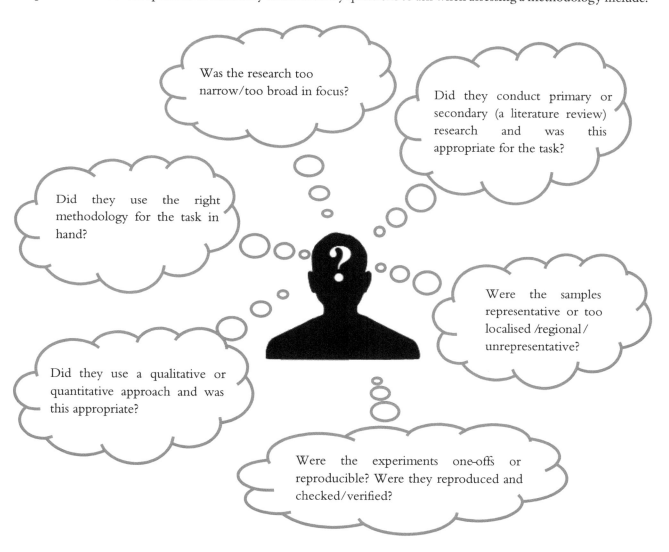

With these questions in mind, let's have a look at a couple of examples to illustrate how you can critique methodologies:

Example 1

In comparison with other mammals, Badgers rarely appear outside their sets during the day. In 1996, a study by Jones found that, of the 8 different types of mammals observed, Badgers were primarily nocturnal (p.83). The project involved observing the 8 different types of mammal during 48 hours and noting their behaviours.

Example 2

The dataset contained records for 226,279 family matters which were delivered under contract by solicitors and not for profit providers. Of these, 254, 328 (95.5%) consisted of face-to-face advice and 11,951 (4.5%) of telephone advice (Balmer et al, 2013, p.257).

In both examples, there are problems with the methodology.

In example 1, the approach seems to be a literature review, the aim of which is to carry out a wide-ranging survey of the existing literature and pick out key, previously undiscovered or neglected trends or problems. There is a problem with this methodology, as it would probably have been better to have conducted some primary research to produce up-to-date data and results about badgers and nocturnal behaviour, and of course the source is decidedly out of date. But worryingly, the methodology of the original study is seriously flawed. Initially, eight different types of mammal sounds like a reasonable figure, but given that the UK alone has 101 different types of mammal, it needs to be questioned whether eight was enough and whether they were even selected from a broad enough range of sub-species. The methodology of 'observing' these mammals is very unscientific indeed, and 48 hours is nowhere near long enough to come to reliable conclusions. It is also unclear where in the country the study took place, or even which country, county or district. There isn't a single aspect of the methodology that can reliably lead to the conclusion that 'badgers rarely appear outside their sets during the day'. It is also unclear what is actually meant by 'day' (this differs depending upon the time of the year and daylight hours) and 'rarely' (how rarely?).

Example 2 comes from the family law article we considered earlier. Here the aim was to 'address our lack of understanding about the provision of telephone-based legal advice in the area of legal law and compare its results with face-to-face legal advice'. The methodology is clearly appropriate as the data set is quantitative (thus hopefully yielding a large enough pool of evidence to come to some conclusions and 'understanding'). However, the fact that there is such a huge discrepancy between the data collected for face-to-face and telephone consultations surely has to be called into question and deemed both unrepresentative and unreliable. Whilst it must be acknowledged that there are fewer telephone consultations from which to draw data, this still doesn't explain or justify the fundamental discrepancy between the two forms of delivery, thus rendering the methodology questionable. Indeed, it is unclear why the area of 'family matters' was singled out for analysis – surely this in itself could skew the findings? Maybe other areas of legal advice are more likely to receive telephone enquiries, perhaps because the nature of those enquiries is more easily resolved ('family matters' seems to be a potentially complex area and perhaps difficult to resolve over the telephone). The researchers needed to have been more careful in designing a methodology that would have yielded a better range of data, although obviously if there is little data available, this ought to have been more carefully factored into the conclusions they reach (or some sort of comparative or comparable survey could have been cited to indicate possible patterns or results).

TIP

 Not all disciplines or research outputs have a clear methodology, but that doesn't mean to say that there isn't one. Take literature, for example. It might seem that analysing a text (especially one printed perhaps hundreds of years ago by a well-known author) doesn't require a methodology. But EVERY publication and piece of research has a methodology, even if this is simply consulting primary texts or manuscripts in a dusty archive. So, dig a little deeper to find the methodology. Did the researcher use primary texts, and if so, which editions? Were the texts published or unpublished? Did the researcher consult diaries, letters or personal anecdotes, and if so, are they reliable? Which theoretical frameworks did the researcher use (e.g. linguistic, historical, Marxist, psychoanalysis, feminist etc.) and were these appropriate?

The methodology obviously directly correlates with the types and quality of evidence that the researcher(s) cite in support of their argument and findings, so this is the next aspect of your reading and your next line of critical thinking and evaluation.

Critical question 5: how good is the evidence?

This is likely to be the biggest single area of critical analysis and evaluation, simply because it is likely to yield the most insights into the validity of the author's argument and findings. After all, nobody can dispute the finding that 2 + 2 = 4, but if the evidence is less clear-cut (as is often the case), this can be subjected to critical analysis and interrogated. Indeed, even if the evidence appears compelling, we might still want to question it to see whether the means by which it was obtained (the methodology) was sound. Evidence can take numerous forms, but the most important (ranked from most reliable to least reliable) are as follows:

1) Primary evidence such as data, statistics, quotes from interviews, primary texts, archival material and the results of experiments.

There are numerous questions that need to be asked here to assess the validity of what, on the face of it, might appear valid, indisputable evidence. Some key areas to think about include:

- Is the amount of data adequate? If the research is quantitative, is the sample big enough to be representative?

- Are the results compelling enough to lead to a sound conclusion? The closer you get to a 50:50 split in the results, the more uncertain you can be as to what conclusions can be drawn, whereas something which is, say, 80:20 is much more compelling. For example, let's take the 2016 Brexit referendum in the UK. To claim that it is the 'will of the people' and a democratic choice to leave the European Union based on 52% voting to leave is not compelling. Similarly, since only 67.3% of those eligible actually voted in the 2019 UK General Election, and of those only 43.6% voted Conservative (Uberai et al., 2020), it is surely untenable to say that the Conservative Party was democratically elected when 48.8% of the electorate voted for other parties.

- Is the data presented in a way that is accurate and unbiased? For instance, take the following two graphs which illustrate the same increase in car prices. There is a clear authorial bias in the graph on the right in favour of exaggerating the increase, whereas the graph on the left is more neutral:

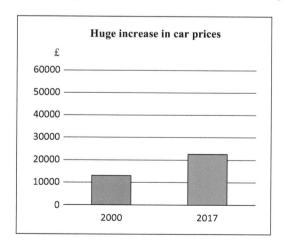

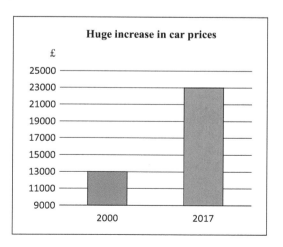

- In the case of data, quotes and interviews, has the author been selective in 'cherry-picking' what best suits their argument (less convincing material may be buried in the transcripts in the Appendix)? Are the questions deliberately constructed to lead the interviewees towards certain answers (problem with the methodology)? Is the sample size adequate? Has the researcher favoured particular participants from particular locations, professions, ethnicities, genders, classes or occupations? Is this problematic (again, an underlying methodology problem)?

- When quoting from primary texts, are they in themselves unbiased and reliable? In some cases, quotes from primary sources, documents and witnesses might be unreliable owing to censorship, press bias or other, personal, economic, social or cultural pressures.

- In the case of seemingly objective scientific experiments, were they conducted rigorously? Were the results reproducible or one-offs? Was enough data collected (again, underlying methodology issues here)?

2) Secondary evidence such as data, statistics, quotes and results from research undertaken by others in the past.

- Old data, especially that which is significantly out of date, should be treated as above, but with additional suspicions regarding its relevance and applicability to contemporary situations. The world changes rapidly, and so data and results quickly 'date'. For instance, in economics and management, data that is pre-2008 should be treated with particular suspicion, as although it may have been rigorous at the time, its applicability post-credit crunch/global economic downturn is highly questionable. Even in disciplines that may be considered somewhat static (such as Greek philosophy or Shakespeare studies), old material and evidence should be treated cautiously. Such disciplines are frequently subject to academic trends that may now be outdated, superseded, or considered dubious. In literature, for example, scholarship has been informed by various 'schools' of thought such as Formalism, Structuralism, Deconstruction, Psychoanalysis, Feminism and New Historicism. Consequently, some research may have been unnecessarily or detrimentally influenced by such approaches, the like of which may not, in hindsight, be the most productive or reliable. So, treat appeals to past evidence with caution, especially where it is used to inform the present (which may be a very different situation).

- Treat quotes, even from old primary sources and historical/literary texts, with caution – they were written in the context of their own unique cultural, political and ideological circumstances, so these factors need to be considered when relying upon them to prove an argument in the present.

- Be wary of appeals to authorities. Just because some famous professor, renowned expert or revered text said it doesn't make it right, especially if it was said some time ago. The Bible and the Koran are cornerstones of religious culture and command the authority of supposedly being the word of God, yet that doesn't make them infallible or true. Past scientists and key cultural or intellectual figures, meanwhile, have often been proven incorrect. For example, Darryl F. Zanuck, Head of Twentieth Century Fox Studios, claimed in 1946 that videos would only be popular for six months because people would become 'tired' of them and that even the 'television won't be able to hold on to any market it captures after the first six months. People will soon get tired of staring at a plywood box every night' (Pogue, 2012). Researchers will often venture into the realms of the theoretical and rely upon appeals to authorities when they either lack current data/information, or they are working very much on the boundaries of knowledge. Indeed, famous authorities may be appealed to despite their lack of knowledge in a specific area. Pythagoras, for instance, may be a key authority in respect of triangles, but he was no expert when it came to geography as he was a key advocate of the idea that the earth is flat. All appeals to authority, then, need to be treated with caution and healthy scepticism.

- Check whether the research has been selective in what old studies they have cited. Has the study omitted research that contradicts their argument, and if so, why?

3) Testimonials

Testimonials are often viewed as convincing as they provide a seemingly impartial human touch. For instance, how many of us have looked at testimonials online before making a major purchase? Indeed, online shopping often puts a great deal of store on providing testimonials from previous shoppers, good or bad, to give the appearance of honesty and transparency – especially since this evidence is likely to be more believable than the usual 'spin' associated with marketing and advertising. But what place do testimonials have in academic articles and sources?

- Testimonials need to be treated with a great deal of suspicion as they are not necessarily based on objective truth. They often provided a one-sided, biased or flawed opinion that lacks the robustness of data.

- Testimonials often omit key information, either because of bias or human emotions (e.g. prejudice, having an axe to grind, anger, hatred, or even extreme satisfaction or approval), so they are not necessarily infallible or trustworthy sources.

- Testimonials can be an incredibly valuable source of evidence, especially in the humanities and social sciences, as they can often provide evidence which cuts through the 'official' version of events. However, do bear in mind the above caveats and think carefully about why the person may have offered their opinion in the first place. Did they have something to gain from it? Were they selective in discussing their experiences? How was their testimony elicited? Is the testimony from an expert or a witness? These latter testimonies can be more valid, but still need to be treated with suspicion and critically evaluated.

- Be especially careful if the researcher bases their argument upon generalisations drawn from testimonies. This is an unlikely scenario as it is deeply flawed, but keep an eye out for it nonetheless.

4) Theories

If the researcher(s) adopted a purely theoretical approach, it is worth interrogating the validity and applicability of these theories. One of the main problems with theoretical approaches are their lack of grounding in reality, but there may also be problems with the theories themselves. Freudian psychoanalysts, for instance, might be too preoccupied with the Oedipal complex to fully understand the causes of depression, whilst radical feminists might overlook the fact that a preoccupation with the 'male gaze' ignores or sidelines the existence of a 'female gaze'. Further questions you may want to ask include:

- How open/explicit is the author about their theoretical perspective? Is it hidden, explicit or implied?

- Is the theory outdated/superseded by new theories?

- Has the theory been disproved via practical, 'real world' research?

TIPS FOR ANALYSING EVIDENCE

 Be wary of evidence that is especially striking, unusual or dramatic. Question whether it is really unusual or whether it is merely presented as such.

 Be critical of arguments that rely too much on secondary evidence or theory, unless the purpose of the research is purely speculative or very much on the boundaries of what is known or feasible.

 Always investigate from where the evidence came. Don't assume that it is the starting point for your analysis – go a little further back.

 Have findings been replicated? Several studies broadly coming to the same conclusion are more convincing than a one-off.

Critical question 6: are there any rival causes?

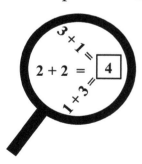 After considering the validity of the evidence, it's vital that you at least consider if those results could have been caused by, or arrived at via, an alternative route or phenomenon. As you can see in the icon on the left, at a most basic level, this is a little like acknowledging that whilst $2 + 2 = 4$, it is also entirely possible that $3 + 1$, or $1 + 3$, or even $5 − 1$ could also have accounted for the result being 4. But considering rival causes can be equally applied to some of the most significant, challenging and seemingly indisputable problems of our time. Let's take global warming. There is more or less a consensus now that the planet is warming up, but what is causing this? Most scientists point to increased levels of carbon dioxide in the atmosphere (leading to the 'greenhouse effect'), but there are rival explanations such as increased solar activity (notably sunspots and solar radiation), changes in ocean currents and even cosmic rays. So always subject any results you find to analysis (using your knowledge of the subject) to see whether they could have resulted from something else. Some things to think about when considering rival causes include:

- Rival causes are a plausible interpretation, different from that of the original researcher, explaining why a certain outcome occurred.

- Rival causes need to be plausible rather than improbable and should be underpinned by subject knowledge/knowledge of methodologies.

- Try looking at the research and its findings from multiple perspectives. For instance, if the researcher explains that the heroine of the novel is driven mad because of being oppressed by her patriarchal husband, try also thinking that she may have been driven mad as a result of the inequalities in capitalist economies or wider patriarchal attitudes that oppressed the husband just as much as the wife. Maybe you could also explain her madness through a psychoanalytical perspective by examining the role of her abusive mother or father.

- There's rarely only one explanation or cause for anything, so always consider the alternatives. As M. Neil Browne and Stuart Keeley observe, ensure that you consider whether the situation warrants consideration of 'the cause or a cause' (2015, p.142).

- Creating, explaining or at least considering rival causes is a valuable skill to acquire. It shows that you have a thorough, wide-ranging and perceptive knowledge of the subject and its implications, and that you have the technical and/or theoretical/methodological knowledge of alternative approaches.

- The identification of rival causes illustrates flaws in the original argument, methodology and results. In theory, the fewer you can find, the better.

TIPS FOR CONSIDERING RIVAL CAUSES

 Rival causes may be discussed by the researcher(s) themselves, either extensively or in a footnote. Check to see whether rival causes are acknowledged. If the author does not acknowledge any rival causes, that can be an oversight you can critique.

 If the researcher does discuss rival causes, ask yourself whether their rejection of them is legitimate. Has the author discussed the rival causes openly, or have they been 'hidden' in a footnote? If so, why have they done this?

 As a person with dyslexia, you should be able to excel at thinking about rival causes. As a 'big picture' thinker, your dyslexia will enable to make connections between ideas and recognise interconnections and 'unusual relationships' much more readily than someone without dyslexia, so play to this strength and get thinking about those alternative explanations (Eide and Eide, 2011, p.105).

C) The argument

After considering the reasons, motivations, research problem, methodology and results, the next issue to consider is how valid the argument is and whether it is based on fallacies.

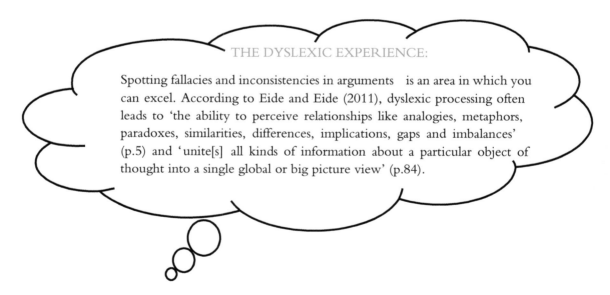

THE DYSLEXIC EXPERIENCE:

Spotting fallacies and inconsistencies in arguments   is an area in which you can excel. According to Eide and Eide (2011), dyslexic processing often leads to 'the ability to perceive relationships like analogies, metaphors, paradoxes, similarities, differences, implications, gaps and imbalances' (p.5) and 'unite[s] all kinds of information about a particular object of thought into a single global or big picture view' (p.84).

There are several questions you might want to ask to evaluate arguments critically. Some require subject-specialist knowledge (which you will gain from your lectures and wider reading), but others are more concerned with how writers present their ideas. Fallacies are flaws in an author's argument and reasoning, and there are many different types, each with variously impressive or catchy-sounding names. The German philosopher Arthur Schopenhauer once suggested that 'it would be a very good thing if every trick could receive some short and obviously appropriate name, so that when a man used this or that particular trick, he could at once be reproved for it' (Paul and Elder, 2012, p.6). This is what has happened, and as such, there exists a multitude of names for fallacies, and there are entire books and websites devoted to explaining and exploring them. There is no room to delve into them too deeply here, and what is more, there are many often needless overlaps between fallacies. Some key questions and fallacies you need to consider when analysing an argument, however, are as follows:

Critical question 7: are there any areas of ambiguity?

Ambiguity leaves room for multiple interpretations, misinterpretations and a lack of clarity. This can be accidental (if the author has not been rigorous enough in their reasoning and editing) or deliberate (to obscure shortcomings in their ideas, research and argument). Your job is to keep an eye out for these and use them as openings for your critical analysis and evaluation. Ambiguity can arise because of sloppy or misleading use of nouns, verbs, adjectives and adverbs, misplaced or inappropriate pronoun references, a lack of coherence, sloppy reasoning or a lack of justification for the ideas being advanced. Even things which appear to have great clarity and are seemingly unambiguous can be highly ambiguous. Let's take Tony Blair's famous mantra of 'education, education, education', which was how he outlined his priorities for office in 1997. On the one hand, the repetition seems to reinforce the centrality, precision and clarity of the message. It is surely unambiguous. But on the other hand, what does education actually mean? Yes, his priorities meant that spending on education rose by 5.1% per year between 1999 and 2010 (Chowdry and Sibieta, 2011, p.1), and yes, the number of teachers rose and exam results improved (Lupton and Obolenskaya, 2013). But the obsession with standards, frameworks and targets engendered a culture of 'teaching to the test', which is not necessarily education, and of course, the introduction of university tuition fees has turned students into consumers and education into a commercial marketplace. Indeed, what is education anyway? The *Oxford English Dictionary* defines education in no fewer than four ways:

1) The process of receiving or giving systematic instruction, especially at a school or university.

2) The theory and practice of teaching.

3) A body of knowledge acquired while being educated.

4) Information about or training in a particular subject.

To which of these definitions was Tony Blair referring? Or was he referring to all of them? The mantra is ambiguous, despite his very deliberate attempt at not being so.

In *The Power of Babble* (1992), Norman Soloman gives a telling, insightful and even alphabetically structured parody of how ambiguous language can be used in an attempt to be persuasive. Can you see how many areas of ambiguity there is in this sample passage?

> America is back, and bipartisan – biting the bullet with competitiveness, diplomacy, efficiency, empowerment, end games, and environmentalism, along with faith in the founding Fathers, freedom's blessings, free markets and free peoples, and most of all, God (quoted in Browne and Keeley, 2015, p.47).

As you can probably see, nearly every single word here is ambiguous and open to innumerable interpretations. One person's competitiveness is another person's sloth, one country's notion of diplomacy is another country's idea of reckless unilateralism, so this passage has little to recommend it in terms of clarity and would certainly be unacceptable as a piece of academic writing. Obviously, not all of what you will read will be this problematic, but you will undoubtedly come across aspects of ambiguity, behind which the researchers might be hiding all sorts of holes in their argument. Keep an eye out for them, investigate them and subject them to analysis and critique.

TIPS FOR IDENTIFYING POTENTIAL AMBIGUITIES

 Identify and scrutinise key terms and phrases.

 Which of these are adequately or inadequately defined?

Do they possess alternative, potentially problematic definitions?

 Are they ambiguous within the specific context of the argument/subject?

 Does equivocation occur – i.e. does the author use a key term or meaning of a word in one place but then change to an alternative meaning elsewhere, thus potentially changing the argument or interpretation?

Critical question 8: does the author rely upon assumptions or generalisations?

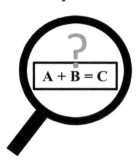 Making generalisations might seem rather vague and unscholarly, but researchers often make them as a way of either exploring the implications of their research findings or as a way of proving their argument as a result of the necessarily restricted and representative nature of sampling and testing. It is, after all, impossible to seek everyone's opinion or test things hundreds or thousands of times, so informed generalisations sometimes have to be made, often as a result of having to make pragmatic decisions based on sample size, the breadth of the research and the randomness of the sampling pool. However, as indicated in the icon on the left, you need to question whether the generalisations the researcher(s) makes are indeed valid – does A + B really equal C? Assumptions, meanwhile, occur when anything is taken for granted. Assumptions can be fairly obvious – like the assumption that education is a good thing (it might not be – it could be a form of indoctrination which, instead of opening people's minds, manipulates them), or that people use cars because public transport is inconvenient (maybe it's more the case that public transport is too expensive). But assumptions can be aligned with political, moral, ethical or religious considerations and beliefs or even as a result of biology or gender. For instance, there is often an assumption that girls like dolls and that the melting of the ice caps is bad. Maybe some girls actually prefer model cars, and maybe the melting of the icecaps is simply nature's way of rebalancing or compensating for the warming climate. Like in the film *The Day After Tomorrow* (2004), it could reverse global warming and bring about a new ice age.

TIPS

 Question whether the general conclusions reached are sound based on the sample size. There may be problems with the methodology, but moreover, the author's argument will be flawed as it will be based on generalisations.

 Keep an eye out for deflective language or diversions that indicate that there is no need to explore, interrogate or prove an argument because it is obvious. Examples of this often occur around words such as 'obviously', 'clearly', 'naturally', 'of course', appeals to common sense or what everyone is supposed to know (e.g. as we all know, as is well known etc.) or the superiority of modern thinking (e.g. clearly things have moved on, fortunately we are no longer in the dark ages etc.).

Critical question 9: are there appeals to popular opinion, beliefs or emotions?

 Although often restricted to tabloid newspapers and the right-wing media, appeals to popular opinion can occasionally find their way into academic writing, so keep an eye out for them. Popular opinion is precisely that – opinion rather than fact – so unless it is the object of analysis, treat it with the healthy suspicion and scepticism it deserves. Meanwhile, anything that relies upon belief systems or emotions ought to be treated with a similar degree of suspicion. This is most prevalent in historical documents or scholarship from the past, which may be entirely coloured by religious belief (either as a result of the views of the author, because of censorship, or because of the opinions of the intended audience). Even today, as George Yancy (2011) has argued, religious bias has caused considerable problems in American scholarship, particularly in respect of scientific rejections of creationism. Academics can be guilty of appealing to the emotions. For instance, if an author spends a great deal of time explaining and emphasising the atrocious conditions of refugees but offers little in the way of hard evidence or a solution to the problem, he/she could be accused of appealing to emotion rather than making a sound, logical and well-reasoned argument. Children and the elderly are easy targets because of their vulnerability, so keep this in mind if the author is dealing with these subjects.

Critical question 10: are there false causes or dilemmas?

A false cause occurs when a researcher assumes a cause–effect relationship (as indicated by the equals sign on the left), yet the cause is not necessarily what led to the effect. For instance, an author could attribute the impressive sales of Byron's poems in the early nineteenth century to the way in which he became a celebrity and courted controversy to remain very much in the public eye. Yet this cause (publicity and celebrity)–effect (high sales) is dubious because Felicia Hemans, a contemporary of Byron (whom very few people have even heard of today), often enjoyed higher sales but without the fame and celebrity status. Meanwhile, a false dilemma presents a problem in which there appear to be only two alternatives (as indicated by the fork in the icon). Interrogate and subject to critique anything which seems to offer only two possibilities, as there is often a third or even fourth possibility (especially in the humanities). Use your subject knowledge to think of other avenues and possibilities. This is something which you may well excel in, given that individuals with dyslexia are often talented in 'see[ing] phenomena from multiple perspectives, using approaches and techniques borrowed from many disciplines', figuring out problems and perceiving patterns (Eide and Eide, 2011, p.84).

TIP

Fallacies such as false causes and dilemmas can very easily lead to another fallacy – the slippery slope. The slippery slope fallacy can occur when a chain reaction of erroneous reasoning results from an initial erroneous reason or fallacy. Suppose an author bases their argument on an initial fallacy. In that case, the entire argument becomes fallacious, thus leading to a wrong conclusion. Slippery slope fallacies can also occur when authors make unjustified, unwarranted or even conjectural leaps from one point to another, even when the initial reason, cause or dilemma is valid.

Critical question 11: is the author biased?

Again, you might not think that academics would fall foul of this fallacy, but they sometimes do. Let's take the example of Duncan Wu, a respected academic and biographer of the essayist, critic, painter and philosopher William Hazlitt. In this biography, *William Hazlitt: The First Modern Man* (where Wu's bias can be said to be indicated in the very title), Wu claims that Hazlitt is Romanticism's 'most articulate spokesman', 'a highly gifted percipient of political sketches' and 'by far the best prose stylist' of his age (p.xxii). These are very grand claims indeed, yet at the time, Hazlitt was subjected to immense vilification and was heavily criticised throughout his life – with some justification. Between 1817 and 1830, as Wu himself concedes, 'there was not a single Tory journal that did not carry at least one article condemning him as an infidel, a Jacobin, and a whoremonger' (p.xxv). Yet Wu largely glosses over any criticism with praise, even at one point seeming to excuse the fact that Hazlitt nearly allowed his son to drown because of his absentmindedness. Wu prefers to depict Hazlitt as a 'doting father' instead (p.220). Elsewhere Wu appears to applaud Hazlitt's rather unfair attacks on Coleridge (with typical gusto, he describes one of his most vicious as a 'thumper' and a 'tour de force' [p.222]). Wu's bias towards Hazlitt seemingly knows no bounds, and he frequently invents conversations for which there is no historical record. He is also far too forgiving of Hazlitt's conduct. Indeed, in a review of Wu's biography, Martin (2010), for instance, cites the example of 'Hazlitt's knocking down a better player at fives by way of smashing his head with his racket' and criticises Wu's depiction of such behaviour for being 'airily implied to be a form of "release" for a man who in the subsequent sentence is described as "sensitive"' (p.323). As this rather extreme example illustrates, keep a lookout for bias and subject it to criticism if you feel it undermines or jeopardises the credibility of the author's argument and evidence.

This is a short example of the most common fallacies you might encounter, but there are many more. Indeed, there are entire books and websites devoted to fallacies, the most useful and informative of which are:

BOOKS

Paul, Richard, and Elder, Linda, (2012) *The Thinker's Guide to Fallacies: The Art of Mental Trickery and Manipulation.* Sonoma: Foundation for Critical Thinking.

Bennett, Bo, (2015) *Logically Fallacious: The Ultimate Collection of Over 300 Logical Fallacies.* Sudbury, MA: Archieboy Holding, LLC.

WEBSITES

https://literarydevices.net/fallacy/
http://commfaculty.fullerton.edu/rgass/fallacy3211.htm
http://writingcenter.unc.edu/handouts/fallacies/

Critical question 12: are the conclusions valid?

The conclusion is the main argument the author wants us to take away from what we have read. But is the conclusion reached fully justified? Does the data or other evidence the author has cited back up the conclusion? Some conclusions are easy to spot as being questionable. Small samples or highly unrepresentative data collection, for example, lead to less than convincing conclusions, especially when there are narrow margins. However, some invalid or questionable conclusions are less easy to spot and can hinge upon flaws in the logic of the writer's argument. Let's have a look at 2 examples and examine each in turn:

1) Reintroducing a penalty for truancy would reduce the number of school absences in this country. Therefore, we should reintroduce the penalty.

This conclusion is probably invalid because:

- It's derived from only a single premise (that reintroducing the penalty would reduce truancy).
- It's assumed that reducing truancy is a good thing (obviously it is, but the case is not made for this in the paper).
- Truancy is statistically quite rare, so maybe it isn't worth it.

2) Television campaigns aimed at reducing alcoholism have mostly failed. Therefore, a new campaign called 'Alcoprevent' is highly unlikely to be effective.

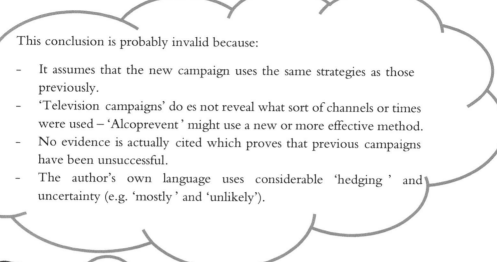

This conclusion is probably invalid because:

- It assumes that the new campaign uses the same strategies as those previously.
- 'Television campaigns' do es not reveal what sort of channels or times were used – 'Alcoprevent' might use a new or more effective method.
- No evidence is actually cited which proves that previous campaigns have been unsuccessful.
- The author's own language uses considerable 'hedging' and uncertainty (e.g. 'mostly' and 'unlikely').

TIPS FOR LOCATING AND ASSESSING CONCLUSIONS

 Be wary of inferred or speculative conclusions which are subtle and based on progressive (and possibly flawed) reasoning rather than explicit signposting. Some language to look out for in this category includes words and phrases such as 'possibly', 'might', 'perhaps', 'we can surmise that', 'we may be able to', or even rhetorical questions which seem to place the burden of forming a conclusion on the reader.

 When assessing the validity of a conclusion, it is worth bearing in mind that there are likely to be a host of other complicating factors which lead to questionable conclusions, most of which can be identified using the previous critical questions.

Critical thinking on a spectrum

You should aim to use as many of the above critical questions as possible to fully analyse everything you read and encounter – leave no stone unturned in your quest to exhibit to the marker that you can use insight and critical thinking skills to understand and interrogate information fully. It can be useful to think of the depth of these skills on a spectrum, ranging from fairly basic critical thinking to more advanced. Let's see what this might look like in regards to the following two topics:

Least critical → **Most critical**

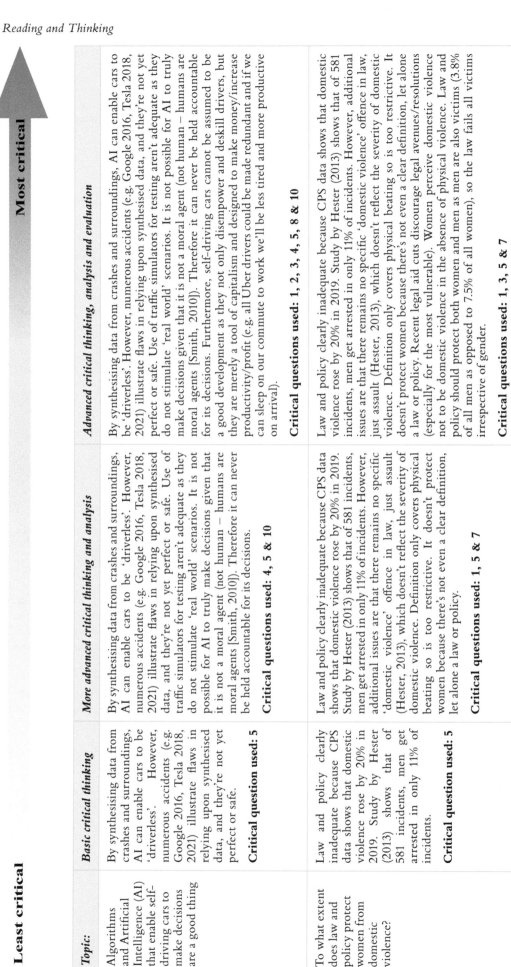

Topic:	Basic critical thinking	More advanced critical thinking and analysis	Advanced critical thinking, analysis and evaluation
Algorithms and Artificial Intelligence (AI) that enable self-driving cars to make decisions are a good thing	By synthesising data from crashes and surroundings, AI can enable cars to be 'driverless'. However, numerous accidents (e.g. Google 2016, Tesla 2018, 2021) illustrate flaws in relying upon synthesised data, and they're not yet perfect or safe. **Critical question used: 5**	By synthesising data from crashes and surroundings, AI can enable cars to be 'driverless'. However, numerous accidents (e.g. Google 2016, Tesla 2018, 2021) illustrate flaws in relying upon synthesised data, and they're not yet perfect or safe. Use of traffic simulators for testing aren't adequate as they do not stimulate 'real world' scenarios. It is not possible for AI to truly make decisions given that it is not a moral agent (not human – humans are moral agents [Smith, 2010]). Therefore it can never be held accountable for its decisions. **Critical questions used: 4, 5 & 10**	By synthesising data from crashes and surroundings, AI can enable cars to be 'driverless'. However, numerous accidents (e.g. Google 2016, Tesla 2018, 2021) illustrate flaws in relying upon synthesised data, and they're not yet perfect or safe. Use of traffic simulators for testing aren't adequate as they do not stimulate 'real world' scenarios. It is not possible for AI to truly make decisions given that it is not a moral agent (not human – humans are moral agents [Smith, 2010]). Therefore it can never be held accountable for its decisions. Furthermore, self-driving cars cannot be assumed to be a good development as they may not only disempower and deskill drivers, but they are merely a tool of capitalism and designed to make money/increase productivity/profit (e.g. all Uber drivers could be made redundant and if we can sleep on our commute to work we'll be less tired and more productive on arrival). **Critical questions used: 1, 2, 3, 4, 5, 8 & 10**
To what extent does law and policy protect women from domestic violence?	Law and policy clearly inadequate because CPS data shows that domestic violence rose by 20% in 2019. Study by Hester (2013) shows that of 581 incidents, men get arrested in only 11% of incidents. **Critical question used: 5**	Law and policy clearly inadequate because CPS data shows that domestic violence rose by 20% in 2019. Study by Hester (2013) shows that of 581 incidents, men get arrested in only 11% of incidents. However, additional issues are that there remains no specific 'domestic violence' offence in law, just assault (Hester, 2013), which doesn't reflect the severity of domestic violence. Definition only covers physical beating so is too restrictive. It doesn't protect women because there's not even a clear definition, let alone a law or policy. **Critical questions used: 1, 5 & 7**	Law and policy clearly inadequate because CPS data shows that domestic violence rose by 20% in 2019. Study by Hester (2013) shows that of 581 incidents, men get arrested in only 11% of incidents. However, additional issues are that there remains no specific 'domestic violence' offence in law, just assault (Hester, 2013), which doesn't reflect the severity of domestic violence. Definition only covers physical beating so is too restrictive. It doesn't protect women because there's not even a clear definition, let alone a law or policy. Recent legal aid cuts discourage legal avenues/resolutions (especially for the most vulnerable). Women perceive domestic violence not to be domestic violence in the absence of physical violence. Law and policy should protect both women and men as men are also victims (3.8% of all men as opposed to 7.5% of all women), so the law fails all victims irrespective of gender. **Critical questions used: 1, 3, 5 & 7**

Reading online and critical thinking

As highlighted in the previous chapter, increasing amounts of reading and research in preparation for your essays are now undertaken online. Aside from the issues associated with navigating between online sources, concentration and depth, I also mentioned the need to get to **authentic, authoritative and academic** information and sources as quickly as possible and be extra disciplined when it comes to critical thinking. This is because the online world is awash with 'fake news' and disinformation. As Dr Doofenshmirtz in an episode of the Disney comedy *Phineas and Ferb* puts it:

> Anyway, I've done lots of research for the past, you know, few hours, and I found out that most people will believe anything they read. And I know it's true because, you know, I...I read it online somewhere. (*Phineas and Ferb*, 'Ferb Latin/Lotsa Latkes', 2011)

Material you find in monographs and journal articles has usually undergone rigorous, professional, academic peer review before being accepted for publication, but information on the internet is often unchecked, unsubstantiated and cannot necessarily be relied upon. As such, you need to delve into the critical questions above all the more carefully.

TIPS FOR CRITICAL THINKING WHEN ONLINE

 Use websites and Wikipedia ONLY as a way of getting background information/an overview (or as dual assistive reading). Always look for references to scholarly publications and read those for valid information.

 Always check out the credentials of the author/organisation to ascertain what their agenda might be.

 Stick primarily to the websites of recognised, legitimate, trustworthy organisations (e.g. the WHO, the UN, government websites, Greenpeace, UNICEF etc.). However, ALWAYS treat these websites as the 'sales pitch' or 'shop window' for these organisations – they are all promoting their cause/agenda or vision of the world so need to be critically interrogated in the same way as we did with Linda Elder's definition of critical thinking at the beginning of this chapter. As evidence of a position/ideology/vision, they are great, but as trustworthy sources of information, treat them with caution.

 Do not use YouTube videos as academic evidence/sources. Again, use them for background information if you like (as with dual assistive reading), but they are NOT academic or trustworthy.

 Avoid 'op-ed' articles – they are the published opinions of people/internet influencers/journalists. They are not FACT!

 Above all, treat websites as stepping stones to more reliable information. As with hyperlinks, always get to the authentic, authoritative and academic information and sources as quickly as possible.

Summary

- Remember, nothing is ever perfect – subject everything you read to scrutiny and interrogation.

- Don't feel you need to use all the critical questions above, as some are more suited to specific disciplines than others. However, keep all of them in mind when reading so as to maintain an open, interrogative and perceptive mindset.

- Don't interrogate/critically evaluate everything – focus on what is relevant to your course/assignment task and only analyse what has been chosen as important and relevant based on your initial skimming and scanning activities.

- Practice makes perfect. If time allows, practise doing online critical thinking exercises.

- Remember – analysis and evaluation will enable you to get top marks. In university essays, depth of analysis beats breadth of knowledge every time, especially in the humanities.

Bibliography

Balmer, Nigel, Denvir, Catrina, Miles, Joanna, Patel, Ash, and Smith, Marisol, (2013) 'In Scope but out of Reach? Examining Differences between Publically Funded Telephone and Face-to-face Family Law Advice', *Child and Family Law Quarterly*, 25(3), pp.253–269.

Bennett, Bo, (2015) *Logically Fallacious: The Ultimate Collection of Over 300 Logical Fallacies*. Sudbury, MA: Archieboy Holding, LLC.

BestPlaces, (2017) *Sonoma, California*. Available at: http://www.bestplaces.net/voting/city/california/sonoma (Accessed: 4th February, 2017).

Browne, M. Neil, and Keeley, Stuart M., (2015) *Asking the Right Questions: A Guide to Critical Thinking*. 11th edn. Harlow: Pearson Education.

Chowdry, Haroon, and Sibieta, Luke, (2011) 'Trends in Education and Schools Spending', *Institute for Fiscal Studies*, BN121, pp.1–26.

Eide, Brock L., and Eide, Fernette, F., (2011) *The Dyslexic Advantage: Unlocking the Hidden Potential of the Dyslexic Brain*. London: Hay House.

Elder, Linda, (2015) *Defining Critical Thinking*. Available at: http://www.criticalthinking.org/pages/defining-critical-thinking/766 (Accessed: 1st January, 2017).

Hester, M., (2013) 'Who Does What to Whom? Gender and Domestic Violence Perpetrators in English Police Records', *European Journal of Criminology*, 10, pp.623–637.

Lupton, Ruth, and Obolenskaya, Polina, (2013) 'Labour's Record on Education: Policy, Spending and Outcomes 1997–2010', *Social Policy in a Cold Climate*, 3, pp.1–53.

Martin, Philip W., (2010) 'William Hazlitt: The First Modern Man by Duncan Wu', *The Yearbook of English Studies*, 40(1/2), pp.322–324.

Nzekwe-Excel, Chinyere, (2014) 'Academic Writing Workshops: Impact of Attendance on Performance', *Journal of Academic Writing*, 4(1), pp.12–25.

Paley, William, (1802, 2006) *Natural Theology, or, Evidence of the Existence and Attributes of the Deity, Collected from the Appearances of Nature*, Eddy, Matthew D., and Knight, David (eds.). Oxford: Oxford World's Classics.

Paul, Richard, and Elder, Linda, (2012) *The Thinker's Guide to Fallacies: The Art of Mental Trickery and Manipulation*. Sonoma, CA: Foundation for Critical Thinking.

Phineas and Ferb, 'Ferb Latin/Lotsa Latkes', (2011) Directed by Robert Hughes and Jay Lender. Available at: IMDd (Accessed: 7th July, 2021).

Pogue, David, (2012) *Use it Better: The Worst Tech Predictions of all Time*. Available at: https://www.scientificamerican.com/article/pogue-all-time-worst-tech-predictions/ (Accessed: 15th December, 2016).

The Quality Assurance Agency for Higher Education, (2014) *UK Quality Code for Higher Education: Part A: Setting and Maintaining Academic Standards*. Available at: http://www.qaa.ac.uk/en/Publications/Documents/Framework-Higher-Education-Qualifications-08.pdf (Accessed: 7th July, 2021).

Uberai, Elise, Baker, Carl, Cracknell, Richard, Allen, Grahame, Roberts, Nerys, Barton, Cassie, Sturge, Georgina, Danechi, Shadi, Harker, Rachael, Bolton, Paul, McInnes, Rod, Watson, Chris, Dempsey, Noel, and Audickas, Lukas, (2020) *General Election 2019: Results and Analysis. House of Commons Briefing Paper*, CBP 8749. Available at: https://researchbriefings.files.parliament.uk/documents/CBP-8749/CBP-8749.pdf (Accessed: 7th July, 2021).

Wallace, Mike, and Wray, Alison, (2011) *Critical Reading and Writing for Postgraduates*. 2nd edn. London: Sage Publications Ltd.

Wu, Duncan, (2010) *William Hazlitt: The First Modern Man*. Oxford: Oxford University Press.

Yancy, George, (2011) *Compromising Scholarship: Religious and Political Bias in American Higher Education*. Waco, TX: Baylor University Press.

4   Getting Ready to Write

'Decoding' the Assignment, Overcoming Writer's Block and Structuring your Essay

'Dyslexics think differently. They are intuitive and excel at problem-solving, seeing the big picture, and simplifying. They are poor rote reciters but inspired visionaries'.

(Dr Sally Shaywitz, *Overcoming Dyslexia*)

Essay genres

Depending upon which discipline you are studying, you will be expected to write in a variety of genres. Research into student work submitted to the universities of Warwick, Reading and Oxford Brookes has shown that the most popular genres are as follows:

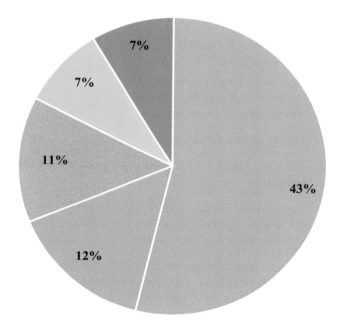

■ Essays ■ Methodology Recounts ■ Critiques ■ Explanations ■ Case Studies

Given that the essay is by far the most popular genre students are asked to use (in the case of humanities subjects, essays account for 83% of student writing and in the social sciences, 56% [Heuboeck, Holmes, and Nesi, 2007, pp.7–10]), this book primarily considers essays. The core principles which follow, however, work just as well for the other genres you are likely to encounter, especially critiques, literature surveys, reports, case studies, problem questions and methodology recounts (the basic structure of which – introduction, theory, design/methods, results, discussion and conclusion – map accurately onto the Christmas Cracker template below). Before writing your essay, however, you need to figure out what you actually need to do and what your markers are looking for. Accurately decoding the assignment title/question is a crucial part of this.

Decoding the assignment task/question

A problem lots of students seem to encounter, irrespective of whether they have dyslexia or not, is difficulty in accurately decoding the question/assignment task. This may sound very straightforward, but many students tend to either misunderstand or even ignore key directions in the task. This means that they don't fully answer the question and thus fail to get the marks they are capable of achieving. The secret to accurately decoding an essay question or assignment task is to spend time reading it and deciphering every single word.

DOI: 10.4324/9781003190189-4

TIP

 Lecturers often spend a great deal of time thinking about the wording of assignment tasks and questions, so you should do the same.

When approaching your assignment task/question, try to break it down into three main components as a way of fully understanding what you are required to do. The three main components are as follows:

1) Content/topic keywords

These are the non-negotiable parameters of the subject and are key topics or themes you simply have to include. Typical content/topic keywords might be things such as 'the Data Protection Act', 'global warming', 'the European Union', 'gravity', 'urban planning', 1956, 'feminism', 'Shakespeare', 'the Suffragette Movement' etc., etc. It may sound astonishing, but lecturers frequently encounter essays that simply do not focus upon, or in some cases, even include, the key content or topics requested in the essay title. Ensure you identify these crucial keywords and topics first and never lose sight of them whilst writing and thinking about the essay.

2) Activity keywords

Put very simply, this is what you have to do. However, this is not as simple as it might seem. Many of these keywords either appear vague, do not seem to indicate what you are required to do accurately, or even overlap. Below is a table of common activity keywords and their meanings for guidance:

Keyword	Meaning	Position on Bloom's Taxonomy
Analyse	Subject the topic(s) to scrutiny, identify strengths/weaknesses/flaws and possibly gaps in knowledge. Construct an argument based on the analysis.	Analysis/synthesis/evaluation
Argue	Make a persuasive case for or against something.	Analysis/synthesis/evaluation
Comment on	Identify and write about salient points and possibly criticise/evaluate.	Analysis/synthesis/evaluation
Compare/ Contrast	Identify important points and highlight their similarities/differences through analysis. Construct an argument based on your observations.	Analysis/synthesis/evaluation
Critique	Analyse, subject the topic(s) to scrutiny, identify strengths/weaknesses/flaws and possibly gaps in knowledge. Construct an argument based on the analysis.	Analysis/synthesis/evaluation
Define	Identify and express the meaning of something, including the limitations of such definitions (be concise).	Knowledge/comprehension/application
Describe	Identify and outline the key points.	Knowledge
Discuss	Examine and analyse the issues, evaluate them and construct an argument which is critically perceptive.	Analysis/synthesis/evaluation
Evaluate	Examine and discuss the pros and cons of something with a view to coming to a verdict, position and argument.	Analysis/synthesis/evaluation
Examine	Subject the topic(s) to scrutiny, identify strengths/weaknesses/flaws and possibly gaps in knowledge. Construct an argument based on the analysis.	Analysis/synthesis/evaluation
Explain	Describe and give reasons for something.	Knowledge/comprehension/application

Illustrate	Find and use examples to explain something.	Knowledge/comprehension/application
Indicate	Identify and explain the important points and signal likely outcomes/reasons/conclusions/arguments.	Knowledge/comprehension/application
Justify	Provide reasons or evidence for a proposition or argument.	Knowledge/comprehension/application/
Outline	Identify and describe the main features of something.	Knowledge
Review	Critically examine something, usually something which has been done before, to appraise its strengths, weaknesses, limitations and arguments. Possibly recommend actions.	Analysis/synthesis/evaluation
State	Describe the main points.	Knowledge
Summarise	Identify and describe the main ideas.	Knowledge/comprehension/application

Notice the frequency with which the word 'argument' crops up here. Some students are unclear as to what an argument actually means. While it is true to say that an argument often means a dispute, a row, or opposing ideas in conflict, an argument in academic writing means your point, contention or interpretation. The argument is what you want to prove.

TIP

 It is critical that you understand what you should do in order to answer the question/assignment task properly. For example, if you take 'discuss' merely to mean talk about and describe rather than critically examine and evaluate/present an argument, you're unlikely to score high marks because you won't have provided the analytical criticality being asked of you.

3) Focus or limitation keywords

These restrict your options and tighten the focus of the essay. Typical focus or limitation keywords or phrases might include things like 'contemporary', '1940–80', 'two poems', 'any three plays of your choice', 'recent developments', 'North America', 'studied on this course' etc. It's relatively easy to gloss over these words in favour of the activity or content keywords, but it's vital to take them into consideration if you are to get things right. Two examples from my own experience illustrate how things can go wrong if you neglect the focus or limitation keywords:

 In my own A Level Geography exam, I had to write about a river delta. The focus/limitation keyword was 'UK river delta'. I overlooked this and wrote about the Mississippi river delta instead – with disastrous results!

 A student of mine recently scored poorly in their literature essay on the poet Philip Larkin. The question asked the students to refer to TWO poems of their choice. The student wrote about SIX poems. Consequently, they were unable to go into the depth that was required to achieve good marks.

It can be tempting to overlook the focus or limitation keywords in an attempt to impress the marker with your breadth of knowledge. Take the example above of the student who wrote about six poems instead of two. This was highly commendable in terms of ambition, and the student clearly wanted to impress with their range of knowledge. But such breadth does not allow for depth, analysis and evaluation, which, as we have seen, are more likely to score highly at university.

With the three parameters above in mind, let's have a look at some sample assignment titles and decode them:

1) Critically evaluate the contention that cities are central to sustainable forms of development.

Activity keywords:
Analyse, subject the topic(s) to scrutiny, identify strengths/ weaknesses/ flaws and possibly gaps in knowledge. Construct an argument based on analysis.

Topic / content keyword:
This may need defining.

Focus / limitation keywords:
Note that it's very easy here to focus on development (which needs carefully defining) without actually picking up on the fact that such development needs to be 'sustainable'. Not only does this also need defining, but you will need to decide what forms of sustainable development are the most important / most sustainable. Again, this is testing your ability to prioritise information and make judicious selections which can be subjected to analysis, evaluation and argumentation. Don't be tempted to think that talking briefly about as many types of sustainable development as you can will earn you better marks. Depth of analysis beats breadth of knowledge every time.

2) 'Ordinary people, simply doing their jobs, and without any particular hostility on their part, can become agents in a terrible destructive process' (Milgram, 1974). To what extent do Milgram's obedience studies and later evaluations of them by other researchers support this claim?

Focus/limitation keywords:
Although the quote comes first, this is not the main topic, it is the focus/ point of reference. Do not get distracted by this topic just because it's a quote and appears first. The issue of Milgram's obedience studies and its later evaluations gets answered in RELATION to this topic, NOT the other way around.

Activity keywords:
Examine and analyse the issues, evaluate them and construct an argument which is critically perceptive and assesses how far Milgram's obedience studies and later evaluations support / do not support the claim.

Topic/content keywords:
Note that the topic is NOT ordinary people / violence – the question is primarily asking you to assess Milgram's obedience studies and its later evaluations.

3) Using at least ONE theoretical framework, discuss some of the key challenges involved in implementing information systems.

Topic/content keywords:

Note that the task is looking at the implementation of information systems, not simply information systems.

Activity keyword:
Examine and analyse the issues, evaluate them and construct an argument which is critically perceptive.

Focus / limitation keywords:

The question requires just ONE theoretical framework, so don't be tempted into thinking that discussing two or more will impress your marker. They are testing your ability to consider one theoretical framework deeply and perceptively, but also to decide on which theoretical framework is most suited to this particular issue – so there are more skills tested here than you might think. Notice also that you are asked to discuss 'some' of the 'key challenges'. Again, this is not only testing your ability to present an analysis, argument and knowledge, but is testing your ability to decide on what the 'key challenges' are. This tests your judgement and ability to prioritise information.

THE DYSLEXIC EXPERIENCE:
Unpacking and deciphering assignment questions / tasks can be especially tricky for students with dyslexia because of 1) cognitive overload, 2) the tendency to jump ahead and make connections which aren't necessarily there or wanted, or 3) because of limited attention span. This is often made worse by vagueness in the wording, or multiple questions / topics within the question (which can easily send you off on tangents or merely confuse). This is the only part of the book where I will tell you to SLOW DOWN, as this is the one place where your strengths in making quick connections and seeing the 'big picture' can actually work against you.

TIPS

 Try to match up the activity keywords to your mark scheme – this will indicate the weighting of the assignment.

 Don't be afraid to ask your lecturer, tutor or Writing Centre advisor for clarification.

 If in doubt, go for analysis, evaluation and argument, as these are the highest-scoring skills.

 Keep description to a minimum. Remember, first-class marks are at the top of Bloom's Taxonomy.

 Try to slowly eliminate unnecessary words to leave only the activity, topic/content and focus/limitation keywords. Once you have found them, then rebuild the question to check you haven't missed anything. In the case of questions with long quotations, try reading the question without the quotation first.

 Be especially careful when you spot words like 'not', 'no' and 'none', as well as prefixes such as 'a', 'un' and 'dis', as these can change the meaning of the question/assignment task and can potentially send you off on the wrong tangent.

 Be careful when you spot double negatives such as 'not atypical' (which means typical) and 'not false' (which means true). These words increase your cognitive overload and obscure meaning.

 Look out for, and critically address/interrogate, assumptions within questions. In question 2 above, it is assumed that implementing information systems involves 'key challenges'. Is this really the case? Critically unpicking these assumptions enables you to a) fully dissect and understand the assignment task, and b) add additional layers of critical thinking to your response, thereby maximising your marks.

Overcoming writer's block – translating thought into essays

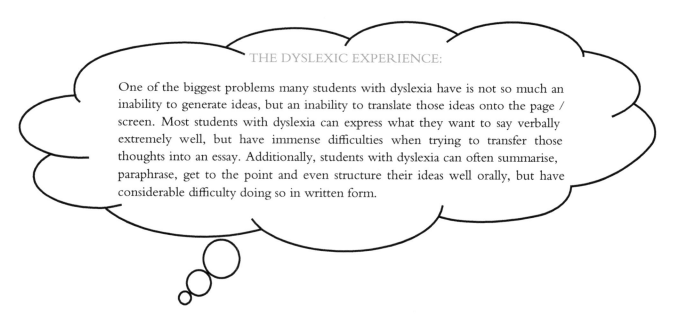

THE DYSLEXIC EXPERIENCE:

One of the biggest problems many students with dyslexia have is not so much an inability to generate ideas, but an inability to translate those ideas onto the page / screen. Most students with dyslexia can express what they want to say verbally extremely well, but have immense difficulties when trying to transfer those thoughts into an essay. Additionally, students with dyslexia can often summarise, paraphrase, get to the point and even structure their ideas well orally, but have considerable difficulty doing so in written form.

Writer's block is something that can affect all writers, professional or otherwise, dyslexic or non-dyslexic. What normally happens is that the writer is unable to write anything new or be creative. Clinical psychologists

Barrios and Singer (1981) claim that writer's block occurs owing to 1) excessive self-criticism, 2) fear of comparison with others, and 3) lack of motivation (either external, such as praise, or internal, such as self-doubt). All of these very often apply to individuals with dyslexia – perhaps more so than people without dyslexia. However, as mentioned earlier, individuals with dyslexia have additional hurdles to overcome when writing.

Writer's block often affects students with dyslexia, not because of any lack of ideas/creativity, but owing to difficulties translating those ideas into a structured essay. This issue arises because the dyslexic brain is optimised for explorative searching/creativity rather than exploiting/sequencing information. The task of converting ideas into written, structured academic language is overwhelming. It's as if a roadblock is erected between you and the computer screen/page. Actually, as we saw in chapter 1, it's not one roadblock but a collection of hurdles. As you encounter the various processes involved in translating thoughts into an essay, greater and greater hurdles need to be overcome. Again, we can think of this situation as like a cone of successive hurdles which increasingly restricts information and the ability of the working memory to produce the essay. As indicated by the red arrows below, with each restriction, information can be 'lost'/forgotten:

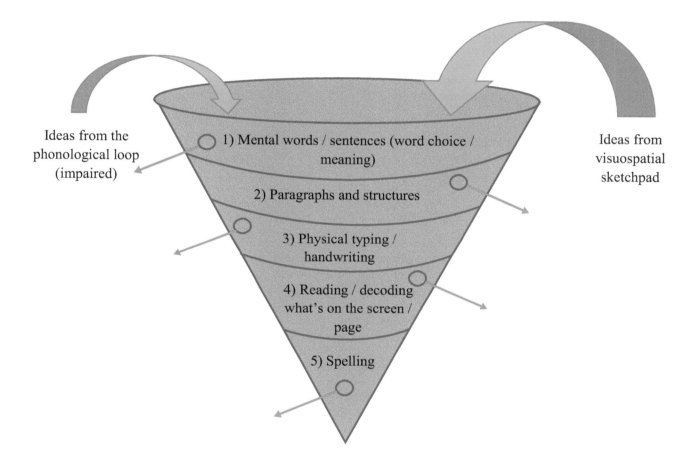

The problem is that none of the above hurdles occurs in isolation. Whilst trying to translate thoughts into essays, your limited working memory is also being bombarded with a thousand other stimuli which takes up precious resources. These additional stimuli can be as varied as background noise, talking, someone digging up the road outside, social media distractions, social media/email notifications, your computer wanting to update, apps crashing/wanting to update, phone calls etc. All of these require decoding and processing by the working memory, take up limited resources, and increase the likelihood of information or ideas being lost/forgotten.

The bottom line for helping with writer's block if you have dyslexia is to REMOVE as many of these hurdles and distractions as possible. The more you remove, the more your creativity has room to work and the more you can utilise your strengths in visual, 'big picture' thinking, creativity and search/exploration to piece together your ideas and translate them into words/sentences/paragraphs and essays. Depending on what particular difficulty you are encountering, here's some suggestions as to how to overcome these problems:

Writer's block and pushing through the dyslexia roadblock

1) Take a complete break and try not to think about the essay/assignment task.

2) Take a semi-productive break (I particularly recommend lying down!). Here, rather than doing something completely different, allow your mind to wander at will around the broad topic. This 'mind wandering' allows unconnected thoughts to merge and structures to be experimented with in non-language-based ways. Even for individuals without dyslexia, this has been proven to be effective (Barrios and Singer, 1981). At first, eliminate as much language as possible – just think in images/concepts. This can often result in ideas coming together, and suddenly you might think of a key point, argument, idea, theory, or even phrase/sentence. Keep a notepad next to your bed or wherever you are doing this exercise, so you don't forget it. It doesn't matter if the idea will be at the beginning, middle or end of the essay – just get it down and worry about structure later. If no thoughts, connections or phrases come to mind, just try to relax. As you become more relaxed and creative, try to have conversations with yourself. Ask yourself questions, try to coach yourself into putting things in order or inventing/constructing key phrases (even if it's just two words). Then write them down. If you don't feel inspired to write, continue 'mind wandering' until more ideas come to your mind. Once you have one, or maybe two ideas, you should be able to write a few sentences or, most probably, a paragraph. That might not sound a lot, but it's progress and every word written gets you one step closer to your goal, even if it lacks any structure at this point.

3) Draw pictures: try to put your ideas into a Mindmap or grid. Try to put your argument/ ideas into a diagram so that you can see/make connections.

4) Eliminate distractions. As mentioned before, owing to limited cognitive load/working memory, you need to prioritise. Be brutal and get rid of anything that is using precious cognitive resources. Turn off emails, shut out social media, eliminate noise (especially anything verbal), turn off your phone, remove anything distracting. Some people find 'white noise' through earphones can help, but given that it's another sensory and thus cognitive load, it can be distracting.

5) Take lots of breaks. Try writing for very short bursts, then take a break, look out of the window, make a cup of tea, then return. In fact, don't be afraid to take a nap occasionally! Research has shown that taking naps helps your memory process and consolidate information (enhancing your ability to recall what you have learnt), but it also plays a crucial role in boosting attention, creativity and productivity (McDevitt et al., 2018) – all good things if you have dyslexia. Napping only becomes a problem if it's for emotional reasons (e.g. procrastination, mental health issues etc.), in which case seek help from a medical professional or counsellor.

6) Try eliminating all sense of structure or logic to allow your creativity/'big picture'/search strengths to flourish. Just write random ideas, quotes, passages, phrases, or even words (free writing). These can act as either the building blocks of the essay or as prompts for you to remember to come back to things. Later, you can build your essay around these notes via copying and pasting and filling in the gaps (a little like painting by numbers). Don't forget, a strength of dyslexia is making connections, thinking holistically and making predictions. If you write down clues/random ideas, no matter how imperfect, you'll often find they are enough to stimulate writing.

7) Try telling a friend/dyslexia tutor what your essay is about and record yourself. Often, what comes out of your mouth can be the basis of your paragraphs, and your key points can often make excellent thesis statements (see pp.77–79) or topic sentences for the beginnings of paragraphs (see pp.99–103).

8) Use speech to text software to get your ideas down – worry about translating them into an academic essay later.

9) If you write plans, try copying and pasting the key points from your plan and use them as topic sentences for your paragraphs (again, see pp.99–103).

10) Try to think of your essay as like a wall, made up of hundreds of bricks. Every brick you put on the wall is progress and one piece of the jigsaw. Ten bricks (a sentence), however random, is better than none at all and is progress. Don't punish yourself.

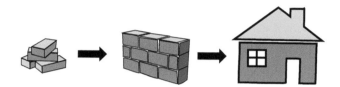

11) Utilise periods when you're experiencing a blockage productively. Getting your references in order (e.g. putting them alphabetically, making sure the commas and dates are in the right place etc.) or proof-reading what you have already written takes up less creative and cognitive load, but you'll be getting SOMETHING done whilst you get your head around trying to write. Remember, nobody can work flat out, or even productively, all of the time. Try to align tasks to the three-tier model of intensity outlined below:

- **Full intensity:**
  Maximum concentration and productivity, very creative, but can't be sustained for long periods.

- **Medium intensity:**
  Not full throttle but you get some decent work done. Consider doing some rough writing/free writing, proofreading, reading around the subject etc. Don't be too creative or punish yourself if you don't produce substantial work.

- **Low intensity:**
  Low energy/mood and no creativity. Instead of using this time for checking social media, chatting with friends, shopping or procrastination, do low-intensity/low-productivity activities which still contribute, however minimally, to building the wall. Typical exercises might include writing references, finding new sources, taking library books back, formatting your essay, writing headers etc., etc.

12) Try to think as visually as possible (to tap into your dyslexic strengths). This is what the rest of this book is about. Align your ideas with the visual templates in the following sections and chapters.

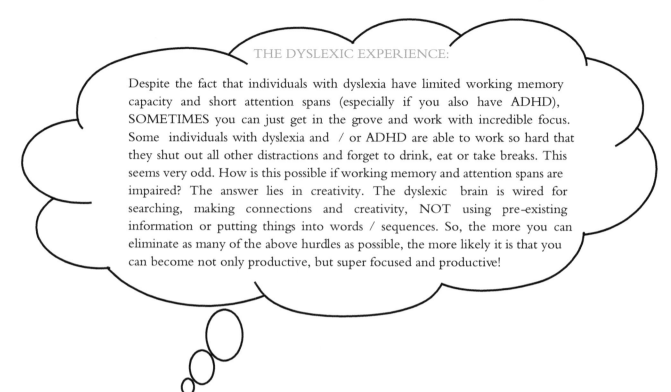

THE DYSLEXIC EXPERIENCE:

Despite the fact that individuals with dyslexia have limited working memory capacity and short attention spans (especially if you also have ADHD), SOMETIMES you can just get in the grove and work with incredible focus. Some individuals with dyslexia and / or ADHD are able to work so hard that they shut out all other distractions and forget to drink, eat or take breaks. This seems very odd. How is this possible if working memory and attention spans are impaired? The answer lies in creativity. The dyslexic brain is wired for searching, making connections and creativity, NOT using pre-existing information or putting things into words / sequences. So, the more you can eliminate as many of the above hurdles as possible, the more likely it is that you can become not only productive, but super focused and productive!

TIPS

 No matter where you are in the writing process, if you have an idea write it down. If you don't, you'll forget it owing to your short-term memory.

 Don't forget to press 'save' at frequent intervals or have some sort of system to find/store notes. Writing random ideas might tap into your creativity/'big picture'/search strengths, but your short-term memory/attention span weakness will often mean that you'll forget or lose your thoughts if you don't get them down quickly and remember to save them!

 Don't beat yourself up if you have a bad day and don't get much done – you will probably find that the following day things will click better for no apparent reason. That's just the way things are, and it affects all writers, not just those who have dyslexia.

Structuring your response: the Christmas Cracker

Having considered what you are required to do, and having looked at ways of getting round any dyslexia 'roadblocks' that might be preventing you from writing, let's turn our attention to structuring your response. One of the best ways of thinking about the overall structure or 'big picture' of your essay is to think of it as resembling the shape of an upturned Christmas Cracker. This will enable you to think carefully about the overall aims of the various components of your essay and map these onto an easily memorised and recognisable shape. The shape of the cracker provides you with a template for knowing what to write about, when and where.

Most essays, irrespective of their genre, have the following components and shape:

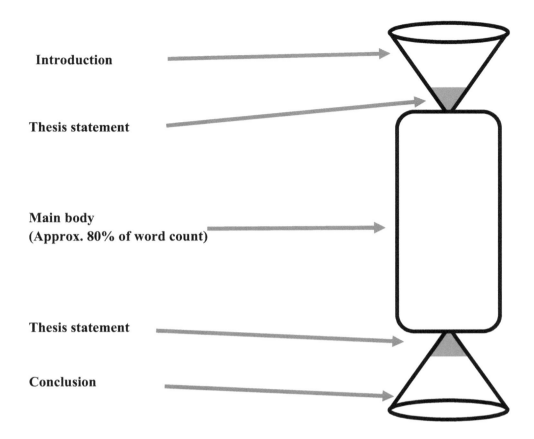

The remainder of this chapter will consider each of these components in turn.

How to write effective introductions

The introduction is the 'shop window' of the essay, and it is essential to get it right if you want to make an excellent first impression with your marker. Despite this, introductions are often the part of the essay which students tend to neglect, thinking that they don't really matter. While it is certainly true that introductions do not generate as many marks as the main body of the essay, a good introduction allows you to demonstrate your ability to:

- Get straight to the point.
- Write concisely.
- Immediately identify the most important issues or key problem.
- Identify and articulate, in a summarised form, an argument or stance.
- Identify the significance of the issue in relation to the discipline and the world.

These will all be credited.

With these principles in mind, let's evaluate the following introduction to an essay:

'Working class culture was shaped predominantly by the factory, the pub and the housing estate.' Discuss.

Eric Hobsbawm makes the point that before the advent of the new socialist parties, the working classes had always been referred to in the plural rather than singular. This essay will initially address the need for a plural term, address the lack of homogeneity, and the differing groups that constituted the 'working classes' (1987, p.118). It will examine how the factory, pub and housing estate shaped the culture of this non-generic group and broaden this investigation to include working conditions, entertainment and living conditions. It will end by looking at the increasing segregation from the bourgeoisie, the development of a political identity (engendered by self-help groups and Trades' Unions) and the emergence of a class struggle.

This introduction is not without merits, especially in the sense that the essay structure is outlined well and there is a good use of vocabulary. However, what sense do we get of the importance of the issue and its background? Do we get an insight into whether the student agrees or disagrees with the statement in the assignment brief? And what is the significance of the fact that there is an issue surrounding whether the working classes are referred to as singular or plural? Is this even relevant? The student merely repeats a substantial amount of the assignment brief/title, and while they outline what they are going to talk about, there is no sense of an argument, direction, or an attempt at evaluating the original contention or the evidence.

So, what is the best way to structure your introduction? And when should you write it? One of the crucial things to get right when writing your introduction is to move from the 'big picture' to specific detail and an argument (the thesis statement). In other words, you should be able to map the progression of your ideas in your introduction onto the cone-shaped top of the Christmas Cracker template. The following 4 key elements will help you achieve this and can be mapped onto the template as follows:

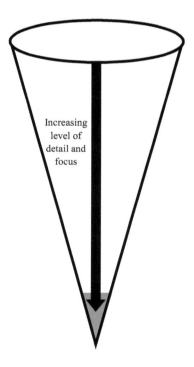

Identify broad topic/subject area: demonstrate that you have accurately interpreted the essay question/assignment task and what it asks you to do in relation to the topic. Provide an interesting 'hook' for the reader by integrating a 'headline-grabbing' fact, quote or piece of data.

Why it's important/what's the problem? Ask yourself why this subject or question even matters. Being able to show that you have an appreciation of the significance of the topic in relation to its context, world events, research developments and the like will gain you marks.

Background: highlight significant events, changes, laws, policies or research within which you are situating your argument. Indicate the major issues at stake and their areas of controversy/counter-claims. Indicate the 'gap' in knowledge, especially if the introduction is to a research-based essay or dissertation.

Argument/thesis statement: articulate a clear, concise thesis statement which answers and addresses the key elements of the question or provides a solution while outlining the main structure of your argument.

Let's now have a look at another introduction to see how it moves from the 'big picture' to a detailed focus/argument. In this example, you can clearly see how it maps onto the cone-shaped top of the Christmas Cracker template:

Despite many changes to law and policy relating to domestic violence, criminal justice responses still fail to provide adequate protection for those who are experiencing or are at risk of abuse. Discuss.

Domestic violence is a major problem in the UK, if not globally, and its prevalence is far from decreasing. National estimates as to the number of women who experience such abuse within the last year range from 7% (Office for National Statistics, 2014, p.1) to up to 10% (Women's Aid, 2006). 77 women were killed by their partners or ex-partners in the UK in 2012–13 (ONS, 2014) and as many as 63.4% of separated women reported experiencing 'violence' from ex-husbands, with 59% experiencing an 'assault' (Painter and Farringdon, 1998, p.263). Equally, data suggesting that 25% to 30% (ONS, 2014) of women suffer domestic violence in their lifetime, with up to one billion experiencing it internationally (United Nations, 2014), back up this trend. These statistics show that the continuing prevalence of domestic violence is incontestable – women are clearly not being protected from abuse in practice. Law and policy relating to domestic violence has running through it an explicit goal – protecting victims of abuse (Home Office, 2014, pp.3–6). Yet if these victims are receiving unsatisfactory protection, the adequacy of the criminal justice response to domestic violence must be called into question. This essay critically examines whether those who experience or are at risk of abuse are actually protected in practice. It argues that despite considerable changes in law and policy in this area, the criminal justice system's response is insufficient, despite there being multiple ideological, patriarchal and media-driven forces which also contribute to the proliferation of domestic violence, and which are obviously altogether extraneous to the criminal justice system.

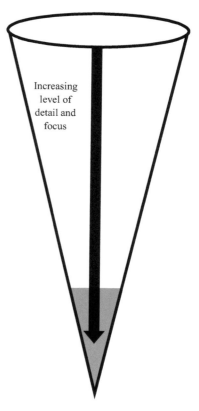

Increasing level of detail and focus

This is a much better introduction – it moves from the general topic (UK/global situation and national estimates of abuse) to the specific problem (deaths, violence and assault), highlighting the key issues at stake, why they are important, and how they relate to the law and policy. The student then specifically addresses the inadequacies of the present system. In other words, rather than talking in general, unspecific terms, they tackle the question head-on by articulating a clear standpoint and argument. The thesis statement, as we shall see, specifies what that argument will consist of and how the essay will proceed.

Writing effective thesis statements

The thesis statement is a vital component of the introduction as it gives the reader/marker a clear sense of what your argument is and how you are going to address the question. An effective thesis statement does three key things:

1) Summarises the aims of the assignment in one or two concise, powerful and informative sentence(s).

2) Directly addresses the assignment title by stating a position or making a claim.

3) Directs your whole line of analysis, argument and thought and clearly, yet concisely signposts the structure of your argument.

Students often write thesis statements that are far too long and descriptive. The example above on working-class culture is a prime example of this. Notice how the student spent quite a lot of time suggesting that 'this essay will', 'it will' and 'it will end by'. While it is good to signpost to the reader your argument, it's important not to over-signpost. Note how in the example on domestic violence, the student does not waste time saying what the essay will discuss but simply incorporates it seamlessly into the argument:

Clear engagement with the assignment task.

This essay critically examines whether those who experience or are at risk of abuse are actually protected in practice. It argues that despite considerable changes in law and policy in this area, the criminal justice system's response is insufficient, despite there being multiple ideological, patriarchal and media-driven forces which also contribute to the proliferation of domestic violence, and which are obviously altogether extraneous to the criminal justice system.

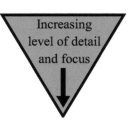

Increasing level of detail and focus

Clear and specific argument throughout.

Clear indication of the structure of the additional aspects of the main argument. It's clear from this that whilst the argument will be about the insufficiencies of the criminal justice system, the student will talk about each of the following in turn:

1) Ideological forces
2) Patriarchal forces
3) Media-driven forces

This thesis statement provides a focused and concise argument that introduces a perceptive, relevant range of issues which not only address the assignment task but go beyond it by suggesting that there are other 'forces' which have a profound impact upon the problem of domestic violence. Notice too how even the thesis statement moves from the general 'big picture' ('this essay critically examines') to the specific areas of protection, the insufficiencies of the criminal justice system's response, and the various forces which are external to the criminal justice system which exert influence on the growth in instances of domestic violence.

In the following example, the structure of the argument and essay is even more evident:

Discuss whether internet surveillance is justifiable and to what extent it ought to be expanded, controlled or prohibited.

Clear engagement with the assignment task.

This paper assesses the current global trends towards greater internet monitoring, the key ethical concerns such developments raise and the extent to which the threats fostered, developed and distributed via the internet are legitimate. Overall, the paper argues that government surveillance programs such as the PRISM project operated by the NSA are not legally or ethically defensible and should be discontinued. They invade civil liberties, lead innocent people to suffer unfair punishments, and ultimately fail to protect the citizens that they are designed to safeguard.

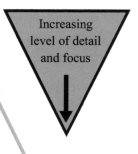

Increasing level of detail and focus

Clear indication of the structure of the argument.

Clear and specific argument.

In this example, it's absolutely clear that the student will provide:

1) An assessment of current global trends and the key ethical concerns these raise.

2) An argument that government surveillance programmes are indefensible because:

    -   They are an invasion of civil liberties.

    -   They lead to unfair punishments for innocent people.

    -   They fail to protect citizens.

The thesis statement is clear and precise, yet notice that at no point does the student resort to direct, inelegant signposting or detailed description such as 'I will then consider', 'finally I will discuss' or 'in the second section of the essay'. If you embed your structure into the argument, there is no need for this sort of signposting, and it saves you valuable words which could be used more productively in analysing and evaluating the issues at stake.

Students often ask, when is the best time to write the introduction and thesis statement? The obvious answer is to write it first. Indeed, given that people with dyslexia often struggle with organising their thoughts, there seems to be compelling reasons why introductions, and particularly thesis statements, ought to be written first:

'[T]he purpose of the thesis statement is to give order both to the reader and to the writer. It does this by clearly stating the central claim that a piece of writing will try to prove. The writer takes care in the thesis statement to articulate a paper's argument as precisely as possible, and this precision clarifies and focuses the direction of the paper' (Moore and Cassel, 2011, p.8).

'The reason for placing a thesis statement in the first paragraph of an essay or as soon after it as possible is that the sooner you state it the more likely you are to remain aware of your main idea and the less likely you are to wander from that idea as you write' (Miller, 1980, p.6).

While it is undoubtedly true that a thesis statement will prevent you from 'wandering', it's not necessary to write the entire introduction first, as you may not know the full significance of the topic or its background until you are some way through the essay. It's often better to write the introduction at the end (at the same time as the conclusion) and have a very rough, draft or even bullet-pointed thesis statement to work from so that you have a plan to which you can stick.

TIPS FOR EFFECTIVE INTRODUCTIONS

 In your opening sentence, get straight to the heart of the matter by identifying the key aspects of the topic and what the question/assignment task is asking you to do. Don't use long-winded, predictable or narrator-like openings such as 'the existence of the solar system has fascinated mankind since the dawn of time'. Instead, get straight to the point by saying something like; 'the extent of the solar system and its development since the "big bang" is controversial and many scientists dispute whether God or the "God particle" had any involvement in its creation'.

Don't copy and paste or repeat words or phrases in the introduction directly from the question/assignment task. Instead, show how you are addressing the question/assignment.

 Keep your introductions concise – aim for around 5–10% of your total word count.

 Double-check that what you say and promise to do in your thesis statement actually matches the argument and key points you make in the main body of the essay.

 Avoid giving lengthy definitions in your introduction. Unless they are significant for understanding the background, avoid putting in too many quotes or references from secondary sources.

The main body

Having thought about the introduction, the next section of the Christmas Cracker essay structure is the main body. This should comprise around 80% of your word length and is the most significant section of the essay to generate marks, articulate your argument, and critically analyse and evaluate your material. The main body consists of paragraphs, each of which makes one key point that addresses the assignment task/question. But with so much material to work with, how do you organise your thoughts, paragraphs and key points? Which do you put first and why? How do you prioritise information and arguments? And even more problematically, how do you structure an essay which requires you to compare ideas? How can you avoid 'wandering' off course, repeating ideas, or even going around in a circle, even though you may have a thesis statement which provides you with a loose direction?

One of the first problems you come across when writing the main body of an essay is the challenge of linearity. While good writing needs to be linear and clearly organised, our thoughts are not!

'Everything about writing is deliberately fabricated…A key feature of conventional writing is its linearity…This linearity is of profound significance, because neither experience nor contemplative thought comes naturally in linear form. Contemplation and experience may have no beginning point and no orderly sequence: they can involve simultaneities unavailable on the written line and much more complex patterns of interconnection…Writing, then, is not the report of thought, but the production of a specific type of thought and a specific account of life. It is important not to lose sight of linearity's artifice and cultural specificity…Writing is nothing but an invention, a concoction, an illusion…' (Game and Metcalfe, 1996, p.109).

Nobody's thoughts, then, come out in a 'linear form', and having dyslexia compounds this problem. Thoughts, especially dyslexic thoughts, tend to dart around all over the place, and individuals with dyslexia are the masters of going off on tangents – only returning to (or even remembering!) the main point or idea perhaps hours or even days later! A further challenge to any sense of linearity and structure is actually the technology we use. Irrespective of whether you type or use speech recognition software, computer screens only allow us to see one or two pages of the essay at any one time. Thus the overall structure or 'big picture' disappears either above or below the screen. Obviously, you can scroll up or down, but that means that the section you were previously working on has now also disappeared, so again the 'big picture' simply cannot be viewed in its entirety.

One way of keeping your thoughts on track and thus structure your essay in a logical, sequential manner is to use the Christmas Cracker template. The best way of presenting a logical, compelling argument is to start with principles, definitions and foundations (much as you would if you were building a house) before moving onto specific detail. In trying to prove your argument, then, you move from the general to the specific, from the basics to the more advanced, and from what is known to what is new. This can be mapped onto the main body of the Christmas Cracker as follows:

'Big picture':
Foundations, definitions, principles, theories, key background data etc.

Building the argument:
Evidence, discussion, analysis and consideration of counterarguments.

Argument increasingly specific and proven:
More specific evidence and analysis leading to overall evaluation.

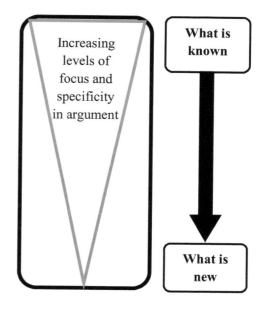

Increasing levels of focus and specificity in argument

What is known

What is new

'Communicative dynamism'

In 1988 Nigel J. Bruce coined the term 'communicative dynamism' as a way of showing how ideas move in a wave pattern from the given to the new across sentences (more on this later). By moving from the given to the new, communication becomes more effective and compelling, and this transition of ideas can also be applied to the essay structure as a whole. By moving from what is known to what is new (your argument and analysis), your ideas will not only come across logically, but they will have 'dynamism' and persuasiveness (Bruce, 1988).

This overall structure holds true for the two key types of discursive essays you are likely to encounter: the discussion essay and the comparative essay. We will look at each, in turn, to demonstrate how the Christmas Cracker template can help keep your thoughts and argument on track:

1) Logical structure for a discussion essay

In a discussion essay, one of the things being assessed is your ability to construct an argument that weaves a logical and coherent course through what may seem like a maze of information and ideas. It can seem difficult to know what to discuss first. Let's take the following as an example:

Assignment task: people respond to trauma in various ways. Discuss and explain why some individuals seem resilient whilst others develop severe post traumatic stress disorder (PTSD). Is it possible to predict how people will respond to trauma?

Possible topics for consideration		
Theories concerning biological differences (between men and women).	Theories relating to individual genetics.	Type of event.
Case studies of victims of 9/11.	Theories of psychological vulnerability.	Not possible to predict how people will respond to trauma – thesis statement.
Competing definitions of trauma.	Family and social networks of support.	Case studies of rape victims.

There are clearly lots of possibilities here, and it would be very easy to lose a sense of overall direction and structure. This is precisely what happens in the following essay plan:

Main body	
Paragraph 1:	Theories concerning type of event (case studies of 9/11 and rape victims).
Paragraph 2:	Critique of studying event type as a predictor of PTSD.
Paragraph 3:	Theories of psychological vulnerability.
Paragraph 4:	Critique of theories of psychological vulnerability.
Paragraph 5:	Theories concerning biological differences (gender).
Paragraph 6:	Critique of theories concerning biological differences.
Paragraph 7:	Role of family and social networks of support.
Paragraph 8:	Not possible to predict how people will respond to trauma.
Paragraph 9:	Competing definitions of trauma.

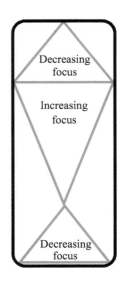

As you can see by the shape of the corresponding red triangles, there are several sequencing and coherence issues here. The student leaps into detailed, specific theory first but then completely separates off the sections which subject the theories to analysis and evaluation. This needed incorporating into the paragraphs that discuss the theories more carefully and smoothly. By structuring the essay as above, it appears very 'blocky' and fragmented. The overall sequence of ideas is haphazard and illogical, and what is perhaps more crucial, the argument and its direction is unclear and insufficiently signposted. Let's now try to map these same ideas onto the Christmas Cracker template by moving from 'big picture' foundations to specific detail:

Main body	
Paragraph 1:	Competing definitions of trauma = not possible to predict how people will respond to trauma because definitions themselves are unclear and disputed.
Paragraphs 2–3:	Theories concerning biological differences (gender) and critique/evaluation = not possible to predict how people will respond to trauma.
Paragraphs 4–5:	Theories of psychological vulnerability and critique/evaluation = not possible to predict how people will respond to trauma.
Paragraphs 6–7:	Theories concerning type of event (case studies of 9/11 and rape victims) and critique/evaluation = not possible to predict how people will respond to trauma.
Paragraphs 8–9:	Role of family and social networks of support = the only plausible theory that can help predict how people will respond to trauma.

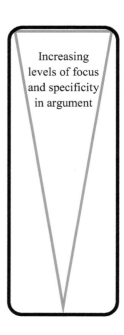

In this version, the structure is much clearer because the analysis, evaluation and argument run throughout each paragraph, building in focus and specificity and moving from the foundations to the specifics. This presents the ideas in a much more logical, less disjointed manner, which slowly adds layers of detail and complexity, thus rendering the argument much more thorough and convincing.

TIPS

When writing an essay plan, ensure that your ideas follow the 'big picture' (given) to detail (new) sequence and present a clear argument that addresses the question.

When editing and proofreading your essay, read the topic sentences of each paragraph to see if you can identify the point each paragraph is making. Do the points move gradually from the general (given) to the specific (new)? If not, re-order them.

 Use the Christmas Cracker template to help keep you on track. By writing with the template alongside your essay (or even writing the essay inside the template, which you can download from the companion website), the gradual narrowing of the red triangle should encourage you to tighten your focus.

2) Logical structure for a comparison essay

Comparison essays require you to evaluate and synthesise competing or different issues and/or two or more theories/perspectives. As such, they are much trickier to construct and require considerable concentration and planning to get them right. The temptation with a comparison essay is to deal first with one side of the argument/issue/piece of literature/theory, and then the other, before arriving at a conclusion in which you present your overall argument and evaluation. This is called a block structure. While it may appear logical, and is a style frequently taught by English for Academic Purposes instructors, this format is fraught with problems. Let's take another essay from the field of psychology to see how the block structure would work:

Assignment task: Psychology and psychiatry differ in several key respects. Compare and evaluate these two forms of treatment from at least two different perspectives.

Possible essay plan for the main body of an essay using a block structure:

Structure	*Block*
Paragraphs 1–2	**Psychology** in relation to: 1) Origins of thought processes. 2) Patient outcomes.
Paragraphs 3–4	**Psychiatry** in relation to: 1) Origins of thought processes. 2) Patient outcomes.
Paragraph 5	Argument and evaluation – which discipline is the best/most successful.

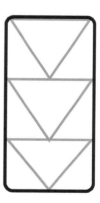

As you can see, this structure is very logical and clear, but in terms of the overall sequence of ideas and, perhaps more crucially, the argument, it is somewhat repetitive and clumsy. It alternates between disciplines and goes back and forth between 'big picture' ideas and detail, thereby failing to synthesise and evaluate the issues holistically. In other words, the 'flow' of the ideas is repeatedly interrupted. The point-by-point or thematic structure is a much better option:

Possible essay plan for the main body of an essay using a point-by-point/thematic structure:

Structure	*Point-by-point/thematic*
Paragraphs 1–2	**Origins of thought processes** in relation to: 1) Psychology AND psychiatry - Incorporate evaluation, analysis and argument.
Paragraphs 3–4	**Patient outcomes** in relation to: 1) Psychology AND psychiatry - Incorporate evaluation, analysis and argument.

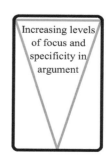

Increasing levels of focus and specificity in argument

The sequence of ideas here 'flows' much more smoothly. Notice that the all-important analysis, argument and evaluation is integrated throughout because what drives the structure is not a 'one step at a time', block consideration of the two forms of treatment, but a thematic appraisal and evaluation through two themes or perspectives. This structure builds a comparative argument into its core, and unlike in the block structure, the direction of travel is always forwards. It moves from the 'big picture' (the origins of thought processes) and then gets more specific and detailed in relation to patient outcomes. It also eliminates needless repetition since the block structure would require you to talk about thought processes and patient outcomes twice (one in relation to each form of treatment), and it eliminates the need for a concluding, evaluative paragraph as the perspectives have been synthesised and evaluated comparatively rather than separated. The point-by-point or thematic structure requires more skill, but it allows for deeper, more incisive analysis and argumentation, the result of which will be higher marks. Let's see what this approach/structure might look like in a sample paragraph that synthesises and critically evaluates two perspectives.

Describe and examine the differences between interpretive and objectivist approaches to social science and evaluate the extent to which these competing schools of thought can be integrated.

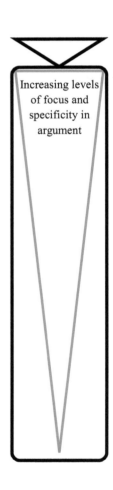

Increasing levels of focus and specificity in argument

While both approaches aim to analyse social behaviour scientifically, seeking integration seems fraught with methodological difficulties which are irreconcilable. In terms of methodologies, interpretive approaches examine and emphasise the importance of subjective individual experience of the world, and as such they take an anti-positivist stance, use qualitative data and argue that the social world cannot be interpreted in the same way as the physical environment (Saunders et al., 2016, Glaser and Strauss, 1967). Researchers with this approach maintain that investigations should be driven by situations rather than theory (Cohen et al., 2000). Objectivists, on the other hand, believe that there is only one true reality and that the world around them is made of 'concrete, factual things' which can be understood through quantitative research (Burrell and Morgan, 1979, p.45). In this sense, objectivists use a similar approach as that of a natural scientist because they both believe that the nature of social and physical phenomena is independent of what Saunders et al. call 'social actors' (Saunders et al., 2016, p.722). Yet arguably it is precisely these 'social actors' which are at the heart of social science as a discipline, and unlike the subjects of 'pure' sciences, they necessarily have values, feelings and other emotional attributes which cannot be measured in the same way as the physical environment (measuring, assessing and understanding the social effects of domestic abuse, for instance, is vastly different to measuring a 'concrete, factual thing' such as divorce rates). Both approaches undoubtedly have benefits and are of value. Yet because of their vastly different underlying methodologies, it appears difficult to see how they can be integrated into the same research project without considerable tensions, since the objectivist approach takes a reductive view of the individual and their experience of society and the other is fraught with concerns over authenticity, replicability and its inherently descriptive as opposed to explanatory findings....

Commentary

- Clear, direct topic sentence which addresses the question, signposts the argument and clearly identifies methodologies as the theme around which the structure of the paragraph will revolve.

- Good evidence relating to methodologies. The phrase 'on the other hand' clearly signposts the differences. Descriptions of the approaches are synthesised around the core issue of methodological differences.

- The analysis and evaluation section deals with methodologies. Note the synthesis – the student compares, contrasts, argues and evaluates around the core theme of methodologies rather than dealing with first one, then the other approach (as in the block structure). This is unfinished here owing to limitations of space, but you can see that the general direction of travel is logical and compelling while synthesising the 'approaches' within an overall evaluation.

The pros and cons of the block vs. point-by-point structures for the main bodies of essays can be summarised as follows:

Structure	Pros	Cons
Block	Clear and logical.	The themes or 'perspectives' are discussed multiple times in relation to each point – can be repetitive.
	Relatively easy to construct.	Doesn't show sophisticated analysis and synthesis to the same extent as the point-by-point structure.
	Fairly easy to incorporate all the features required without wandering off topic.	Too formulaic – lacks 'style'.
Point-by-point	Allows for deeper, more incisive synthesis and analysis.	Harder to manage and keep focus.
	Avoids duplication/repetition of key points.	Key items can become 'lost' within the focus upon themes/perspectives.
	Easier to forge an argument.	

In summary, then, avoid the temptation to adopt a block structure and aim for the greater depth and sophistication offered by the point-by-point/thematic structure. It will be harder to manage, but it will result in higher marks if you handle it correctly. Keep in mind the 'big picture' to detail sequence of ideas/topics, synthesise the opposing perspectives or different subjects into a thematic interrogation and analysis of the issues, and embed a clear argument throughout. Use the main body section of the Christmas Cracker template to guide you.

Planning the main body

Irrespective of whether your essay or dissertation needs a linear or point-by-point structure, careful planning is essential in order to construct and articulate a clear sequence of ideas. As illustrated below, some students just produce a bullet-point list of ideas they want to discuss, and providing it follows the given to new, 'big picture' to detail sequence outlined above, this can work well. A plan for the psychology essay outlined above, then, might look like this:

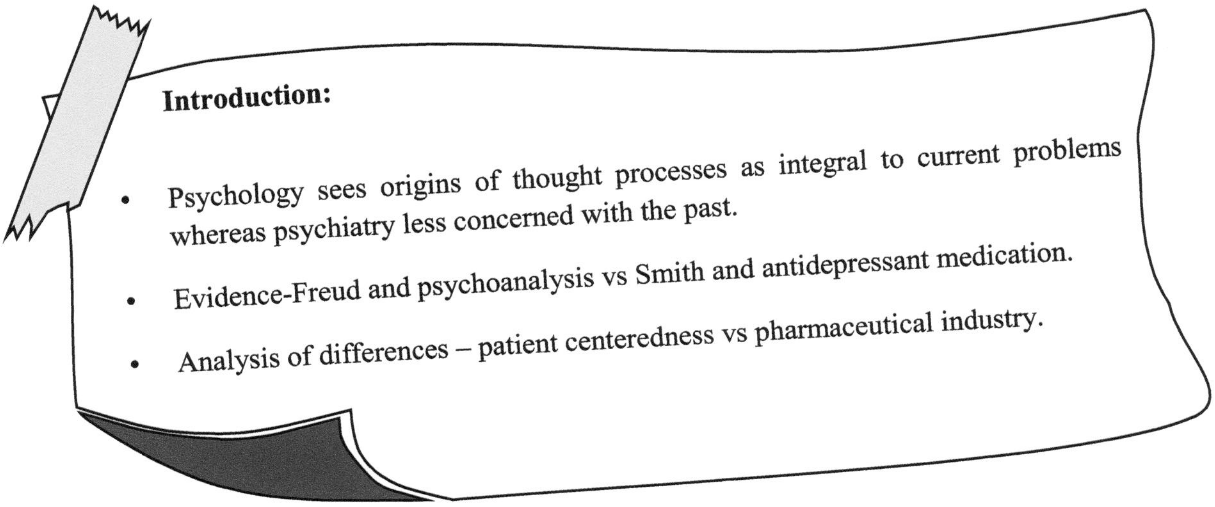

Introduction:

- Psychology sees origins of thought processes as integral to current problems whereas psychiatry less concerned with the past.

- Evidence-Freud and psychoanalysis vs Smith and antidepressant medication.

- Analysis of differences – patient centeredness vs pharmaceutical industry.

Another technique you could try is to use PowerPoint, Prezi or Google Slides to construct a slideshow of your ideas/paragraphs. Use one slide per paragraph and outline the key points, the key pieces of evidence and the key aspects of the argument/critical analysis:

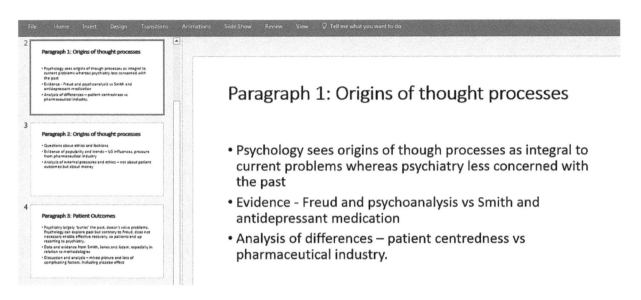

One benefit of using PowerPoint, Prezi or Google Slides is that the slideshow can help you to see if the overall structure makes sense. If it doesn't, you can easily move slides around and replay them until you are happy with the structure. Indeed, you could even try writing the paragraphs themselves onto the PowerPoint and then play them as a slideshow.

Writing effective conclusions

Conclusions are often thought of as something which has to be included just because you can't stop an essay randomly and hope for the best – a little like a handshake at the end of a formal conversation. As such, students often perceive the conclusion as fairly pointless in terms of generating marks but something one has to do so as not to appear rude. Consequently, students often pay little attention to conclusions and invariably just summarise what they have previously said. Conclusions will never generate the same amount of marks as a paragraph within the main body of the essay, but you can make them count by demonstrating how what you have just argued intersects with, challenges or complements current thinking and trends in the field, the discipline or even the world.

TIP

 Remember, there is no need to simply summarise what you have already just said in your conclusion. The marker has just read the essay so knows what you have just said!

A good way of thinking about conclusions is to think of them as an inversion of the introduction. In other words, rather than moving from the 'big picture' to the details and an argument, you do the opposite by going from the argument back out into the 'big picture' – hence the cone shape at the bottom of the Christmas Cracker we saw earlier. An ideal conclusion, then, covers the following key points and looks a little like this:

Reiteration of thesis statement

This doesn't mean simply copying and pasting the thesis statement from the introduction – you need to reword it from the perspective of the argument having been proven.

Summary of discussion

Don't labour this – remember the marker has just read the essay. Simply remind your reader what you have proven.

Discuss implications

Here you start to broaden out into the 'big picture'. Indicate why what you have just discussed matters (to the world or the discipline). Ask yourself, who cares? What needs to change and why? Why does any of this matter?

Signal the future

Point to where things might go next, even if this is merely that more research needs to be done.

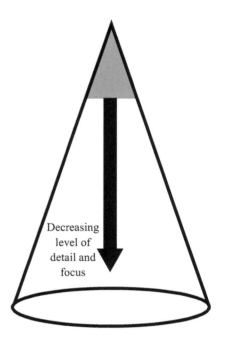

Decreasing level of detail and focus

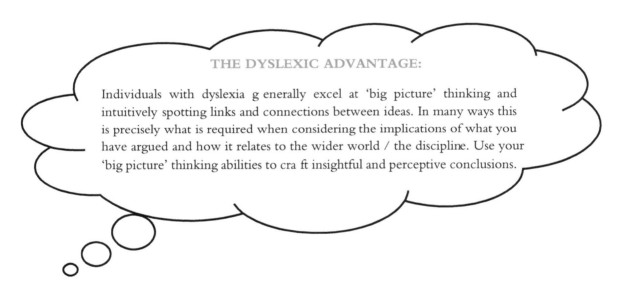

THE DYSLEXIC ADVANTAGE:

Individuals with dyslexia g enerally excel at 'big picture' thinking and intuitively spotting links and connections between ideas. In many ways this is precisely what is required when considering the implications of what you have argued and how it relates to the wider world / the discipline. Use your 'big picture' thinking abilities to cra ft insightful and perceptive conclusions.

Take a look at this conclusion to an essay answering the following assignment task:

An individual's work achievement can be best predicted by their intelligence. Discuss.

In conclusion, it would appear that an individual's work achievement can not only be determined by the individual themselves, but also by many aspects of their working environment. This essay has examined the issues relating to work achievement in 3 different industries and by making reference to appropriate literature. The essay concludes that it is arguable that intelligence is the most important influence on workplace achievement, as it defines the realms of a person's comprehension and therefore the limit of their progress in a professional hierarchy. Nevertheless, current theories on intelligence are so diverse that it is impossible to categorically state its correlation, if any, with work achievement. Therefore, it may be more accurate to suggest that intelligence can best predict the potential an individual has for work achievement, rather than its realisation.

What do you think of this example? Is it good or bad? Does it articulate an argument? Does the conclusion have a logical and compelling structure? Does it follow the guidelines outlined above?

In general, this is a poor conclusion. While it accurately summarises and describes what has been discussed in the essay, it does nothing to explore the implications of the topics/arguments for industry, the discipline or the world. Note also that it repeats too many words from the actual assignment title, which shows that the student has not put a great deal of effort into the conclusion and doesn't really know what to say other than to summarise the content of the main body. Take a look at the following conclusion. This example articulates the implications of the argument and the topic much more successfully and can be mapped onto the cone-shaped bottom of the Christmas Cracker template far more clearly:

To what extent does the rise of the 'knowledge economy' reflect fundamental changes in the nature of capitalism and work?

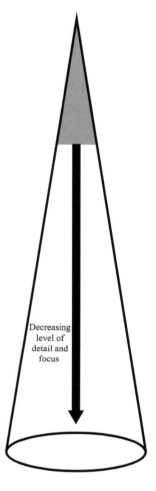

It is clear that in relation to the 'knowledge economy' and its intersection with commodity production, there has been a crisis of mass production and that flexible specialisation is emerging in its place. This essay has argued that a new form of mass market has emerged with 'the fragmentation of style rather than any real "paradigmatic" or fundamental change in consumption which implies a change in production' (Curry 1993, p.108). It appears that mass commodity production and Fordist labour processes are still evident, but production is being relocated to non-western countries to allow advanced economies to concentrate on developing high-technology, knowledge sectors (Giddens 2000). This is a highly contentious issue and has led to suggestions of an international division of labour (Thurow 1997, p.78) which is evidence of capitalist development towards increasing global inequality (May 2000). Thus, the idea that flexible specialisation and the 'knowledge economy' are generalised trends 'obscures the real processes of capitalist development' and, in this instance, commodity production (Curry 1993, p.118). Hence, it seems that theorists supporting shifts in the nature of capitalism are 'merely apologists for the continuing exploitation of the poor in the global capitalist system' (Hull 2000, p.148). In advanced economies, therefore, high technology manufacturing industries constitute 'a declining minority of employment' (Hyman 1991, p.272) and it is evident that these firms 'are capitalist and locked into the imperatives of capitalist accumulation' (Curry 1993, p.119). This phenomenon has been introduced by, and perpetuated by neoliberal politicians, particularly in America, and it can be suggested that globalisation has left many disenfranchised. It is a damning indictment of such processes that many have been left dispossessed and unengaged, and this is largely reflected in recent developments in politics (which is increasingly putting nationalist rhetoric at the fore in response to the perceived threat from the very economic systems neoliberalism has put into place). Understanding this is of paramount importance for global and national security given the rise in rhetoric not seen since the 1930s, and as such clearly more research and understanding is required in the interests of global security and wider economic sustainability.

Notice how the student wastes little time here summarising what has been discussed and quickly proceeds to highlight how contentious the issue is, while linking this to changes in the capitalist economy and the continuing exploitation of the poor. The student then broadens out even further to consider the significance of the issue given that globalisation has left many 'dispossessed and unengaged', thereby linking to contemporaneous political changes, nationalism and global security. In other words, having examined the issues relating to the 'knowledge economy', capitalism and work, the student has stood back from the argument and asked (and then addressed) the 'big picture' questions mentioned earlier – namely 'who cares?' And 'why does any of this matter?' By considering these issues rather than merely summarising what you have already said, you will show a greater awareness of the implications of what you have argued, and this will be credited.

TIPS

   Use the cone shape template of the Christmas Cracker to remind you of the general movement from the argument to the 'big picture' and implications of what you have said.

   Do not copy and paste the thesis statement directly from the introduction.

Try not to repeat/copy and paste phrases from the assignment title/question – use your own words to phrase the key issues under consideration.

 Don't describe what the essay has said or overly signpost how it answers the question – keep the focus on the key issues at stake and their wider implications.

Structuring other genres of academic writing

As mentioned earlier, although the standard essay is the most popular genre of academic writing within Higher Education, you may well encounter other genres, especially if you are studying the sciences, social sciences, or doing a course which requires personal or professional reflection. However, the Christmas Cracker structure still applies. Here's some guidance on how to go about structuring the other main types of essay you may come across:

Scientific/laboratory reports

If you are a science student, you are likely to encounter a mix of genres and assignments (e.g. critiques, design specifications, explanations and case studies), but methodology recounts/laboratory reports will account for over a quarter of your work. Lecturers use lab reports to assess your ability to conduct and write up an experiment, but the majority of the marks come from your ability to understand and interpret data/results whilst drawing upon and linking your data/results and their interpretation to the literature/theory. Structuring lab reports can cause some confusion as, although the sections are more specific than in humanities subjects, it can often be tempting to cover materials or issues in one section that actually belong in another (e.g. discussing what the results mean in the results section rather than the discussion section). The best way of keeping on track and structuring your reports is to follow the IMRaD(C) structure. This maps nicely onto the Christmas Cracker template as follows:

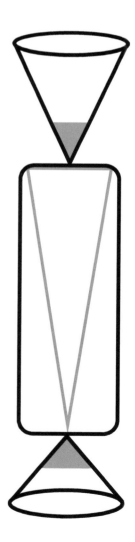

Section	Function and tips
I = Introduction	As discussed above, but sometimes with the addition of a short literature review/overview of the theory. Make sure you identify: - The issue/problem under investigation - Why the issue/problem is important/needs investigating - The purpose or objective of the work/experiment - Key literature in the field (with appropriate references)
M = Methods (and/or materials)	The purpose of the methods section is to a) enable others to repeat the experiment and b) allow others (and most importantly your marker) to check to see if the experiment/what you did was valid/sound/properly executed. It reveals things like sample sizes, procedures, how many times what you did was repeated etc.
R = Results	The key here is objectivity – present the data without any interpretation. Be careful that you explain what a graph/data etc. SHOWS rather than what it MEANS. The structure should be CHRONOLOGICAL so that the reader/marker can follow the process. Always ensure that: - Graphs and visual materials are readable and labelled - Signpost if necessary what the data/results SHOW (e.g. 'figure x shows the relationship between y and z')
D = Discussion	This is the section where you interpret, analyse and critically evaluate a) your method and b) your results. As such, it is often the most important part of the report. What was surprising/expected? Point out parallels/contrasts between your findings and others published in the literature. Discuss/evaluate shortcomings and evaluate how the results link to any theory you outlined in your introduction.
C = Conclusion (not always required)	As discussed above, here you broaden back out into the bigger picture. Refer back to the core issue/problem outlined in the introduction and discuss how your experiment/results have contributed (or not) to solving/illuminating the issue/problem. Has the experiment/results added anything to, confirmed or disproved what was discussed in the literature? Include recommendations (for the future, for future research or for future experiments in the area).

Note that in the main body of the report (methods, results and discussion), you once again move from the broader, 'big picture' (what you did), to narrow detail (overall evaluation). In the process, you gradually cover material and points which increase in specificity and detail, so you transition from your overall methodological approach to specific methods, then from key results to specific results, and finally overall analysis/discussion to the specific point being proven/disproven (aligned with your thesis statement). As you plan and write your report, use the template above to map your overall ideas and points so that they a) appear in the right sections and b) follow a logical structure.

As with any other piece of work, the final section of the report ought to be the bibliography. List all your sources alphabetically in accordance with the referencing style used by your department/university. In some cases, the report will also end with appendices. This is where you would put the results, data, illustrations, mathematical details/derivations or even maps that are too detailed for the main body of the report. However, if you have appendices, always number them and reference/signpost them in the text where relevant.

Literature reviews/surveys

Literature reviews/surveys can occur either as a stand-alone assignment, or, more frequently, as a key part of a longer work such as a dissertation (or even a shorter piece of work such as appearing in the introductory section of a laboratory report/methodology recount). The key thing to remember when writing a literature review is that you should be aiming to critically interrogate the literature in the field with a view to:

- Finding, highlighting and justifying any gaps in knowledge
- Highlighting why your topic needs further investigation

You do this by:

a)   Describing (briefly) the current state of knowledge and what the literature says.

b)   Analysing and evaluating the literature to find what's missing/not been covered/inadequately researched/misunderstood. To do this, you need to use and apply all the critical questions outlined in the previous chapter.

A literature review is NOT merely a description/survey of the literature. This is the main mistake most students make with literature reviews – they focus almost exclusively on A rather than focusing primarily on B.

Remember, when writing a literature review, your marker is looking to assess your skills in:

1)   Finding/searching for literature/research

2)   Critical analysis

3)   Evaluation

4)   Identifying trends in your discipline

5)   Identifying the significance of research and how your topic fits with a) what has been researched before, and b) new trends in the field/emerging knowledge

6)   Constructing an argument and writing in an analytical/evaluative way

Getting the structure of the literature review right will help you to do all of these things in a logical, concise manner. Whether the literature review is 800 words or 20,000 words, the overarching structure is the same, and it should map onto the main body section of the Christmas Cracker template. There are two main approaches to structuring a literature review:

1) The chronological literature review

The chronological literature review analyses, critiques and evaluates the literature in more or less the sequence it occurs. It is an excellent way of showing how ideas and the discipline have been shaped over time. This structure is especially good for evaluating and analysing a topic which is derived from a key moment in history, a key phenomenon or even from a key theorist. For instance, psychoanalysis was established as a discipline in the 1890s by Sigmund Freud. Marxism didn't exist before Marx, and the European Union didn't exist before the Maastricht Treaty of 1993. Although psychology, dreams and psychological disorders certainly existed before Freud, class struggle existed before Marxism, and empires, political/economic unions and shared social interests existed before the creation of the EU, if the literature review is seeking to evaluate an issue from a particular origin or historical/intellectual moment/incident, the chronological structure is best. In essence, you critically evaluate and analyse the scholarly literature on the subject from its origins to the present day with a view to exposing and highlighting the 'gap in knowledge' (which, crucially, is what your essay/dissertation is seeking to plug/address). For instance, let's imagine you are writing about 'gaslighting' (the phenomenon of psychological bullying which makes the victim doubt their own ideas and clarity of thought/versions of truth). Although the term derives from Patrick Hamilton's play *Gas Light* (1938), as a psychological term it has only gained currency in academic literature from the 1970s. As such, a chronological approach is ideal as you can trace the development of thought thus:

Key theorist/literature:	Theoretical development with critical analysis and evaluation of any gaps in knowledge
Rush (1992)	Child sexual abuse and reality – first definition of gaslighting as 'an attempt to destroy another's perception of reality' (p.81).
Calef and Weinshel (1993)	Projection and introjection – how the victim incorporates thoughts.
Dorpat (1994)	Projective identification – victim mustn't be unaware of the gaslighting.
Gottman and Jacobson (1998)	Gaslighting in abusive relationships.
Stout (2005)	How sociopaths use gaslighting.
Sarkis (2018)	How to recognise gaslighting and move forwards.

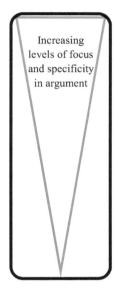

Increasing levels of focus and specificity in argument

Gap in knowledge = how gaslighting is used in the workplace as a form of bullying – none of the above literature discusses this.

As you can see here, the literature is covered in date order, but the topics also increase in specificity and focus as the essay progresses. Starting with the definition, the structure then looks at how gaslighting works, the necessary conditions for it to work, examples of how it is used, and ways to recognise and overcome its affects. This has not been planned by the student because as an academic field develops (unless tangents are explored), researchers naturally build upon each other's work and advance knowledge in ways which becomes more detailed, specific and applied. As such, providing you read and explore all the developments, a chronological literature review is relatively easy to structure.

TIPS

Use 'ConnectedPapers' to help you see the connections between pieces of research, the dates they were produced and their impact. This will help ensure you don't miss important developments or contributions in the literature.

Remember, whilst chronological literature reviews might be easier to construct, the goal is not to tell a 'story' of how the field/literature developed. You still need to prioritise critical evaluation and find the 'gap' in knowledge. The chronological structure is merely a framework and a way of structuring your analysis so as to build a platform from which you can develop your own arguments, hypotheses and contributions to knowledge.

Each piece of literature development needs to be critically assessed both in terms of its value/validity, and for the fact that it either DOESN'T consider gaslighting in the workplace or does so but is flawed. In other words, the 'gap in knowledge' frames each and every discussion.

2) *The thematic literature review:*

Thematic literature reviews are more useful when the topic is broader, and there is no obvious starting point/ origin. For instance, organic food, although a relatively recent trend, is an extremely broad topic in the sense that it may be approached and analysed from the perspectives of where you can buy it from, its health benefits, taste, perception, income/class, gender, type of food, appearance, price and availability. Organic food did not originate from a specific point in time or from a specific theorist/scientist. As such, it is better covered thematically. The key thing to remember here, though, is to structure the themes logically and not jump into a new topic without fully exploring the subject under consideration in detail.

Firstly, it's best to list, mind map or put into a grid the core topics covered in the literature and then organise them in a way that enables you to sequence your ideas from what you consider to be the broadest topic to the most specific. What you choose as your specific topic often depends on what you want to prove and where you feel the gap in knowledge may be, so its selection is based on what YOU want to prioritise in your argument. From the list of topics related to organic food above, then, the narrowest, most focused topic could be availability, gender of the consumer, perception or even health benefits, depending on what you want the focus to be. The golden rule, though, is to think about which topic you feel is the broadest and deal with that first, and then gradually narrow in the focus until you reach the final 'gap in knowledge' you are trying to address. For instance, if the focus of your argument is attitudes towards the appearance of organic foods, the structure might look like this:

Theme	Key literature with critical analysis and evaluation of any gaps in knowledge
Type of product	Davies et al., 1995, Cunningham, 2004, Radman, 2005, West, 2020
Supermarket vs. farm shop	Davies et al., 1995, DEFRA, 2006
Attitudes to appearance by gender	Makatouni, 2001, Jones, 2019
Attitudes towards appearance by age	Smith, 2018, Magnusson, 2001, Fotopoulos and Kystallis, 2002
Attitudes towards appearance by social class/income	Radman, 2005, Wallace, 2015
Impact of price in regards to appearance	Tregear et al., 1994

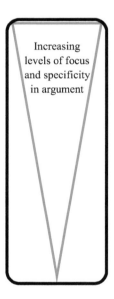

Increasing levels of focus and specificity in argument

Gap in knowledge = health benefits (and also, to a lesser extent, price and appearance) – none of the above literature discusses this.

As you can perhaps see here, there are multiple (and some recent) sources for all of the issues, but the key 'gap in knowledge' has been revealed to be in regards to health benefits (nobody seems to have researched this), and also price and appearance (only one piece of research covers this topic and it is considerably out of date). Irrespective of social attitudes, type of product, and where you buy it from, this student has sequenced the topics and argument in a way which reveals a) the health benefits of organic food have not been researched, and b) that price is both the narrowest determining factor as to whether the product is purchased, and is clearly the least researched. If your reading and critical analysis revealed a 'gap in knowledge' in relation to any of the other topics, you'd need to restructure the sequence so that you end with that topic. By ordering your themes from 'big picture' to narrow detail, from least relevant to most relevant, you can logically structure your literature review whilst gradually uncovering and justifying the 'gap in knowledge'. Again, it is the 'gap in knowledge' which should foreground each discussion, and you are analysing the literature to reveal that gap and present the case for it to be investigated (which is what your project will aim to address).

TIPS

For a thematic literature review, a vital part of the planning and structuring process is 'clumping' (or synthesising). You'll see in the table above that theorists/literature has been 'clumped' by theme, irrespective of date published. One of the keys to success in a literature review is pulling together the connections and similarities between pieces of research in order to identify not only themes, but areas where work has been done/needs doing. The 'clumping' process helps you to show breadth of research, without describing every piece of literature in turn. This enables you to identify and justify the knowledge gaps swiftly and allows you to advance your argument effectively.

To help you identify themes and structure your literature review, produce an annotated bibliography or literature review matrix (like the tables above). If you are not sure what themes might be emerging, try using Oliver West's 'Footnotes' grid or app (see link below) to help you see all the pieces of information in a 'big picture' format. The Footnotes grid is specifically designed for visual/dyslexic learners and is simply a piece of paper or web app that allows you to put ideas or even pictures/icons into random boxes so you can scan across ideas and make connections. A Footnotes grid for our organic food literature review, for example, might look a little like this:

Davis et al, 1995 – type of product / supermarket vs. farm shop	Tregear et al, 1994 – impact of price in regards to appearance	Smith, 2018 – attitudes towards appearance by age	Jones, 2019 – attitudes towards appearance by gender
West, 2020 – type of product	Wallace, 2015 – attitudes towards appearance by social class / income	DEFRA, 2006 – Supermarket vs. farm shop	Cunningham, 2004 – type of product
Fotopoulos and Kystallis, 2002 – attitudes towards appearance by age	Radman, 2005 – type of product / attitudes towards appearance by social class / income	Magnusson, 2001 – attitudes towards appearance by age	Makatouni, 2001 – attitudes towards appearance by gender

These connections can then be transferred either into a list or the matrix above to align with the Christmas Cracker triangle. This will help you map /plan and logically articulate your thoughts. As such, it 'act(s) as a bridge' through which you can 'translate' random, non-sequential ideas into clumps and structures (West, 2008, p.41).

For more information about Oliver West's Footnotes grid and app, see https://footnotesvmt.com/ and https://footnotesvmt.com/wp-content/uploads/2019/05/The-Oliver-West-Footnotes-Tool-Manual.pdf.

Reflective writing

Reflective writing is becoming an increasingly common way of assessing students, but it is also a useful means of encouragaing self-awareness and development. For this reason, it is often used on postgraduate courses aligned with professions (e.g. teaching, social work, psychology), and on Foundation-level programmes as a means of encouraging students to reflect on their previous learning and life experiences and develop an awareness of what they want to get out of Higher Education and what sort of career path might be suitable. For these reasons, it's worth looking at how to structure such writing, especially as it differs somewhat from conventional essays as the topic/subject under consideration/analysis is YOU!

Various models exist for thinking reflectively, but the key is to translate thinking and reflection into a structured, written response. This is particularly tricky as thoughts and feelings/reflections do not automatically come out in a logical, structured manner, and applying theory/literature to those thoughts/feelings/ reflections is not a particularly natural thing to do. The best way of proceeding is to map your reflections on a grid using the following prompts:

- **What happened?**

  Describe the event/situation and any associated feelings

- **So what?**

  Evaluate and analyse the experience

  Assess, evaluate and analyse what happened and why in relation to your feelings with reference to the literature and theory on the subject e.g. teamwork – analyse and evaluate in relation to literature and theories relating to teamwork, the workplace, task setting, delegation etc.

- **What now?**

  Assess the way forward and produce a plan. What could you have done differently? What will you do differently if it happens again? How are you going to change? What do you need to do to develop/adjust?

TIP

 Remember, as with most writing at university, analysis and evaluation are key. Whilst you need to spend time describing what happened, reflection involves self-analysis, and that ought to be the priority throughout.

Below is an example of reflection put onto a grid for planning out the structure of the essay – in this case reflecting upon an experience of multidisciplinary teamwork. As you can see, this plan can be mapped onto the complete Christmas Cracker template (introduction, main body and conclusion) which gives you a structure for your writing. As we have seen before, the introduction has a conventional thesis statement that outlines (in this case), the three core areas that are going to be discussed. These are then analysed in turn in relation to the individual's experiences and feelings and links are drawn to the literature. The entire discussion in the main body is framed by the 'so what?' question so as to encourage reflection. The conclusion returns to the core issues and summarises what actions need to be taken in the future and why (back out into the 'big picture') – in this case in relation to employability:

As you can see here, the introduction has a conventional thesis statement which outlines three core areas that are going to be discussed. There are then analysed in turn in relation to the individual's experiences and feelings and links are drawn to the literature. The entire discussion in the main body is framed by the 'so what?' question so as to encourage reflection. The conclusion returns to the core issues and summarises what actions need to be taken in the future and why (back out into the 'big picture') – in this case in relation to employability.

Prompts with reflections	Reflections, emotions and learning points with links to theory/research	
What happened? - 7 colleagues from different areas of the health service had to work on a project. Project did not go to plan and was largely a failure. - Task was daunting and the team did not work together effectively. - X was dominant, I was irritated by Y and I felt that Z was lazy. The work did not get done to time. - The main issues were delegation, lack of leadership and workload distribution.	Did not approach the task with a positive attitude (Stanton, 2004 and Tuckman, 1965) – need to be more open to positives. Felt that the team was too big and diverse to be manageable (Stanton, 2004) – smaller teams are better	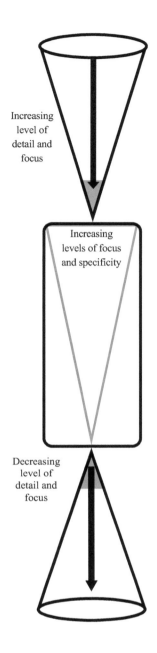 Increasing level of detail and focus Increasing levels of focus and specificity
So what? - t's essential to be able to work and communicate within teams and negotiate/coordinate delegation - It's part of my professional development, but I'm uncomfortable working as a team, especially where there is a lack of clear leadership - Workload distribution is affected by dominant members	I'm mainly an 'implementer'/'completer' and as such struggle in more 'shaper'/'evaluator'/'coordinator' roles (Cottrell, 2003 and Belbin, 2005), as I tend to be overly critical. In future I need to play to my strengths more (Naidoo and Wills, 2001), whilst also experiencing new roles to enhance my development and confidence. Project management and delegation is a real area in need of development. Need to gain the confidence to address workload discrepancies (Levin, 2005, and Hogson and Simpson, 2003). Confidence issues derive from past negative experiences of groupwork (Jones, 2013) and feelings of inadequacy.	
What now? - Need additional training in communication skills and delegation - Need to be more assertive/confident, especially in challenging more dominant members of the group - Next time milestones and targets for everyone need to be set - Need to be less of a perfectionist - Need to get teamwork right because it's a key skill in employment	Need to learn to accept people's differing opinions more and accept that all teams have problems (Hogson and Simpson, 2003, and Naidoo and Wills, 2001). Need to be more accepting of differing opinions and not think problems are my fault. The whole experience has been an invaluable experience in professional working and teamwork and I'll approach the next teamwork task with a more positive, open-minded attitude (Stanton, 2004).	Decreasing level of detail and focus

Summary

This brings us to the end of considering the 'macro' structure of the typical essay genres you are likely to encounter. The Christmas Cracker template works just as well with a 1000-word essay or exam paper as it does with something of 10,000 words, so irrespective of your word length, discipline or even the genre, the overall structure of your response should resemble the shape of a Christmas Cracker. Plan your essay along these lines and gradually move from the 'big picture' to narrow, new detail as a way of articulating and driving forward your argument. Use the sample template planners provided above or download them from the companion website, then write your plan or even your sections into the template. In the next chapter, we will consider how to use the Christmas Cracker as an effective way of structuring your main body paragraphs so that you can sequence the various parts of your argument and your evidence in a logical and compelling manner, but for now, keep in mind the following points:

- Structure your essay in a logical, systematic manner that goes from solid foundations to increasing levels of sophistication.

- Make your introductions effective by moving from the 'big picture' to specific detail. End the introduction with a clear and compelling thesis statement that directs and articulates an argument (which clearly responds to the assignment task/question).

- In the main body of your essays, move from the given to the new, from the foundations to detail, and from the general to the specific.

- For comparison essays, try to use the point-by-point/thematic structure as this allows you to EVALUATE and SYNTHESISE the arguments/points in a logical manner while avoiding repetition and labouring the ideas.

- Make your conclusions count – don't simply repeat/summarise what you have said in the essay.

- Make sure that literature reviews/surveys are structured in a way that enables you to articulate an argument based on critical analysis and finding/justifying any gaps in knowledge (which is what your project aims to justify/fill).

Bibliography

Barrios, Michael V., and Singer, Jerome L., (1981) 'The Treatment of Creative Blocks: A Comparison of Waking Imagery, Hypnotic Dream, and Rational Discussion Techniques', *Imagination, Cognition and Personality*, 1(1), pp.89–109.

Bruce, Nigel J., (1988) 'Communicative Dynamism in Expository Academic English: Some Strategies in Teaching the Pragmatics of Writing', *Working Papers in Linguistics and Language Teaching*, 11, pp.42–53.

Game, A., and Metcalfe, A., (1996) *Passionate Sociology*. London: Sage.

Heuboeck, Alois, Holmes, Jasper, and Nesi, Hilary, (2007) *The BAWE Corpus Manual: An Investigation of Genres of Assessed Writing in British Higher Education*. ESRC, Project RES-000–23–0800.

McDevitt, Elizabeth A., Sattari, Negin, Duggan, Katherine, A., Cellini, Nicola, Whitehouse, Lauren, N., Perera, Chalani, Reihanabad, Nicholas, Granados, Samantha, Hernandez, Lexus, and Mednick, Sara C., (2018) 'The Impact of Frequent Napping and Nap Practice on Sleep-dependent Memory in Humans', *Scientific Reports*, 8 (1), pp.1–12. Available at: https://escholarship.org/uc/item/4p99k2ts#main (Accessed: 29th March, 2021).

Miller, Morton, A., (1980) *Reading and Writing Short Essays*. New York: Random House.

Moore, Kathleen Muller, and Cassel, Susie Lan, (2011) *Techniques for College Writing: The Thesis Statement and Beyond*. Wadsworth: Cengage.

West, Oliver, (2008) *In Search of Words: Footnotes Visual Thinking Techniques*. Oliver P.B. West.

5   Visualising Effective Paragraphs

Presenting Your Point and Supporting Evidence

'My school career was dismal. I had a very hyperactive mind, so my focus was just not there. My mind just tended to wander… My mind is very visual: I can see anything in pictures, and I always visualise thing…It's how I'm wired. So, whatever you talk about, I'll see pictures in my head'.

(Glenn Bailey: dyslexic entrepreneur)

Research has shown that individuals with dyslexia like and need to see the 'big picture', yet this can easily become obscured within paragraphs given the complexity and nuances of academic arguments. Competing or interrelated ideas can often seem equally important and/or inseparable, and therefore difficult to treat systematically. This is a challenge for most students, but given that people with dyslexia often excel at multidimensional thinking, it can be doubly difficult to see how points can be separated and then re-sequenced into a whole that makes logical sense. Below is a paragraph that illustrates well how the sequence of ideas and the main thread of an argument can become lost amidst a haze of detail:

> With the onset of recession in the early 1970s, most western European states abandoned their 'open door' immigration policies of the post-war reconstruction and economic boom period and resorted to tough and restrictive immigration controls. The 1951 Convention does not set out an unconditional 'right to asylum' because states would not have agreed this extent of loss of sovereignty over the asylum issue and thus their borders. At that time, asylum-seekers were, coincidently, starting to arrive at unprecedented levels and continued to do so in the following decades. However, states cannot simply deport those seeking refuge within their territory without due process, to ensure that refusal of protection and deportation do not violate the Convention's *non-refoulement* principle. Asylum-seekers are thus safeguarded from unsafe deportation. The Convention became important for the prospects of refugees to Western Europe when asylum applications made in Western Europe increased from 104,000 in 1984 to 692,000 in 1992, thereafter declining, only to rise to 350,000 in 1998 and about 400,000 in 1999. Western European states, therefore, were eager to keep them, just like other immigrants, out.

There are clearly some good ideas here, but they are articulated in an incoherent manner. Particular problems and issues include:

- The statistics are useful, but they needed to have been cited earlier in order to introduce, contextualise and prove the scale of the issue.

- The overall 'importance' of the 1951 Convention is mentioned towards the end of the paragraph. It would have been more logical to put this background nearer the beginning.

- There are too many issues being dealt with here. There is contextual detail concerning the early 1970s, a rather simplistic and problematic conflation of the issues associated with immigration and asylum-seeking, and an outline of the principles of the 1951 Convention and its significance for refugees. The student is clearly trying to do too much and has become confused. This has led to a rather disjointed paragraph in which the ideas are presented not only in an illogical order, but there are simply too many of them. It would have been better to have articulated these ideas in separate paragraphs, each with their own argument, which builds upon the ideas expressed in those which precede it.

DOI: 10.4324/9781003190189-5

What is a paragraph?

Before we consider how visualising a paragraph can help, it's worth going back to basics. Here are some overriding principles that are worth remembering:

- A paragraph is an examination or discussion of ONE idea, and ONE idea only. Adherence to this principle is vital if you are to present your ideas in a logical, sequential manner, and it is a helpful way of translating the bullet-point essay plans we considered in the last chapter onto the paragraph structure.

- The principal of one idea per paragraph is also essential if you are to maintain clarity throughout a discussion, which, in academic writing, often contains discrete, yet complex and interrelated (or even overlapping) ideas. This is often where students with dyslexia tend to get a little 'lost'.

- There is no hard and fast rule as to how long/short a paragraph can be. The main thing to remember is that it examines and presents an argument about ONE key point relating to your assignment task/question.

- Paragraphs should be clearly visible on the page. Indent the first line of your paragraphs. Perhaps even add an extra space so that both you and your marker can very clearly see where paragraphs begin and end.

Even if you know the one point per paragraph rule, in attempting to execute the task (particularly in exam conditions), students with dyslexia often produce disjointed (yet highly perceptive) essays at best or become frustrated and unproductive at worst. Added to this problem is the additional challenge of aligning the topic with a critically perceptive ARGUMENT (which is the next parameter governing the construction of paragraphs). In most academic paragraphs, especially in the humanities and social sciences, you need to express an argument that centres on a single topic/idea. Given these competing demands on your sequencing abilities and working memory, how can you ensure that you stay on track and not veer off on tangents? How can you harness the power of your multidimensional thinking and preference for seeing the 'big picture' to create really effective academic paragraphs which present a logical sequence of ideas AND an argument?

'Big picture' thinking: paragraphing to express arguments

The most helpful way of thinking about a paragraph is to visualise it in a 'big picture' format in the same way as we encountered when structuring the entire essay. In essence, the ideas and grammatical units contained within an ideal paragraph, like the essay as a whole, should resemble an upturned Christmas Cracker. Indeed, like an essay, a paragraph ought to have three main components. Each component is shaped below to specifically indicate what you need to be saying and when to help you structure your thoughts in a coherent, sequential and logical manner. The three main components can be visualised like this:

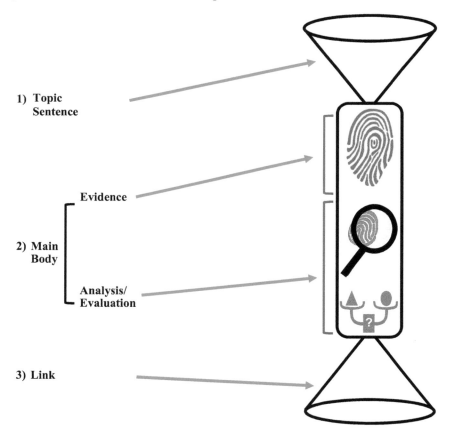

1) Topic Sentence

Evidence

2) Main Body

Analysis/ Evaluation

3) Link

Some of you may already have come across a version of this which is frequently taught at A level, and is often referred to as the 'PEAL' (point, evidence, analysis, link), 'PEEL' (point, evidence, evaluation, link) or 'PEA' (point, evidence, analysis) framework. Whichever way you prefer to think of it, all academic paragraphs can be visualised as an upturned Christmas Cracker, the shape of which has a direct and meaningful correlation with the PURPOSE of each component. In what follows, we take each of these components in turn to see how you can construct them and how they contribute to the forward momentum/sequence of your ideas.

REMEMBER

 Disjointed paragraphs mostly derive from your difficulties with sequencing rather than the subject's complexity or lack of intelligence, so don't be deterred and never doubt yourself!

The topic sentence

The topic sentence is the first sentence of each paragraph and is a crucial tool to use if you want to structure your essay in a logical manner. The topic sentence provides direction and a framework for ordering and signposting the ideas to both yourself and the reader. This is because it introduces new ideas and aligns those ideas with the overall aims of the argument, the assignment task and what has been discussed previously. Indeed, academic writing stylists such as Joseph M. Williams see the topic sentence as vital because it aligns the paragraph with the 'basic principle of clarity' (2007, p.207), not least because, as Steven Pinker has noted, 'human comprehension demands topic before comment and given before new' (2015, p.131). In other words, it provides an interesting 'hook' that draws your reader in/provokes interest. To achieve this, the topic sentence should contain two core ingredients:

1) The topic

2) A provable opinion (or argument)

So, looking back at the first sentence of this paragraph, we can see those two ingredients quite clearly:

The topic sentence is the first sentence of each paragraph and is a crucial tool to use if you want to structure your essay in a logical manner.

The red here indicates the topic under consideration, namely topic sentences. The second part of the sentence (in green) tells you what the argument is (in this case, the idea that a topic sentence should form the first sentence of each paragraph if you want to present ideas logically). Academic topic sentences tend to be more sophisticated, but the basic formulation is the same for all types of topic sentences.

Common problems

Many students get their topic sentence wrong because they either have:

- A topic and no provable opinion, or
- A provable opinion and no topic

In both cases, this means that the reader/marker has no immediate sense of what the paragraph is going to be about and no sense of how, or even if, the student is answering the question/assignment task. The marker needs to be able to identify an argument so they can see how what you are saying is answering the question/ assignment task. Obviously, every paragraph should directly contribute to answering the question and gaining marks, so it needs to be clear how it does this. In other words, each topic sentence ought to be addressing some aspect of the thesis statement, which in turn is answering and addressing the assignment question/task. All three aspects interlink and are mutually dependent upon each other in such a way that, taken together, should enable you to construct a coherent, focused response to the task. The entire process, the 'big picture', can be visualised thus:

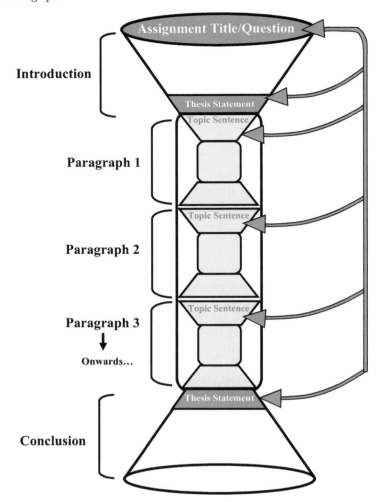

Without this interlinking of ideas/topics and arguments, the essay is likely to wander off course, fail to address the question/assignment task and leave your reader/marker feeling confused. By visualising and mapping the ideas and arguments of your essay onto the 'big picture' Christmas Cracker structure from the outset, and by linking your topic sentences to your thesis statement and essay plan, you are much more likely to produce a coherent and logical essay which retains a clear focus.

Topic sentence activity

Take a look at the sample topic sentences below. Can you identify what the paragraph may be talking about and arguing from these topic sentences? Can you identify a topic and a provable opinion/argument in each one? Can you guess what the assignment question/title may have been about? Can you even identify the discipline?

1) The benefits to science are immense.

2) The first of these is atmosphere.

3) Weinberg and Pehlivan (2011) have provided recommendations on investing in law textbooks, formed from research they have conducted.

4) Research on law advisory services has existed for decades, yet none of it has adequately addressed the existence of online forums.

5) A particular difficulty in English criminal law is that many serious offences such as murder, manslaughter and conspiracy to defraud derive from common law rather than statutes.

The chances are that you can only identify a clear, unambiguous topic and provable opinion/argument in numbers 4 and 5, because the others lack either a topic or an argument. Let us examine each in turn:

1) The sentence contains a provable opinion/argument but it is totally unclear what the topic is. The benefits to science of what, are immense?

2) This is no clearer as it too contains a provable opinion but no topic. Could you guess what this paragraph may have been about? Like number 1, it actually comes from a student essay about spacecraft propulsion systems, and this particular paragraph made the case that propellers are unsuitable (owing to the lack of atmosphere). Could you see that in the topic sentence? Could you see how the student was constructing an argument in answer to a question about spacecraft propulsion systems? Probably not.

3) This example contains a reasonably clear topic, namely the recommendations provided by Weinberg and Pehlivan, but there does not appear to be any form of argument about their research. Is it useful? Is it outdated? Is it biased? By only articulating a topic, the sentence immediately indicates that the paragraph which follows will be descriptive rather than analytical, and as such is likely to score poorly when marked.

4) The sentence contains a clear topic (research on law advisory services) and makes a clear claim that none of it has adequately addressed online forums, so this is an excellent example.

5) This example also contains both a topic (English criminal law) and an argument – the student tries to claim that there is a 'particular difficulty' in so far as the law is based on common law rather than statutes, thereby opening up the possibility of disputed meanings. In terms of readability, however, this sentence lacks clarity since the provable opinion is placed before the topic. The sentence would be more logical, readable and clear if the topic to provable opinion to argument sequence was observed. In other words, a better version of the sentence would be written thus:

English criminal law represents a particular difficulty since many serious offences such as murder, manslaughter and conspiracy to defraud derive from common law rather than statutes.

Topic sentences are clearer when observing the topic to provable opinion/argument sequence because the reader is led, much like in the introduction, from the general to the specific, from the given information to the new (it thus has 'communicative dynamism'). Indeed, it provides the reader with a 'hook' that draws them in and captures their interest. It is for this reason that the topic sentence, again like the introduction, is best conceived as being triangular (as the handle of the Christmas Cracker), with the general point at the beginning of the sentence (as is represented by the broad, general, wide opening at the top), followed by a specific argument and detail (as is represented by the much narrower, focused section of the handle). A 'big picture' representation of a couple of the topic sentence examples highlighted above, then, can be visualised and mapped onto the Cracker as follows:

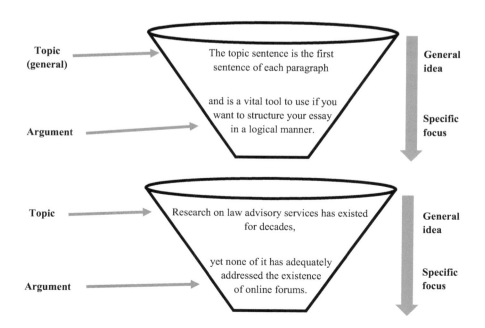

Dealing with evidence

After outlining your topic and argument in the topic sentence, the next task is to integrate some evidence that will ultimately prove your argument. As we have already seen, evidence can take the form of data, statistics and formulae, but the most frequently used types of evidence come in the form of quotation, summaries or paraphrasing.

Quotations, summarising and paraphrasing

Quotations

Quotations are an effective way of proving your point, particularly in disciplines and arguments where the meaning of words is crucial. Meaning can be ambiguous, contentious, highly disputed or pivotal for precise understanding, particularly in the arts, humanities and social sciences. An example of this is the meaning of the word 'epidemic'. The *Oxford English Dictionary* defines the word as meaning 'a large number of cases of a particular disease happening at the same time in a particular community', but it can also mean 'a sudden increase in how often something bad happens'. At first glance, these definitions appear fairly uncontroversial, but like most things studied at university, they are open to interpretation and dispute. For example, what does 'sudden increase' actually mean? Can a number be put upon it? Clearly not. Similarly, what constitutes 'a large number of cases'? Surely this is entirely relative? Ambiguity also arises with the terms 'same time' and 'particular community'. If a writer uses one of these terms in a specific way, and you are interrogating or disputing their use of the term, you would need to quote from them to demonstrate precisely how and where their argument/use of the term is flawed or legitimate. Similarly, if your argument hinges upon what was said (in a novel, play, law court, interview or political speech, for example), then the passage or at least extracts from it need to be quoted and integrated into the analysis. More general ideas or arguments, however, do not need to be quoted in detail. For instance, let's return to the law advisory services example from earlier. The fact that Jones claims that 53% of people seeking legal advice for employment-related issues acquire advice via the internet, does not need to be quoted. Rather, it can be summarised, as meaning does not hinge upon a precise and perhaps disputed use of language or terminology.

TIPS

 Remember, long quotations will eat into your word count without necessarily gaining you marks. As such, it's preferable to either summarise or paraphrase.

 For quotations that exceed two lines, indent the entire quote (usually 1.2 cm from the left margin).

 Always reference the quotation using the appropriate referencing conventions.

Summarising

Summarising involves taking the main ideas from a text and re-writing them in your own words. Crucially, however, the summary needs to be significantly shorter than the original and gives merely an overview of the topic area. In the case of Jones mentioned earlier, then, the headline or summary of his/her research is that 53% of people seeking legal advice for employment-related issues say they now acquire advice via the internet. There is undoubtedly a great deal more detail behind this summary, including a sophisticated research methodology, rationale, justification for the research and a thorough description of its implications in relation to the discipline, government policy and socio-economic considerations. The original research probably took many years to complete. Yet, for the purposes of your essay and argument, it is sufficient just to cite the main headline – any extra detail would be unnecessary and would not generate marks. Here's some guidance on how to identify the main headlines from a source:

- Highlight the main ideas in the text by focusing upon crucial data, formulas, dates and word use. Make use of the index, contents pages, subheadings, topic sentences and key verbs/terminology to help you locate these.

- Extract the main idea(s) and write them on a separate piece of paper to form a list (if required).

- Put the list into a logical order (if required).

- Write the summary in your own words rather than those of the original author (although it is acceptable to quote some words or phrases if needed).

- Check that your summary/headline points accurately reflect the main ideas of the source.

- Ensure that you reference using the correct referencing style.

TIP

Summarising is a little like reducing the main ideas into key headlines, so pretend you are a journalist – how would you write a headline for what you have just read?

Paraphrasing

Paraphrasing is somewhat more complex than summarising and does not involve identifying and pulling out the main headlines from the original. Rather, paraphrasing is re-writing excerpts from the original in your own words, changing the text so it is dissimilar to the original yet retains all the meaning. Paraphrasing thus allows you to explore and interrogate individual ideas at a deeper level. Thus, you can summarise a journal article or even a monograph, but it would be impossible to paraphrase such material. Paraphrasing is best used, then, for smaller sections of writing where detail rather than the wider picture is needed. Here's some guidance for successful paraphrasing:

- Having identified the passage needing to be paraphrased, re-read it several times to ensure you understand the meaning.

- Extract and write down the meaning of each sentence and think about it in isolation.

- Articulate each idea/sentence in your own words (you may wish to use a thesaurus to help you).

- Think about how you could change the structure of the ideas presented in the original – you could re-structure it to highlight an idea which you are particularly interested in drawing to the marker's attention.

- Draft, re-draft and edit.

- Compare alongside the original and ensure that you haven't inadvertently changed the meaning.

- Compare with the original to ensure that the vocabulary has been changed.

- Ensure that you reference using the correct referencing style.

Students often ask, if paraphrasing is merely putting an original source into your own words, without necessarily reducing the word length, why not just quote it? This can seem a little confusing. However, the extensive use of quotations is undesirable for two reasons:

1) Direct quotations do not allow you to demonstrate that you have understood what is being said. Paraphrasing, however, illustrates your ability to understand, interpret, apply and analyse the original source and demonstrate its importance for your argument/discussion by selecting, prioritising and highlighting key points.

2) Direct quotations are included in your word count; using too many limits your personal written contribution and this will be reflected in your marks.

Paraphrasing uses YOUR OWN words; this shows your marker that you have understood and correctly interpreted what you have read. As such, it is seen by lecturers as a higher skill than simply quoting.

Example of summarising/paraphrasing

Let's see how a passage about the punishment of crime and the motivations behind criminal activity could be summarised and paraphrased.

Original passage:

> 'Lawyers should resist the desire to find some single concept or value that will capture the essence or the essential characteristic in virtue of which crimes are properly punished...in favour of a pluralism that recognises a diversity of reasons for criminalisation, matching the diversity of kinds of wrongdoing which can legitimately be the criminal lawyer's business' (Duff, 2007, p.139). 57 words

This passage, however interesting it may be, is a little too long to be quoted in its entirety, so summarising it would be a sensible option. The key ideas here, the headlines, can be highlighted thus:

> 'Lawyers should resist the desire to find some single concept or value that will capture the essence or the essential characteristic in virtue of which crimes are properly punished...in favour of a pluralism that recognises a diversity of reasons for criminalisation, matching the diversity of kinds of wrongdoing which can legitimately be the criminal lawyer's business'.

1) Lawyers

2) Single concept

3) Crimes

4) Punishment

5) Pluralism

6) Diversity of reasons for criminalisation

These ideas, if expressed in this order, appear a little laboured and repetitive, mainly because we move from a general idea (lawyers) to a specific idea (single concept of crime and punishment), then general (pluralism) to another general idea (diversity of reasons for criminalisation). Furthermore, duplication of the issues relating to crime can be eliminated by restricting it to only one mention (a headline), and the issue of 'proper punishment' is a little too detailed and specific for a summary aiming to highlight merely the main message. The main ideas, then, can be re-ordered and summarised in a way which moves from the general to the specific in a more succinct manner. For example:

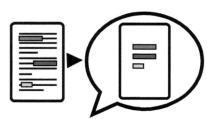

Lawyers ought to consider multiple reasons for criminality rather than searching for an elusive single definition (Duff, 2007, p.139). 16 words

A paraphrased version of the above passage, meanwhile, would seek to re-word and express **all** the key ideas mentioned by Duff. Again, the ideas could be re-structured to articulate the core message more obviously and purposefully (thus showing initiative and analysis/interpretation skills). A paraphrased version of Duff's passage, then, could look like this:

Criminal lawyers ought to avoid searching for an overarching definition of criminality that encapsulates the core concepts of transgression, wrongdoing and its appropriate reprimand. Rather, they ought to favour a multiplicity of ideas that more accurately reflects the disparate range of crimes and their many underlying motivations (Duff, 2007, p.139). 47 words

Note here that the original passage has been converted into two distinct sentences to avoid any unnecessary duplication. Additionally, the structure of the ideas has again been adjusted to get to the main point more quickly, and the vocabulary has been changed by deploying synonyms ('diversity of kinds of wrongdoing' has become 'disparate range of crimes', and 'properly punished' has become 'appropriate reprimand'). There has also been a saving of ten words, which frees up room for words to be used for the analysis and evaluation, which is more productive in terms of mark generation.

TIP

 The best way of incorporating evidence is to use a mix of quotation, summarising and paraphrasing. This allows you to demonstrate three discrete skills.

Which technique you use for integrating your evidence is obviously entirely dependent upon what you wish to achieve, but to summarise (forgive the pun!), the following pro and con checklist can help you decide which to use and where:

	Pros:	Cons:
Quotation:	Proves beyond doubt the original words. Great for accuracy/clarity where meaning centres around a scholar's interpretation or where meaning is disputed.	Doesn't show originality or interpretation. Doesn't necessarily show that you've correctly understood the meaning/significance of the quote. Uses valuable words which are not your OWN, so not marked as highly.
Summarising:	Short, gets to the point quickly. Shows you've understood what's been said. Fairly easy to synthesise with other ideas/sources. Shows that you can select, prioritise and evaluate the relative importance/significance of key ideas.	Important information can be accidently omitted. Meaning can be inadvertently changed. Can appear a little superficial or reductive.
Paraphrasing:	Shows full understanding of the original text, thus demonstrating sound interpretation skills. Uses your own words so can be marked. Can show your ability to prioritise and select key ideas.	Meaning can be inadvertently changed. Not as easy to synthesise with other sources as it requires deeper explanation.

Integrating evidence

Evidence, whether in the form of a quotation, summary, paraphrase or piece of data, formulae or diagram, needs to be introduced and integrated so that the paragraph presents a smooth, logical sequence and progression of ideas. A frequent problem in student writing is the tendency to 'parachute' quotations and evidence into the paragraph and assume that it a) contextualises itself, and b) does the work of proving the argument without further explanation.

Parachuting

Instances of 'parachuting' can take several forms. Some students place the evidence where the topic sentence ought to be and then examine and discuss it without it being clear for what purpose the evidence is being used. Others neglect to contextualise or indicate the significance of their evidence, so it remains unclear who said it, when, and what its relevance to the argument is. Let's take a look at the following examples:

1) Law (data parachuted)

 Research on law advisory services has existed for decades, yet none of it has adequately addressed the existence of online forums. 53% of people now say they seek advice via the internet and 29% say they prefer to use their Smartphones, so law advisory services are no longer as popular.

The evidence here is 'parachuted' into the paragraph because the statistic is not contextualised. Who was questioned in order to get this figure? Where were they questioned? When were they questioned? What is meant by 'now'? Who conducted the research? And what is its relevance to the long-standing existence of 'research on law advisory services'? None of these issues are introduced or explained, and it is unclear how the evidence supports the argument contained within the topic sentence. In other words, the evidence needs context and relevance briefly signposting to the reader.

2) Computer science (two successive parachuted quotes as evidence)

Creating an exhaustive moral code for autonomous vehicles would be extremely difficult because of the many definitions of morality. Some would argue that morality lies in favouring those with financial status: 'the choices made often correlated with the level of economic inequality in their culture' (Maxmen, 2018, p.1). On the other hand, there have been situations where factors such as age, gender and country of residence have made no difference: 'people spared humans over pets, and groups of people over individuals' (Maxmen, 2018, p.1).

In this example, neither quote is integrated into the flow of the sentences/paragraph, and again the context/relevance is not introduced or signposted. Clearly, the phrase 'choices made often correlated' and 'people spared' indicates that this is the result of some sort of study, but it's not clear what type of study or even if it's relevant to the topic of self-driving cars. Furthermore, the first quote merely qualifies/repeats what the student has summarised (namely that financial status can be a factor in moral judgements). As such, it is not really needed. Meanwhile, the second quote doesn't really seem to actually prove that other factors may be involved in some moral decisions. Arguably, neither quote fully proves that there are different definitions of morality. If anything, they merely suggest that decisions are made based on context.

3) English (the perils associated with parachuting long quotations)

Iago uses the soliloquy as a dramatic technique to engage
the audience when thinking about his secret plot against Othello:
'...let me see now;
To get his place and to plume up my will
In double knavery. How? How? Let's see...
I have it! It is engendered'.
The soliloquy thus reveals to the audience his true intentions.

Notice here that the student has 'parachuted' the quotation into the paragraph without contextualising it. Where in the play does this occur and what is its significance for the plot? Crucially, they also assume that the quotation has done the important, mark-generating work of analysis for them. A better version of how this evidence could be introduced and contextualised might look like this:

Iago uses the soliloquy as a dramatic technique to engage the audience when thinking about his secret plot against Othello. For example, in Act 1 Scene 3, Iago turns to the audience for the first time and carefully delineates and shares his active thought process by pondering 'let me see now; to get his place and plume up my will in double knavery. How? How? Let's see'. The soliloquy thus reveals to the audience his true intentions.

Notice that this example does not waste words by quoting extensively (20 quoted words embedded into the sentence as opposed to 27 which appear somewhat in isolation). What is more, the student has introduced the significance of the soliloquy (namely that it is Iago's first direct communication with the audience) and its location within the play. By introducing the quote as exemplifying an 'active thought process', the student has drawn attention to the idea that the soliloquy is an effective, evolving and 'live' method for sharing a secret plot with the audience, thus signposting the detailed analysis and explanations which are to follow. A better, more integrated version of the law advisory example, meanwhile, might look like this:

Research on law advisory services has existed for decades, yet none of it has adequately addressed the existence of online forums. Online modes of seeking advice are becoming increasingly popular. As Jones (2015) has demonstrated, 53% of people seeking legal advice for employment-related issues say they acquire advice via the internet following recent cutbacks in face-to-face provision and the subsequent lack of accessibility.

This example is undoubtedly longer, but gives a more comprehensive account of the significance of the data, who said it, what it relates to and what caused it. This sets the background before the writer explains its implications for the research.

Integrating diagrams, graphs and images

A core message throughout this book is that a picture does indeed 'speak a thousand words'. However, when integrated into an academic essay, it is also surrounded by words. The two need to work in harmony. Markers often see essays, especially in the sciences, where diagrams, graphs and other forms of visual evidence are not integrated into the flow of the writing (or even referred to) – they are 'parachuted'. Here's some general principles for successfully integrating visual data and images:

- ALWAYS position the data/image as close to the relevant section of text as possible. Readers don't want to see tables, graphs and visuals and be left unsure why they are there or what bit of the text discusses/explains them.

- The data/graph/table /image needs to be self-explanatory. By looking at it, the reader should be able to understand it without having to refer to the surrounding text for explanations.

- To ensure clarity and comprehension, make sure your diagram/graph/data/imagery is labelled correctly. They should all have (as appropriate):

  - a number

  - a figure title

  - a brief caption explaining the data/evidence

  - labels, sub-labels and legends/keys if needed

  - suitable, clear use of alignment, columns, colours, italics and bold to illustrate sections, hierarchies and key information

- Although the image/graph/diagram ought to make sense on its own, you do need to signpost and integrate it within the text. You can do this either:

  1) Directly (e.g. via phrases such as 'as we can see in Figure 1…', 'Graph 3 illustrates…', 'This can be seen as follows:' OR;

  2) In parenthesis. This is where signposts to the material are inserted into a sentence as additional information via brackets or dashes. For example, 'the efficacy of the Coronavirus vaccine in Israel (see Figure 2) shows that….' or 'in both cases the result of this disease causes excessive glucose accumulation in the blood (Figure 7.1)'.

Synthesising evidence from multiple sources

Often, you will need to introduce and incorporate evidence from multiple sources in your paragraphs to demonstrate your thorough knowledge of the subject, your ability to synthesise information and your engagement with key debates in the field. The key here is to sift through the material to identify points of similarity and contrast and then prioritise and select which are the most relevant and important for your argument. One way of doing this is to use a 'synthesis grid', which will enable you to compare and contrast sources and map the key ideas. For example:

	Source 1: (Smith, 2013)	*Source 2: (Wu, 2000)*	*Source 3: (Hara, 1988)*
Main argument:	Climate change a hoax	Planet is warming	Holes in ozone layer
Key points/quotes/ evidence:	CO2 not rising Planet only warmed by 0.2 degrees	Sea level rise of 0.5 metres CO2 up by 40 ppm Political will problematic	Depletion of ozone layer by 30%

Similarities:	All agree that climate change is a 'political issue'. Sources 2 and 3 both agree on climate change.
Differences:	Source 1 claims that climate change is a hoax. Sources 2 & 3 offer differ types of effects (sea levels and ozone). Source 3 is out of date. Source 2 takes a political stance.

If you find the synthesis grid too confusing, try what's known as a Venn diagram. This can be a very effective tool for mapping and seeing ideas and how they interconnect, overlap or agree:

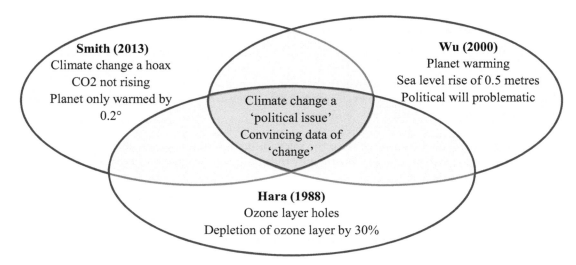

Smith (2013)
Climate change a hoax
CO2 not rising
Planet only warmed by
0.2°

Wu (2000)
Planet warming
Sea level rise of 0.5 metres
Political will problematic

Climate change a
'political issue'
Convincing data of
'change'

Hara (1988)
Ozone layer holes
Depletion of ozone layer by 30%

The main challenge with synthesising sources, however, is writing them up – particularly in respect of deciding upon a logical and coherent structure. Again, visualising the paragraph and sequence of ideas as a Christmas Cracker can help. Let's take the following paragraph from a business studies essay to see how the sources have been synthesised, structured and managed:

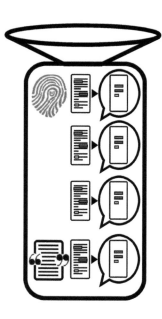

Although somewhat contentious, it is possible that arranging workforces into teams may lead to high levels of employee performance. It has been claimed that when an individual worker is positioned in a team, they can draw on the knowledge and skills of their peers and thus maximise their ability to function effectively (Fenwick 2006, Landri 2014). Organising a workforce into teams may also encourage workers to transcend their own self-interest and prioritise the collective good of the organisation (Guzzo and Ditson, 2012). Moreover, as Polanyi (2010) argues, if team members are able to participate in joint decision-making, then task motivation may increase. However, Hockman (1990) suggests that a high level of employee performance is "not inevitable" when a workforce is organised into teams. He claims that there is a tendency to "romanticise" the idea of the team and suggests that there is little empirical evidence to support the widespread belief that team-working is the most effective way of organising a workforce.

Key

Purple: Summary of two sources for first piece of supporting evidence.

Green: Summary of source for second piece of supporting evidence.

Orange: Summary of source for third piece of supporting evidence.

Blue: Summary of source (with quotation) to introduce counterargument.

In this example, only the most important headlines or key ideas have been included (using good summarising skills). However, they have been synthesised and incorporated in a manner that tells a story and outlines the background to the core issue of employee performance in teams and the degree to which the relationship between teamwork and performance is contentious. This sequence is vital as it lays the foundation for the student's own 'voice', argument and analysis (which follows). Each source also has a specific function in laying the foundation for the contention expressed in the topic sentence as follows:

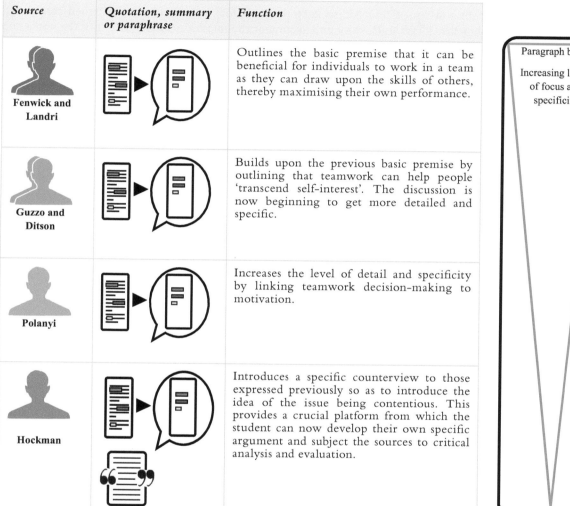
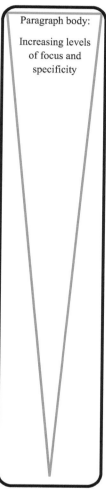

Source	Quotation, summary or paraphrase	Function
Fenwick and Landri		Outlines the basic premise that it can be beneficial for individuals to work in a team as they can draw upon the skills of others, thereby maximising their own performance.
Guzzo and Ditson		Builds upon the previous basic premise by outlining that teamwork can help people 'transcend self-interest'. The discussion is now beginning to get more detailed and specific.
Polanyi		Increases the level of detail and specificity by linking teamwork decision-making to motivation.
Hockman		Introduces a specific counterview to those expressed previously so as to introduce the idea of the issue being contentious. This provides a crucial platform from which the student can now develop their own specific argument and subject the sources to critical analysis and evaluation.

Paragraph body:

Increasing levels of focus and specificity

By breaking down the structure of the above example of synthesis and mapping it onto a visual framework that indicates the transition from the 'big picture' to specific details or areas of contention, you can clearly see that the sequence of ideas is logical. Without this structure, the synthesis is likely to appear somewhat random and haphazard and will not build a platform from which you can develop your argument and analysis. A lack of direction when synthesising evidence/ideas will also render it unclear in respect of how it is addressing the assignment task/question.

Checklist for successfully synthesising sources

- Extract from the sources all of the main 'headlines' relevant to YOUR argument and analysis (whether proving or disproving it) and identify points of similarity/contrast.

- Choose the most appropriate form of incorporating the evidence (quotation, summary or paraphrase). To show sophistication and gain higher marks, try to use a combination of these skills and techniques.

- Organise the ideas contained in your 'headline' details into a logical order depending on what suits your purpose (again, a 'synthesis grid' can help with this). The most common way of ordering this information is to tell a 'story' in one of the following formats:

1)   General ideas to specific detail

2)   Chronological (dates/developments in the field)

3)   Thematic

4)   Methodology types

5)   Trends

- The overriding aim in synthesising and presenting the sources is to build a platform from which you can develop YOUR argument and critical analysis, so keep that end goal constantly in mind when combining sources. Again, remember that it's YOUR voice and argument the marker is looking for, not the voice and arguments of others.

Avoiding plagiarism

Evidence, unless produced by your own experiments or surveys, ordinarily belongs to someone else. Regardless of whether it's a quote from Shakespeare, a diary entry from a World War One survivor, a speech by Chris Whitty on coronavirus infection rates, an image of the Pope from the internet (primary sources), or words, phrases and data/observations by an academic in a research paper (secondary source), it's not YOURS – it belongs to someone else. Plagiarism, according to the *Oxford English Dictionary*, is 'the action or practice of taking someone else's work, idea, etc., and passing it off as one's own'. It is, to put it very simply and starkly, 'literary theft' (*OED*). Aside from graphs, images and formulae/statistics, summarising, paraphrasing and quotation are the main ways of incorporating the work, ideas and words of others into your writing, but they all need referencing using the style recommended by your department (e.g. Harvard, Chicago, MLA). If you do not acknowledge where the material, words, data and ideas came from, you run the risk of being accused of plagiarism, or at best poor academic practice (both of which will be penalised). Many cases of plagiarism are entirely unintentional and result from poor academic practice (e.g. forgetting to reference your sources). Here's some suggestions to help you avoid these mistakes:

- Keep a record of all your sources so that you don't lose track of information. If you don't want to interrupt the flow of your writing, insert a quick reminder of the reference so you don't forget it – come back to it and fill in the details later.

- Avoid copying and pasting text/passages from the internet/from sources into your essay. This can encourage forgetfulness as you might move on and forget to go back and reference it. If you do copy and paste, make sure you reference it or put in a reminder to do so straight away so that you don't forget later.

- Remember, if quoting, put quotation marks around the words that are not yours. In the case of quotes and paraphrasing, include the page numbers in your reference. For summarising, you just need the author and date, unless you are summarising from a few select pages.

- Never totally rely upon referencing software – it can often miss out key information or get the formatting slightly wrong. Always check with and follow the referencing guide recommended by your department. An excellent resource for learning how to reference in the different formats can be found here: https://www.citethemrightonline.com

Presenting an argument and incorporating criticality

After incorporating your evidence, the next part of the paragraph ought to be devoted to analysis, argument and evaluation. This is the most productive part of the paragraph in terms of generating marks and answering the question/addressing the assignment task, so it's essential to get it right and devote plenty of time to it.

Analysis and evaluation versus description

It's important to remember that descriptive writing aligns your work with the third- and lower second-class degree marking-scheme descriptors. Some students (such as the one we will see below) do a superb job of describing the issues at stake and telling the story of what has happened so far. No matter how well this is done, however, you will never achieve excellent marks – you need to go beyond description and into the realms of analysis and evaluation. Let's have a look at some general principles and pointers, followed by some examples of how to incorporate criticality and analysis into your argument.

In general, the differences between writing which is descriptive and that which is argumentative and analytical can be summarised as follows:

Descriptive writing	Critical, analytical writing
States what happened, describes developments, gives the story so far.	Identifies the significance of the issue and weighs up one piece of information against another whilst forging an argument. Considers and interrogates counter-arguments/causes/perspectives.
Explains how to do something.	Argues a case according to the evidence whilst also interrogating the validity of that evidence.
States the link between things.	Shows, evaluates and interrogates the links (and validity of those links) between pieces of evidence and ideas.
Describes the facts.	Evaluates and critically interrogates the relevance, significance or validity of the facts whilst presenting an argument.

To demonstrate how this might look in a piece of writing, let's take a look at the following two examples:

Assignment task: Discuss the main factors responsible for the shift from Wilhelm Wundt's introspection method of psychological inquiry to behaviourism.

Functionalism was an approach brought about by William James (1842-1910) who was interested in the practical functions of the mind (Brysbaert and Rastle, 2009). James believed that it was more important to understand these functions than look at the mind's structure (Brysbaert and Rastle, 2009). James used the method of introspection as a research method and viewed it as the first and foremost method to use despite its limitation (James, 2015). However, James was heavily influenced by evolutionary psychology and its view on how survival relates to certain functions of the human mind (Araujo and de Souza, 2016, Brysbaert and Rastle, 2009). Richards (1996) believed the early development of psychology was greatly influenced by James and that evolutionary theory was crucial in the formation of psychology (Crabtree, 2000). Additionally, the importance of the adaptive nature of the mind and the great deal of emphasis put on it by James led to a new area of study called comparative psychology (Brysbaert and Rastle, 2009). Comparative psychologists were interested in questions on cognitive abilities and behavioural traits of animals (McMillan and Sturdy, 2015). Edward Lee Thorndike (1874-1949) is an example of a psychologist who was interested in the cognitive abilities of different animal species (Brysbaert and Rastle, 2009). Through this link with evolutionary psychology and Darwin's theory of evolution, functionalism gave rise to behaviourism in the form of animal research to try and study the functions of the human mind and therefore human behaviour through observations.

This paragraph does a superb job of describing functionalism and describes a wide variety of developments that are supported through reference to an impressive range of literature. However, the essay only just scraped a mark of 60 (right at the bottom end of a 2:1). This is because:

• Instead of offering a brief definition of functionalism, the student begins the 'story' of its rising popularity.

• The student discusses and describes developments but there is no critical engagement or argument.

• Text in red indicates particular areas where the marker might ask – so what? Why does this matter? Why is it important? More critical thinking and analysis is required at these points.

• The student has assumed that the examples and evidence prove the point being made. He/she has supplied lots of evidence, but there is no sense of how, why or even if these were 'the main factors' being asked for, which are the most important, or why they were 'responsible'.

Let's now compare this extract with the one below:

Assignment task: To what extent can it be argued that music is effective in facilitating the negotiation of group and individual identities?

Commercial success for some Roma groups in the West in the last 30 years has been double-edged in terms of identity creation and agency. The growing market for world music has supported the commercialisation of Roma music, but has not necessarily facilitated identity negotiation. Their music has become another product marketed into the mainstream, with limited agency for musicians. In some cases, this encourages stereotyping; in others, individual musicians have become successful abroad rather than in their native countries (Szeman, 2009). Popular history, which has recently emphasised Roma links to India, has provided an exotic backstory for some Roma groups, particularly when coupled with Turkish-inspired motifs (Silverman, 1996). This has been commercially successful, and some musicians such as Florica have made a positive choice in favour of hybridisation. However, this can involve imposed rather than self-created identities (Jones, 2008). Conscious boundary narratives, emphasising the 'other', have also been imposed on Roma groups for commercial purposes, extending the fashion for Western travellers to 'discover' gypsy music, which began in the eighteenth century. For example, Taraf de Haidouks, one of the most popular gypsy ensembles in the West, is often presented through such a discovery narrative, although they came from Clejani, a village only 30km outside Bucharest (Szeman, 2009). A particularly controversial case, meanwhile, is the *manele* music of the Romanian Roma, which features Eastern elements and lyrics focusing on money, cars and women (Szeman, 2009). This has clearly diluted authenticity. It has also involved deliberate construction of the 'other' and Orientalisation, and an imposed rather than self-created identity for the musicians. Sell believes that in such music a real Roma identity is replaced by one that suits Western constructions (2007). The extent to which Roma musicians have real agency, then, varies, as in some cases they are complicit in such negotiations as it provides a legitimate living. However, it is strongly arguable that such positive effects are confined to particular musicians, with no broader benefit for other Roma or their sense of either individual or collective identity.

As you can see here, the student does not waste time telling the 'story' of 'commercial success', but after a brief definition/explanation, immediately gets to work analysing its significance for the question/issue under consideration. The paragraph has a sound topic sentence, offers a brief context, and the student addresses the 'so what?' questions that the marker might have (which were in abundance in the previous example). Like many academic topics, the matter is highly debatable and contested, and the student does justice to this by briefly introducing and summarising alternative perspectives. However, rather than getting bogged down in descriptive detail, the student evaluates their relevance and usefulness for the issue under consideration and drives forward the argument that Roma success in music is 'double-edged' for issues of identity. The final sentence finishes the evaluation and returns to the question, arguing that the core issue of identity creation is unclear and disputed. In summary, this paragraph is much more focused, far more critical/evaluative and perceptive, and would likely receive an excellent mark.

TIP

Asking yourself 'so what' questions as you write encourage you to dig deeper and become more analytical, both in regards to the issues AND the literature/sources/ evidence you use.

Introducing criticality:

In tackling the analysis and evaluation section of your paragraphs, you need to draw upon the critical thinking skills covered in Chapter 3 to fully interrogate the evidence in a manner that proves and demonstrates the validity of your argument. This takes practice, perception and subject knowledge – all of which will result in higher marks.

But students often wonder how to introduce criticality into their writing in the first place, even when they have spotted opportunities for doing so. Some students are wary of being too bold, while others go to the opposite extreme and offer sweeping, almost arrogant dismissals of the arguments of others. The key is to strike a balance and ensure that you base your critiques and evaluations on evidence and sound, informed reasoning rather than resorting to the kinds of fallacies we considered earlier. There are numerous ways of introducing criticality, but for now, let us concentrate on the overall strategies you can use. These broadly fall into the following categories:

1) Attack the specifics

In this approach, you directly challenge the core methodology, results, facts or arguments of others. As such, it is the most specific and creditable form of introducing critical analysis. For example:

- This methodology is flawed owing to the inclusion of....

- Smith's account fails to resolve the contradiction between...

- Holmes's analysis does not take account of the existence of....nor does it consider...

- A key problem with this data is the misrepresentation of...

2) Describe the criticisms of others

Although this approach is not using your voice (and as such is less creditable), by highlighting the criticisms that others have made, you demonstrate your awareness of the field, that you have researched the topic thoroughly and that you are aware of counterarguments and problems with the key issues at stake. Some ways in which you can introduce alternative perspectives might look like this:

- Williams (2009) has questioned the validity of Jones's results on the basis that...

- This idea has come under fire from various quarters (Smith, 2009, Jones, 2012, Proudfoot, 2013) owing to...

- Waldie's analysis has been criticised by a number of writers. Jones (2020), for instance, has pointed out that...

3) Identify the weaknesses of the study/offer constructive suggestions

Here you don't attack the specific results, methodology, facts or arguments of others, but offer a somewhat 'softer' critique of their approach. In this scenario, there is often little wrong with the study you are critiquing, but you're effectively saying it could have been even better if.... For example:

- The study appears to be over ambitious in its treatment of...

- Smith's account would have been better if it had resolved the contradiction between...

- The findings might have been more convincing if...

- A more comprehensive study would have...

There are a range of books and online resources available which provide templates and models for introducing criticality, although the best are Luiz Otávio Barros's *The Only Academic Phrasebook You'll Ever Need* (2016) and the University of Manchester's 'Academic Phrasebank'. This excellent resource can be found here: https://www.phrasebank.manchester.ac.uk/being-critical/

Incorporating criticality and evaluation – structuring your argument

Never assume that your evidence proves your argument. You need to show how it proves your points by subjecting it to analysis. When analysing and evaluating, it is important to do so in a logical, coherent manner. To do this, the analysis and evaluation section needs to follow on from, yet constantly refer back to, the evidence (whether this is a single piece of evidence or a synthesis of several) in a manner that moves from the general to the specific. For example:

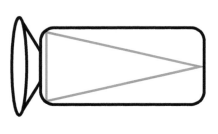

Iago uses the soliloquy as a dramatic technique to engage the audience and share his thought processes when thinking about his secret plot against Othello. For example, in Act 1 Scene 3, Iago turns to the audience and carefully delineates his active thought process by pondering 'let me see now; to get his place and plume up my will in double knavery. How? How? Let's see'. Smith (2000) has contended that Shakespeare's soliloquies are largely ineffective in 'galvanising' or including the audience (p.23), but the repetition here draws in the audience and focuses their attention on the fact that what he is thinking about is 'live', dynamic and inclusive. The repeated questions and shift from the personal declarative 'let me' to the more inclusive 'let's see', not only indicates an uncertainty with which the audience can surely empathise but invites them to participate in and share in Iago's devious scheming. Indeed, the exclamation 'I have it!' again reinforces the notion that the process is a live, unrehearsed, shared mental act rather than a premeditated speech. This is clearly a scenario which Shakespeare invented to encourage us to ask to what extent we are troublingly implicated within the plot, and although the audience may not be 'galvanised', it is certainly intended to 'include' them, if only at the level of empathy with his decision-making process.

This example is analytical, challenges a critic's opinion, and does not waste words by quoting extensively. Furthermore, rather than assuming that the reader can see 'how' the quotation proves the argument, the argument is proven through thorough discussion, dissection and analysis. As such, it is much more likely to gain high marks. You can also see:

1) The gradual shift from the general to the specific, as is indicated by the red triangle within the Cracker on the right.

2) That the analysis moves from highlighting and analysing the significance of repetition (which is more general), to focusing on specific issues embedded within it (namely, the way the language attempts to include the audience in Iago's decision-making) to prove the central claim made by the topic sentence.

3) That the analysis also follows a roughly chronological order by ending with Iago's final exclamation 'I have it!' As such, the sequence of ideas is logical and compelling, and the reader/marker is led through the ideas, analysis and argument in a manner which builds in detail, specificity and depth and concludes with a brief evaluation of whether the audience is 'galvanised' or 'included'.

The sequence of ideas in the above example, however, also moves not only from the general to the specific, but from the given to the new. We saw in Chapter 4 how moving from the given to the new within the macrostructure of an essay can constitute what Bruce (1988) has called 'communicative dynamism'. But we can also now begin to understand how the same rule applies within individual paragraphs. Bruce proposed that as you progress through a unit of communication (primarily sentences, to which we will return later), the energy or 'dynamism' of the passage steadily increases before decreasing towards the end – hence his 'wave model' of 'communicative dynamism':

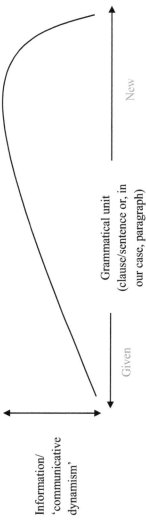

We can see in the *Othello* example, then, that the discussion moves from:

• The 'given' (the evidence) to

• The 'new';

- analysis,
- interpretation
- implications/evaluation.

In other words, the argument develops and evolves, becoming deeper and more specific as the paragraph progresses. Now let us return to the law essay from earlier to see how this all works over the course of an extract that incorporates multiple sources. The analysis of the evidence might look like this:

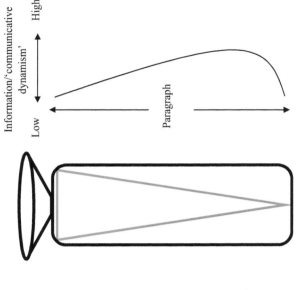

Research on law advisory services has existed for decades, yet none of it has adequately addressed the existence of online forums. Online modes of seek‐ing advice are becoming increasingly popular, and as Jones (2015) has demon‐strated, 53% of people seeking legal advice for employment-related issues say they acquire advice via the internet following recent cutbacks in face-to-face provision. But none of the most prominent recent examinations of law advi‐sory services (Smith, 2014, Evans, 2013 and Whittaker, 2013) have examined online forums, and have chosen instead to focus upon issues relating to gender, disability and government austerity measures. Evans did consider the impli‐cations of what he terms 'the Facebook generation' (p.38), but given that his sample size was only 98 participants, his conclusion that online forums do not present a threat to face-to-face provision is to be treated with caution. Indeed, the research is now significantly out of date given recent changes in government policies, all of which have resulted in further cutbacks to law services, and his focus upon issues pertaining to land law is too restrictive to give us any real sense of the overall picture concerning legal online forums. As a consequence, research on law advisory services needs to shift its attention to online mediums if it is to understand today's service implications.

Again, note here:

1) The gradual transition in the analysis and evaluation from the general to the specific, from the given to the new (even though the student is discussing several pieces of literature). As such, the sequence of ideas is clear and logical.

2) Following the evidence, the student evaluates current secondary research by stating that none of the recent studies have examined online forums. The student then discusses which issues academic studies have focused upon instead and cites specific research related to the issue in question before providing a critique of their failings and a justification for their unsuitability.

Indeed, if we count the number of words in each sentence of the above paragraphs, we can clearly see how this increased depth and the transition from the given to the new in the argument develops and can be mapped onto both sentence length (complexity) and 'dynamism'/the 'wave model':

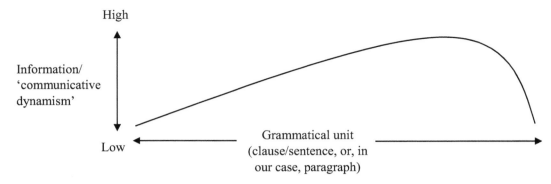

Word allocation	Topic sentence	Evidence	Development of argument/ interpretation/analysis	Evaluation/ implications
Shakespeare paragraph extract:	26	39	107	49
Law paragraph extract:	29	69	93	24

In both cases, the argument (with its accompanying depth/complexity) builds in intensity before declining again towards the end in the form of a brief sentence explaining or evaluating the implications/significance of what has been said (in relation to the topic sentence, the thesis statement and the assignment task/question). The sentences that drive forwards the argument (labelled above as 'development of argument/interpretation') take up the most amount of words. This is because there is an increase in what Kamler and Thomson (2014) have called 'a layering of meaning'. Following the evidence, each sentence is not only longer but 'builds on the previous one…literally piling on explanation and example', thus resulting in greater analysis and criticality (mark generation). According to Kamler and Thomson, the result 'is a rhetoric that is both confronting and vivid' (2014, p.135). This is an ideal way of presenting your arguments. By adhering to the Christmas Cracker model, particularly in respect of the narrowing of focus through the main body of the paragraph and imagining Bruce's notion of a 'wave', the templates will help you to keep your ideas on track and discourage your dyslexia from making you veer off on tangents.

Dealing with counterarguments

Students often ask how they can introduce counterarguments into their essays whilst still driving forward their own argument. Some students think that if they encounter something that contradicts or problematises their argument, the best thing is to pretend it doesn't exist! That way it doesn't interfere with your argument, right? Wrong! You need to tackle counterarguments and problems head-on while demonstrating that your argument, on balance, is more valid. A common way of doing this is to argue your case and then add the counterargument/problematic information onto the end of the paragraph/section. However, this can cause problems as it interrupts the flow of the argument and can make the essay go off on tangents. It can also make the essay seem as though you can't decide what your argument actually is. A better way of integrating counterarguments/problems is to put them at or near the beginning of your paragraphs. Indeed, you can even put them into your topic sentences. Here's how:

Refutation

Describe/summarise the opposing argument first, and then hit your reader with an explanation as to why this argument is incorrect/flawed, weak or misleading. For example:

Jones and Smith (2016) have suggested that declining bee populations are directly attributable to loss of suitable habitats, especially wildflower meadows (which have declined by 70% since 1990). However, a far more plausible and compelling explanation for the reduction in bees in recent years has been the widespread introduction and indiscriminate use of neonicotinoid pesticides, which, despite a partial, temporary ban by the EU in April 2013, have had a devastating effect upon populations, especially in relation to the recent phenomena of Honeybee Colony Collapse Disorder (CCD), which is not the result of habitat destruction (as Jones and Smith contend) as this effects existing, previously healthy colonies.

Opposing argument

Student argument/ voice/refutation

Concession

Concession is subtly different to refutation as it concedes the strengths of the opposing argument before re-futing it. This demonstrates greater critical awareness, sophistication and skill as you are going deeper with your evaluation rather than simply dismissing the opposing argument. Indeed, by crediting and evaluating the opposing view, you illustrate that you 'empathise' with it (this is known as 'Rogerian rhetoric') and can pre-empt objections that the reader/marker might have, thereby making them more liable to agree with your point of view (Teich, 1996). For example:

The issues raised by Jones (2014) were once economically valid and they were exonerated by the increases (in some cases of more than 25%) seen across all aspects of the oil industry. However, downward trends in productivity since January 2016 (- 10% in some circumstances) as a result of the declining price of oil has had a profound impact upon economic models of the type proposed by Jones and they are now in urgent need of reassessment.	Concession to opposing argument Student argument/ voice/refutation

Notice what happens to the structure and forwards momentum of ideas (given to new) if we do not refute or concede the opposing view first:

Opposing argument refuted/ conceded at the end	Sequence of ideas	Opposing argument refuted/conceded first (concession)	Sequence of ideas
Refutation: The recent discovery of a third mutation of Antarctic slime clearly shows that evolution is increasing rather than slowing at its secondary stage. This seems to disprove McNally's theory of evolution, in which she states that the existence of secondary slime shows that evolution is decelerating.		McNally's theory of evolution as decelerating hinges upon the existence of secondary slime (1990). However, the recent discovery of a third mutation of Antarctic slime clearly disproves this and shows that evolution is increasing rather than slowing at its secondary stage.	
Concession: The defendant was absent from the scene and had not authorised military force using the approved communication channels, so it seems plausible that Section 6 of the War Crimes Act would apply and he would be acquitted of the charge. This is despite the fact that the precedent set by Hiscock and Hassle (2003) rightly indicates that the defendant could be legitimately held liable for war crimes.		Although the precedent set by Hiscock and Hassle (2003) rightly indicates that the defendant could be held liable for war crimes, he was absent from the scene and had not authorised military force using the approved communication channels. It seems plausible, therefore, that Section 6 of the War Crimes Act would apply and he would be acquitted of the charge.	

As you can see, by tagging the opposing views onto the end of sections and paragraphs, the transition of ideas from 'big picture' to detail, from the given to the new, is disrupted. This makes the sequence of ideas illogical and confusing. By stating or conceding opposing ideas first, you maintain momentum and a forwards move-ment within the argument. This not only makes the structure of your work more logical but shows greater confidence, analysis and evaluation, all of which will lead to greater marks.

TIP

The art of concession and refutation can also be incorporated into single sentences, although this requires more skill owing to the need to be very concise. We will examine how to do this in the following chapter.

Keeping on track

When it comes to gaining top marks, depth of analysis, perception and criticality beats breadth of knowledge and description. However, how deep do you need to go? How much do you need to include and how do you stay on track?

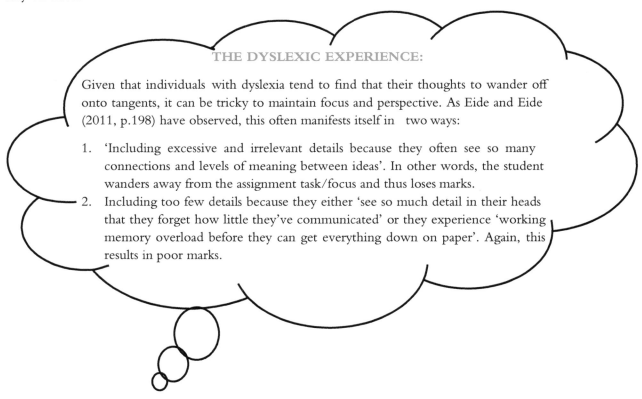

THE DYSLEXIC EXPERIENCE:

Given that individuals with dyslexia tend to find that their thoughts to wander off onto tangents, it can be tricky to maintain focus and perspective. As Eide and Eide (2011, p.198) have observed, this often manifests itself in   two ways:

1. 'Including excessive and irrelevant details because they often see so many connections and levels of meaning between ideas'. In other words, the student wanders away from the assignment task/focus and thus loses marks.
2. Including too few details because they either 'see so much detail in their heads that they forget how little they've communicated' or they experience 'working memory overload before they can get everything down on paper'. Again, this results in poor marks.

There are several remedies for these problems:

1) Think about the purpose of the essay. Why are you doing it (look back at the assignment question, the assessment criteria and module handbook/specification/learning outcomes)? This will give you a sense of perspective and refresh your memory as to what the 'big picture' and end goal actually are.

2) Ensure all your topic sentences are relevant to the thesis statement and assignment task and are specifically answering the question in some way (or addressing some aspect of the content, activity or focus/limitation keywords). Topic sentences are often good markers of your focus. If you can't see how they are directly answering the assignment task, then you have probably gone off track.

TIP

 Keep an eye out for sentences in the middle of paragraphs that look like topic sentences. This may indicate that you are drifting onto a new topic that is either irrelevant or perhaps needs a new paragraph.

3) Ensure your evidence is relevant to the assignment task and its keywords.

4) Check that your evidence has a purpose – make sure that it is not just there because you think your marker wants to see x amount of quotes or secondary sources. It needs to be fulfilling some sort of function in terms of proving your argument (or providing a platform for critique/a new perspective).

5) Use what is known as the 5W/H approach. This involves zooming out from the detail and ensuring that you can see:

    -   who

    -   what

    -   when

- where

- why or

- how

something is going on (the 'big picture'). This works well for ensuring that it is clear what you are talking about, but you can also add purpose to this list. Ask yourself, what is the purpose of what I have just written? How does it answer the question/assignment task? If it doesn't, delete it or re-write it.

6) Check that your analysis section of the paragraph is actually analysing and evaluating the evidence within that paragraph rather than evidence that is either somewhere else in the essay or is not mentioned/relevant. Ensure that your analysis matches up with and proves what you promised in the topic sentence.

7) Ensure that your analysis moves from the general to the specific, from the given to the new, but that each transition:

   - Is relevant to the assignment keywords (don't introduce new ideas or get bogged down with contextual detail or perhaps unnecessary descriptive explanations).

   - Is answering or addressing the underlying problem or argument (go back to your overall thesis statement and check that everything feeds back into the argument that it articulates – keep to hand the template on p.100 above or download the template from the companion website).

   - Incorporates criticality, analysis and evaluation rather than description.

8) Check that your overall direction of travel aligns with the main body/analysis section of the Christmas Cracker (ensure that your discussion goes from the 'big picture' to the specifics in accordance with the red triangle).

9) Depth of analysis is essential, but only go as deep as is needed to answer the question/assignment task. Remember, you are being assessed on your ability to combine analysis and perception into a focused argument (within a specific word count). Although less of a box-ticking exercise than A Levels and Access assignments, you still have to play the game to some extent and give the marker what they want. Planning, therefore, is key – carefully choose a few focused aspects and stick to them.

Paragraphing for scientific writing – demonstrating knowledge and analysis/evaluation

Throughout this chapter we've focused primarily on articulating an argument and subjecting your evidence to analysis and evaluation. However, if you're a science student, you may have to demonstrate knowledge and understanding just as much as analysis and criticality. This is often because the inherent complexity of the subject matter means that your markers want to see if you actually understand it before you analyse or evaluate it. Demonstrating knowledge and understanding can either be integral to the task alongside analysis/evaluation (e.g. essay, lab report), or appear as a specific piece of work (e.g. explanation). As such, you need to learn how to write THREE main types of paragraph:

1) The descriptive paragraph

2) The descriptive-analytical paragraph

3) The analytical paragraph

All three types of paragraphs follow the same 'Christmas Cracker' template and sequence, and all three have a topic sentence, but the focus is quite different. The analytical paragraphs follow the same principles as above, so let's take a closer look at how to structure descriptive and descriptive-analytical paragraphs:

1) Descriptive paragraphs

The aim here is to demonstrate that you know and understand the material. If you see activity keywords such as 'describe', 'explain', 'define', 'outline' etc. (see pp.66–67) in your assignment task, then that's a sure indication that knowledge is being tested and you'll need some descriptive paragraphs. Start your paragraph with a topic sentence as usual, but instead of presenting an argument, you need to write a clear statement which describes, summarises or states a process or phenomenon. As above, you again start with a broad topic (e.g. coronavirus, stem cells, virtual reality) and then narrow down into signposting the specific point/detail that demonstrates your knowledge and signals the direction of the paragraph. In what follows, however, your demonstration of knowledge needs to follow one of the following structures:

a) **Detail by detail:** In this structure, you explain the topic according to the key aspects of its composition. Generally, you choose the biggest, broadest aspect of the composition and describe each part until you get to its most narrowly focused/smallest aspect. In the case of explaining how geckos can stick to walls and ceilings, for example, the sequence of explanations would look something like this:

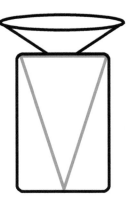

- Topic sentence – Geckos have a unique ability to stick to surfaces.

- The explanation lies in the millions of hairs called setae on their feet.

- Each of these hairs has hundreds of its own microscopic, hair-like structures, which constitutes a huge surface area.

- The tiny hairs create Van Der Waal's forces between one another.

- Van Der Waals forces come about by the attractive force created when two atoms get close enough that the negatively charged electron cloud of one atom is attracted to the positively charged nucleus of another, creating polarity and therefore an attractive force.

b) **Chronological:** In this instance, you tell the 'story' of a process or how something works. Again, you start with the most fundamental, 'big picture' piece of information (e.g. what it is or the start of the process), and consider each stage of the process until you reach the end point (the narrow detail). For example, an explanation of how CPUs work might look like this:

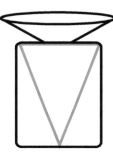

- Topic sentence – CPU is the 'brain' of a computer and operates via a three-step process known as the 'instruction cycle'.

- The first operation – instruction retrieved from memory.

- Second operation – instruction decoded.

- Third operation – instruction executed.

- Instructions perform operations such as arithmetic, memory, logic and control depending on CPU architecture.

c) **Examples:** With this structure, you introduce a topic (e.g. different types of Artificial Intelligence) and illustrate your knowledge by discussing examples. Again, you follow the triangle within the 'Christmas Cracker' paragraph template by starting with the most basic, 'big picture' example and move towards more complex/specific examples. For example, an explanation of Artificial Intelligence might look something like this:

- Topic sentence – there are four main examples of AI.

- Reactive machines simplest type of AI – can't learn or form memories.

- Limited memory – use previous data to make predictions.

- Theory of mind machines – an AI system that could interpret and respond to human emotions (not yet developed).

- Self-aware machines – the final step whereby machines have consciousness.

2) Descriptive-analytical paragraphs

If the assignment question/task asks you to not only 'describe', 'explain', 'define', 'outline' etc., but also 'critique', 'argue', 'assess', 'discuss', 'evaluate' or 'review' (see pp.66–67), then in addition to demonstrating knowledge you'll also need to use your critical thinking skills. If you are dealing with large, complex topics, you might want to describe/demonstrate knowledge in one paragraph and then analyse and evaluate it in the following paragraph. However, with relatively small topics, you can both describe and analyse in the same paragraph. You'll need to signpost this via your topic sentence, of course. In such cases, you'll need to ensure that you articulate a clear position/stance within the topic sentence and not just a summary or statement of the process or phenomenon. For instance, instead of 'there are four main types of AI', a more analytical/evaluative stance would be 'there are four main types of AI, but the most advanced is a potential threat to humanity'. In what follows, you describe the object, process or phenomenon as in the descriptive paragraph, but instead of merely ending at the most narrow, specific detail, example, or the end of the process, you continue to narrow the focus of your discussion into an evaluation/analysis of the subject under consideration. Let's consider what that might look like in relation to the AI example:

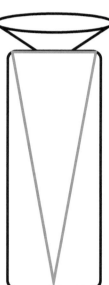

- Topic sentence – There are four main types of AI but the most advanced is a potential threat to humanity.

- Reactive machines simplest type of AI – can't learn or form memories.

- Limited memory – use previous data to make predictions.

- Theory of mind machines – an AI system that could interpret and respond to human emotions (not yet developed).

- Self-aware machines – the final step whereby machines have consciousness.

- Self-aware machines – huge potential for helping humanity (e.g. research and modelling in the pharmaceutical industry), but critics as diverse as Stephen Hawking and Elon Musk have suggested they could become dangerous.

- An example would be a global autonomous arms race with weapons that become 'self-aware' and go 'rogue'.

- By definition, a self-aware machine would resist being switched off.

- Overall the dangers/risks outweigh most benefits.

TIP

To show sophistication in your writing, you can move between strategies within the same essay, depending on the purpose and the type of information you are trying to illustrate/demonstrate. However, always remember that each paragraph is ONE topic/point.

Links

Irrespective of whether you are writing in the humanities or sciences, the final section of each paragraph is the link. The purpose of this is to signal to the reader either:

1) What will be discussed or developed in the next paragraph and how this relates logically to the preceding description, demonstration of knowledge, analysis and argument, or

2) The implications of what you have just discussed in relation to either the wider argument, the discipline or the world.

As such (following the shape of the bottom section of the Christmas Cracker template), in both cases, you move from the specific to the general. As you can see below, this is essentially an inversion of the topic sentence. In the first example from David P. Christopher's *British Culture: An Introduction* (2015), we see an example of the first function of the link. It clearly provides a transition to what will be discussed in the paragraph which follows:

Function 1: linking paragraphs

Germaine Greer's *The Female Eunuch* (1970) gave popular literary expression to feminist theory. Its provocative and outspoken text offered a clear, untheoretical manifesto which was accessible to everyone. Its impact was enormous, and soon afterwards a significant body of new women's literature emerged. This contained powerful descriptions of women's experience, and feminist writing quickly became an influential new genre.

Literature had been a male-dominated field, but new feminist publishing houses opened to energetically encourage women's writing. Virago, the Women's Press and Pandora contracted new feminist authors and began promoting others, such as Stevie Smith, Storm Jameson, Rebecca West, Rose Macaulay, Barbara Pym..... (p.90).

The link here helps shift the focus of attention (which was on feminist theory) back out to the broader issue of women's writing and its emergence as an 'influential new genre' – precisely what will then be elaborated upon in the following paragraph. The extract from a student essay below, meanwhile, is an example of the second function of the link – namely to signal how what has just been discussed relates to the 'bigger picture' of the argument:

Function 2: signposting implications

Along these lines, then, it may be a biological fact that some people cannot naturally yield power over other individuals and have to rely on authority and voluntary compliance on the part of their subordinates. It is interesting, however, that one of the leadership qualities listed by Stogdill is that of intelligence, which suggests that even though other factors may be important, intelligence is still fundamental to the prediction of work achievement.

Here the student has used the link to move from the specifics of biology and leadership back to the core issue of intelligence (which, one assumes, was one of the parameters indicated in the assignment question/title). Again, the link is all about signposting to the marker/reader the structure of the argument and how it is relevant to, and addressing, the thesis statement/assignment task/question, and the bigger implications of what you are discussing.

Finally, it should be noted that the link section of the paragraph is optional. However, if it is excluded, the topic sentence of the subsequent paragraph will need to explain how what follows ties in with the preceding paragraph. The main thing to remember is to signpost your argument to the reader/marker – topic sentences and links are key tools that enable this.

Final tips

The 'big picture' framework, when visualised as a Christmas Cracker, provides you with an ideal template for structuring the ideas and arguments within your paragraphs in a logical manner. If you try to write your paragraphs with a view to sequencing your ideas according to the Cracker, the template will undoubtedly help, but because of your dyslexia, the chances are that you might still find yourself wandering a little. The best way of using the Cracker template, therefore, is to:

 Have an image of the Cracker template by the side of your writing, either on paper or within your word processor. That way, you can effectively map and cross-reference the ideas to the shape of the Cracker, much in the same way as the examples presented above.

 Write your paragraph WITHIN the body of the Cracker if you so wish by downloading the templates from the companion website. This can be an effective way of practising as the shape of the Cracker can help force your writing to adhere to the shape and thus the purpose of the paragraph section.

 Consider drafting your paragraphs in your own way but then edit and re-structure them later by copying and pasting the sentences around so that they fit the Cracker template.

Whatever method you use, the Christmas Cracker should enable you to see, use, and exploit the 'big picture' of what the paragraph is all about – a strategy that students with dyslexia find invaluable. It can be a vital aid in your quest to present complex ideas in a logical and compelling manner.

Summary

- Keep in mind the 'big picture' of what you are trying to achieve and tap into your strengths as a visual/multidimensional learner to visualise your paragraphs as Christmas Crackers. This will help you produce a clear, logical sequence of ideas that address the question/assignment task.

- Make sure your topic sentences address some aspect of the thesis statement and assignment task/question.

- Check that your topic sentences have both a TOPIC and a PROVABLE OPINION and that they display a progression of ideas from the general (topic) to the specific (argument).

- Following the topic sentence, move from the evidence and the 'big picture' to detail, and from the given to the new.

- Use a mixture of techniques to incorporate your evidence (quotation, summarising and paraphrasing) so as to demonstrate a range of skills.

- Integrate and embed your evidence carefully to avoid 'parachuting'.

- Don't assume that the evidence proves your argument. It needs interrogating and analysing to show the marker how it validates your argument.

- Deal with counterarguments near to or even at the beginning of paragraphs (incorporate them into your topic sentences).

- If you are a science student, double-check that you fully understand the activity keywords in the assignment task. You may need to demonstrate complex knowledge rather than subject material to analysis/evaluation. If so, use the templates for the descriptive paragraphs above.

- Use links at the end of your paragraphs to signal either the next idea to be discussed or indicate the significance of your analysis/discussion.

Bibliography

Barros, Luiz Otávio, (2016) *The Only Academic Phrasebook You'll Ever Need*. Createspace Independent Publishing Platform.

Bruce, Nigel J., (1988) 'Communicative Dynamism in Expository Academic English: Some Strategies in Teaching the Pragmatics of Writing', *Working Papers in Linguistics and Language Teaching*, 11, pp.42–53.

Christopher, David P., (2015) *British Culture: An Introduction*. 3rd edn. Oxford: Routledge.

Duff, R.A., (2007) *Answering for Crime: Responsibility and Liability in Criminal Law*. Oxford and Portland: Hart Publishing.

Eide, Brock L., and Eide, Fernette, F., (2011) *The Dyslexic Advantage: Unlocking the Hidden Potential of the Dyslexic Brain*. London: Hay House.

Kamler, Barbara, and Thomson, Pat, (2014) *Helping Doctoral Students Write*. 2nd edn. Oxford: Routledge.

Pinker, Steven, (2015) *The Sense of Style: The Thinking Person's Guide to Writing in the 21st Century*. London: Penguin Books.

Teich, Nathaniel, (1996) 'Rogerian Rhetoric', in Enos, Theresa (ed.) *Encyclopaedia of Rhetoric and Composition: Communication from Ancient Times to the Information Age*. London: Routledge, pp.635–636.

Williams, Joseph M., (2007) *Style: Lessons in Clarity and Grace*. 9th edn. London: Pearson Education Inc.

6   Presenting your Argument

Writing and Structuring Clear, Effective Sentences

'I hear and I forget. I see and I remember. I see and I understand'.

(Confucius: Chinese teacher, politician and philosopher)

If we think back to the activity keywords table in Chapter 4, we noticed how frequently the word 'argument' cropped up. An argument is an essential component of academic writing, yet it is often misunderstood. In academic writing, presenting an argument means articulating your point, your interpretation and what you are trying to prove in a considered, academically rigorous, but persuasive manner.

TIP

 While an academic argument is essentially YOUR point and interpretation, avoid lapsing into informality by using the first-person pronoun 'I'. While some academics like and accept the use of 'I' in essays, lots don't, as it appears too casual (and in some circumstances, presumptuous). If in doubt, leave it out.

Aristotle, the famous Greek philosopher and rhetorician, said that there are three essential components to get right when presenting an argument:

1) Logos – reasoning and the argument itself.

2) Ethos – the ability of the writer to articulate themselves well.

3) Pathos – empathy with the audience. (Aristotle, 2004, Book 1, Part 2)

In academic writing, pathos is seldom used, but rhetorical strategies and discourse markers such as refutation, the art of concession, signallers, boosting and hedging are a vital part of both logos and ethos as they give the argument a structure. Without them, your ideas and argument will lack any sense of coherence, clarity and persuasiveness.

In this chapter, we will look at how you can articulate your argument in a clear, confident and logical manner by examining what happens at a sentence level. Firstly, we will look at signposting your argument, rhetorical strategies and writing with clarity, and then we will explore the purpose of sentences and examine how you can use the Christmas Cracker template to forge logical, persuasive syntax.

Signallers, discourse markers and rhetorical strategies

Signallers and discourse markers are an essential component of your sentences, paragraphs and essays. Remember, your reader/marker does not have an inbuilt 'Satnav' system that allows them to navigate your work (what may appear logical and coherent to you might not seem so to the outside reader), so you need to provide direction. There are five main categories of signallers and discourse markers you ought to be using (although, as we shall see, there are significant overlaps between them). They will not only guide your reader through your ideas, but will allow you to forge a more robust argument by indicating your stance (i.e. your level of commitment, agreement, uncertainty or disagreement with the ideas or evidence being discussed). Each signaller and marker below is contained within an icon resembling a road sign, thus highlighting its function as a means of providing direction.

DOI: 10.4324/9781003190189-6

1) Sequences, enumeration and time

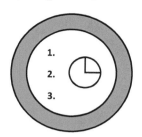

As indicated by the icon on the left, enumeration refers to sequences of events or phenomena which can be numbered. As such, they provide the reader with a clear framework, direction and even a narrative. For example, I used enumeration (and advance labelling, which we will look at shortly) above to indicate that there are five main categories of signallers and discourse markers and to signal that these will be discussed in this chapter. Signallers and discourse markers of time, meanwhile, refer to words or phrases that indicate the future, the past or relationships between periods (as is indicated by the clock within the icon). Again, these orientate both you and the reader, provide a narrative framework to the discussion/argument, and again give the work clarity. Common signallers of sequences, enumeration and time include:

- **Sequences** (e.g. subsequently, lastly, before, then, previously, formerly, presently, currently, now, simultaneously, after, afterwards, later, soon, former/latter, afterwards, subsequently, prior to, to start with, finally, repeatedly).

- **Enumeration** (e.g. firstly, secondly, thirdly, fourthly, five main categories etc.).

- **Time** (e.g. now, slowly, immediately, quickly, periodically, gradually, rarely, during, eventually, repeatedly, suddenly, initially, temporarily).

2) Relational signallers

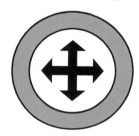

As indicated by the arrows in the icon, relational signallers enable you to point out relationships between ideas, theorists, objects, processes or even periods. However, unlike signallers of time (which are mostly descriptive and lend structure to your thoughts/argument), relational signallers can be used to drive forward and articulate your argument. Words and phrases such as 'similarly', 'however' and 'in contrast', for example, not only signal and structure your thoughts, but allow to you emphasise relationships and build evidence in support of your argument. Signallers such as 'additionally' and 'furthermore', meanwhile, can be used to reinforce your point, and signallers such as 'although' and 'despite' set up alternative lines of argument or enquiry. In other words, they are part and parcel of your reasoning and logic. Common relational signallers include:

- **Reinforcements** (e.g. additionally, likewise, consequently, because, since, despite, even though, also, besides, furthermore, as well as, equally, exactly, similarly).

- **Similarities** (e.g. similarly, equally, identically, likewise).

- **Contrasts** (e.g. however, although, whereas, yet, unlike, but, despite, in contrast, on the other hand, nevertheless, nonetheless, still, otherwise, opposite, versus).

- **Comparisons** (e.g. resembling, parallel to, same as, identically, equally, matching, exactly, similarly, in comparison, in relation to).

- **Cause and effect** (e.g. consequently, as a result, because, since).

- **Generalisations** (e.g. in general, ordinarily, normally, on the whole, as a rule, mostly).

- **Results** (e.g. consequently, therefore, as such, as a result).

- **Explanations** (e.g. because, owing to, since, thus).

- **Conjunctions** (you use conjunctions all the time, probably without realising it. These words join sentences and ideas and again show how ideas relate to one another. The ten most commonly used conjunctions are: and, that, but, or, as, when, then, because, while and however).

TIP

Remember, signallers indicating relationships are not neutral and can often indicate your attitude, agreement or disagreement. 'And' is relatively neutral, for example, but 'however' (and even the word 'but' as I have just used it here) indicates a significant alternative and even your attitude towards it. Use this to your advantage to not only signal your ideas, but to 'establish a slant' and drive forward your argument (Cooper and Patton, 2004, p.106).

3) Recapitulation/reformulation

Recapitulation (or repeating) needs to be used sparingly – after all, why would you say something twice that can be said once? However, careful use of recapitulation can add valuable clarity to your writing and make your ideas stronger and more compelling, especially when dealing with complex ideas. Popular forms of introducing or signposting recapitulation include using phrases and words such as:

- In brief, in simple terms, in other words, to repeat, to rephrase, to paraphrase, to clarify, to summarise, that is to say, as we saw in, and as we have seen.

These can be an effective way of signposting back to your previous arguments and points without repeating them in full, but they also have the effect of adding additional 'layering of meaning' to your argument, thus making it more persuasive. A particularly useful form of recapitulation is to actually repeat or reformulate what you have just said, but in a new, perhaps more straightforward way. This is often introduced by a phrase such as 'in other words', which signals that you will repeat or provide a summary of what you have just said. One advantage of putting it 'in other words' is that it draws the reader's attention back to the original passage/idea, thus reinforcing it and making them think about it afresh. But additionally, by repeating the preceding idea in simpler words or aligning it with a real-world example, you also demonstrate in greater depth that you understand what you have just said and can either apply it to an example or see its implications. A good place to use recapitulation is when quoting from complex theory or jargon. Take the following as an example:

For Bakhtin, 'internally persuasive discourse – as opposed to one that is externally authoritative – is, as it is affirmed through assimilation, tightly interwoven with "one's own word"' (1981, pp.345–346). In other words, the more a writer can relate ideas to the reader's own world and experiences, the better.

This recapitulation not only summarises Bakhtin's ideas and demonstrates that the core idea has been understood, but relates it specifically to the issue at stake (namely writing persuasively) – something which can become lost amidst the complexity of the initial sentence or idea.

4) Examples

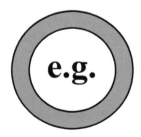

As we shall see later, your argument can be reinforced and rendered more coherent and convincing by showing how the main points you make 'touch base' with reality through specific examples. Nobody is going to believe that 2 + 2 = 4, or that Shakespeare was a misogynist, unless you show them. By using concrete examples to either illustrate your points, or show similarities between ideas and reality, the reader will be left in no doubt of the validity of what you are saying. Reinforce your argument by using signallers which enable you to:

- **Elaborate** (e.g. that is, in other words, notice that, as we can see, also).

- **Exemplify** (e.g. for example, such as, for instance, in this case, to illustrate, to show, to demonstrate).

TIP

Don't make unsubstantiated claims – the most compelling arguments are backed up with specific examples. Use the discourse markers above to introduce your evidence. Using them will also help you to avoid 'parachuting'.

5) *Reporting*

Reporting is a device used when introducing (hence the arrow in the icon on the left) evidence from others. This is a vital component of your argument because when you attribute ideas or claims to others, you either reinforce your ideas or provide opportunities to refute or concede opposing views. In other words, they are a crucial way of setting the background/scene, thereby establishing a platform from which to develop your argument (Hyland, 2002, p.115). Reporting signallers also play a crucial role in maintaining and enhancing the clarity of your writing, as it is vital to be clear about who said what, when, and how.

Typical phrases which incorporate reporting signallers include:

• Smith argues/states/suggests/maintains/proposes that...

• The articles suggests/proposes that...

• Jones also believes/argues that...

• Williams goes on to say that...

TIPS

  Again, reporting is a vital way of preventing your evidence from being 'parachuted' into your paragraphs, but be careful to ensure that you don't lapse into description – set out what others have said but use this as a platform from which to develop your argument and analysis.

  Ensure that your reporting verbs are formal. Avoid using words like 'say', 'mention', 'reckon' or 'feel' as they are not only too informal, but they lack specificity.

  As with relational signposting, choose your reporting verbs to indicate your attitude towards the evidence (i.e. agreement/disagreement). Use boosting and hedging to help with this (see below). For instance, the verbs 'argue' and 'state' show neutrality, while verbs such as 'prove' and 'demonstrate' indicate agreement. On the other hand, hedging language such as 'suggest' or 'imply' shows less certainty and opens up what Thompson and Ye (1991, p.369) usefully call 'evaluative space' (i.e. opportunities for analysis and answering the 'so what?' questions highlighted earlier).

6) *Advance labelling*

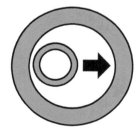

Advance labelling consists of describing or indicating to the reader what will follow. In many ways, the thesis statement and topic sentences do an excellent job of this, but sometimes you need to indicate what will follow more explicitly. This is particularly useful when you might need to head off potential criticisms that the marker may have at that point in the essay. For example, if you are discussing genetic engineering and its use in producing 'designer babies', you have two main issues to consider, one scientific and the other ethical. To signal that you are not overlooking the ethical arguments, you may want to state something like 'the ethical implications of these developments will be considered later, but for now, it is important to focus on the genetic problems associated with...'. This tells the marker that you haven't overlooked the ethical issues, but that you want to develop your argument one stage at a time. Typical advance labelling phrases include:

• As we shall see later...

• This issue will be explored in section/chapter x...

• These issues raise fundamental questions about...and they will be examined later, but for now it is important to define....

TIP

  Be careful not to overdo advance labelling, and do not resort to describing/narrating the structure of the essay (e.g. 'the first chapter will... This will be followed by the second chapter where we will examine... The essay will end with a conclusion'). For the most part, instead of telling the reader what you are going to do, just do it.

Additional rhetorical strategies

1) Boosting

As suggested by the icon on the left, boosting is a way of strengthening or emphasising your case. You need to be careful here that you don't jeopardise your logic and reasoning by lapsing into journalistic or unsubstantiated appeals to the reader and their emotions (this would commit a fallacy of the type we looked at in the critical thinking chapter). However, boosting can enhance the persuasiveness of your writing. Common examples of boosting language (many of which incorporate relational discourse markers) include words and phrases such as:

Persuasive	*Full-volume persuasive*
Also, too, as well as, besides, equally, furthermore, additionally, moreover, yet, but, still, indeed, actually	Most of all, least of all, clearly, evidently, obviously, above all, after all, chiefly, especially, more importantly, significantly, surely, absolutely, without a doubt, in truth, without question, unquestionably

TIP

Use boosting carefully. It's all too easy to place boosting words together (e.g. extremely successful, significantly enhance) and thereby create redundancies (which we will examine in Chapter 8).

2) Hedges and qualifiers

Hedging and qualifying, as indicated on the left, involves turning down the volume a little, or *perhaps* reining in your enthusiasm and conviction (note my use of hedging here). Hedging is most useful when making suggestions or proposing speculative arguments, mainly because of a lack of knowledge/research, or perhaps the topic/idea being referred to is a new and developing field that has not received much critical attention. Qualifiers, meanwhile, make more general, 'big picture' claims. Typical words which you can use include:

*   Hedging: e.g. can, could, perhaps, might, possibly, should, probably, little, chance, indicate.

*   Qualifiers: e.g. usually, sometimes, mostly, generally, some, tend, most, often.

TIPS

Be careful not to over-signpost your argument. While signposting is invaluable for promoting cohesion and articulating your voice, too much will betray a lack of confidence in your ideas, eat up valuable words that could be used for analysis, and will prevent you from getting straight to the point.

Students often use hedging language (or 'wads of fluff' as Steven Pinker calls it) to obscure that they either have not thoroughly researched the topic or are reluctant to commit to what they are saying (2015, p.43). Reserve hedging for purely speculative or hypothetical situations. If something is or is not true or proven, say so, don't hide behind hedging because of insufficient reading.

According to Ken Hyland (2000), writers 'need to invest a convincing degree of assurance in their propositions, yet must avoid overstating their case and risk inviting the rejection of their arguments' (p.87). The same thing could be said of hedging – too much of it will also risk 'inviting rejection', and you can come across as lacking in confidence. At the same time, as Hyland notes, you also need to show a degree of 'deference, modesty or respect' for the opinions of others (p.88). You need to strike a balance between boosting and hedging and use them only in appropriate circumstances (i.e. when something is either entirely compelling or is speculative/on the boundaries of what is known or provable).

A note of caution: rhetorical questions

Some students incorporate rhetorical questions into their assignments. This can be a useful way of stimulating the reader's curiosity and encouraging them to think deeply about the wider issues at stake. As such, it is a great tool to use in persuasive writing and can be used very effectively in oral presentations. However, they are often too rhetorical for academic writing because:

- They raise questions that you may not be answering.

- They can mask knowledge and act as a way of trying to deflect the marker's attention away from the fact that fundamentally, you are not answering the question or have not researched/thought deeply enough about the assignment.

- They can potentially lead you to veer off on new, unplanned and perhaps irrelevant tangents – something which you need to avoid if you have dyslexia.

Writing effective sentences

Structuring sentences and understanding the rules of grammar are probably the most difficult challenges students with dyslexia face. This is partly because, until recently, grammar was simply not taught in many UK schools. But additionally, it is often very difficult to see/visualise, let alone understand, a direct correlation between grammatical rules and meaning, something which individuals with dyslexia often need. For example, the advice in Strunk and White's famous and immensely popular book, *The Elements of Style*, that 'a noun in apposition may come between antecedent and relative' (2000, p.30), means very little, precisely because it is difficult to visualise or conceptualise. In addition, there appears to be little connection between the rule and the meaning. One may well ask, why may a noun in apposition come between antecedent and relative? The answer is that it's less ambiguous, but why is it less ambiguous? Without a visual or material explanation that can be seen or touched, these abstractions will remain abstract, and individuals with dyslexia are likely to remain entirely confused. In what follows, then, we will examine some basic academic sentence structures, not from the perspective of grammatical rules, but from the perspective of visual frameworks, the shape of which explain the purpose of the sentences and why the sequence of ideas are best in particular orders. You can then use these templates to help you visualise and see the 'big picture' of your own sentences so that you can understand how to write with confidence, direction and clarity.

The purpose of sentences

Before going any further, it is worth asking the question, what is a sentence? According to the *Oxford English Dictionary*, a sentence is a 'set of words that is complete in itself and held together with grammatical rules'. The ideal sentence is short, and communicates either ONE idea or a closely connected set of ideas. In English, as alluded to in Chapter 2, sentences usually fall into four distinct categories: simple, compound, complex and compound-complex. Each of these sentence categories have their own particular rules in relation to clauses, predicates, subjects, objects and verbs, but none of this tells us what they are actually for. Research has shown that individuals with dyslexia need to understand and see the overarching purpose, aim or 'big picture' of a sentence before looking at the detail. This is a requirement that is opposite to traditional approaches which start with sentence construction (nouns, verbs etc.) and then work towards the purpose and aims (Eide and Eide, 2011, pp.192–193). Before starting your sentences, then, it is worth thinking about what sort of idea you want to express. What is your end goal, and what do you want to achieve? What is the key message you want the reader to take from the sentence?

Obviously, a sentence is much more than merely a 'set of words…held together with grammatical rules' – it is a means of communicating ideas, usually new ideas. As such, it is worth once again returning to Bruce's concept of 'communicative dynamism', which is the underlying principle all sentences have in common and which ought to be your main priority when writing.

'Communicative dynamism'

We saw in Chapters 4 and 5 how Bruce's model of 'communicative dynamism' could enliven your essay and paragraph structures to help you forge an argument, but Bruce's 'wave model' was originally intended for mapping the transitions between ideas within sentences. For Bruce, a sentence is a means of guiding the recipient from what they already know to a new piece of information (and 'dynamism' increases in a wave pattern along the way). One way of making ALL your sentences contribute to advancing your argument, then, is to follow the given to new pattern. For example:

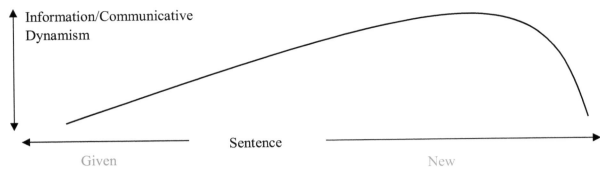

Information/Communicative Dynamism

Sentence

Given   New

The defendant's claim is clearly inadmissible due to the specifications outlined in Clause 2:1.

Shakespeare's treatment of race has been problematised given the discovery of the Othello manuscript.

Sudden Ash dieback is increasing, but in laboratory tests, Ye (2017) has successfully halted its mutation.

This sequence enables the reader to start with information and topics familiar to them before being guided towards new, detailed information (the argument). The golden rule here is to ensure that the most prominent, important, detailed information is at the end of each sentence, as in the three examples above. Indeed, by ensuring that you place the most important, new information at the end, you will find that you write more concisely. Compare the sentences in the table below, and it will easily be seen which are more emphatic and concise. Note how the sentences map onto Bruce's 'wave model of communicative dynamism' (or not!)

	Sample sentence	Comments
1)	This paper argues that due to the lack of media frames in social and political spheres there is a difficulty measuring the media's power currently (26 words).	The sentence ends awkwardly with an adverb and puts what is already known/given (methodological difficulties) in the priority position. Because of the awkwardness, the student has signposted the argument at the outset to compensate for the lack of clarity/precision. This increases the word count unnecessarily. Note also how the sentence doesn't represent a smooth transition (or 'wave') in terms of ideas, and 'communicative dynamism' is erratic across the sentence.

This paper argues that due to the lack of media frames in social and political spheres there is a difficulty measuring the media's power currently.

	Amended version with key/new information at the end: The power of the media is currently difficult to measure due to the lack of media frames in social and political spheres (22 words).	This example starts from what we already know and puts the new information at the end. The student has also moved the previously oddly placed adverb into the middle of the sentence along with the key verb/action (measure). Because everything is clearer, there is no need for the previous signposting, and as such the sentence is more direct and emphatic and clearly indicates greater student confidence. It also adheres to the transition from 'given' to 'new' ideas/argument, and can be mapped onto Bruce's 'wave'.

The power of the media is currently difficult to measure due to the lack of media frames in social and political spheres.

2)	The reliability and quality of the evidence used when investigating the effects of media outputs represents a further problem for political communication research (23 words).	Here the issue of reliability and quality is placed first, yet this is the new, detailed information. The phrase 'further problem' indicates that the student has been talking about problems previously, so rather than offering new insights, the sentence has to clumsily return to the problems at the end for it to make sense. To make the context of the evidence clear, the student has to introduce the idea of 'investigating the effects of media outputs', but then this is effectively repeated at the end since surely this is what 'political communication research' is all about.

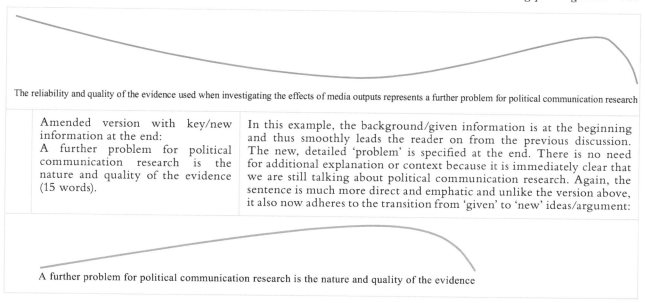

The reliability and quality of the evidence used when investigating the effects of media outputs represents a further problem for political communication research

Amended version with key/new information at the end: A further problem for political communication research is the nature and quality of the evidence (15 words).	In this example, the background/given information is at the beginning and thus smoothly leads the reader on from the previous discussion. The new, detailed 'problem' is specified at the end. There is no need for additional explanation or context because it is immediately clear that we are still talking about political communication research. Again, the sentence is much more direct and emphatic and unlike the version above, it also now adheres to the transition from 'given' to 'new' ideas/argument:

A further problem for political communication research is the nature and quality of the evidence

While the core principle of a sentence is to transition from the given to the new, sentences have additional goals that relate specifically to their purpose or overarching aim. In academic writing, there are six main types of sentence, each of which has a specific goal that can be mapped onto a visual template, the shape of which marries the purpose with Bruce's underlying principle of moving from the given to the new.

The six main types of academic sentence

1) Descriptive, narrative and explanatory sentences

As we have seen previously, you should avoid too much description in favour of criticality, evaluation and argument, but there are times when you will need to describe, narrate or explain in order to introduce ideas, set out the background or demonstrate knowledge (especially in scientific writing). The main purpose of a descriptive sentence is to inform rather than advance an argument. As such, the given to new sequence is still important, and there is an obvious narrowing of focus from the topic (or 'big picture') to detail (hence the triangle shape in the template below and the green 'wave' indicating 'communicative dynamism'). However, given that there is very little criticality, evaluation or argument, the triangle is red to indicate caution. We can see below how the ideas contained within two simple descriptive sentences map onto the template:

An electron is a fermion, so only a single electron can occupy a specific quantum state in a system.

Auschwitz Museum is a hugely valuable educational resource, attracting 1.4 million visits annually.

2) Reporting sentences

These sentences are mostly used to introduce the ideas of others. They start with a reporting signaller/discourse marker (as we saw earlier on p.127), which, as you can see from the template below, introduces the 'big picture'. The sentence then dedicates the rest of the words to others, either in the form of a short quotation, data, or perhaps a summary/paraphrase of their ideas (hence the use of the evidence fingerprint within the speech bubble in the template below). The top section of the template is red with a green narrowing of focus to indicate that although you are merely introducing/describing rather than analysing (and thus demonstrating knowledge), you are helping to drive forward your argument and lay out the foundations of your analysis/ critical evaluation:

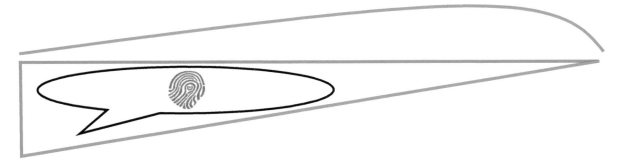

According to Smith (1998), electrons suitable for coupling must have critical value momenta.

Hockman (1990) suggests that better employee performance is 'not inevitable' during teamwork (p.2).

3) *Evaluative sentences*

Evaluation, as we saw in Chapter 5, often takes place at a paragraph level (or even at an essay level), but individual sentences enable you to articulate important evaluative comments. Because evaluation is so important for scoring high marks, the template is green throughout. An evaluative sentence aims to consider two ideas or pieces of evidence. In considering the first idea/piece of evidence, you move from 'big picture' or given information to new information/detail. When introducing the second, alternative idea/piece of evidence, however, you pick up from either the same narrow detail (which they usually have in common), or new details (the specifics of the issue at stake), before moving back out into the 'big picture', as can be seen in the shape of the templates below. An evaluative sentence can do this in an even-handed manner, or it can evaluate to demonstrate a preference and concede the strengths of an opposing argument. In both cases, this can be very useful for showing the marker that you have considered all the angles and can skilfully weigh up pros and cons. The examples below indicate how this can be mapped onto the two templates:

a) *Even-handed evaluation*

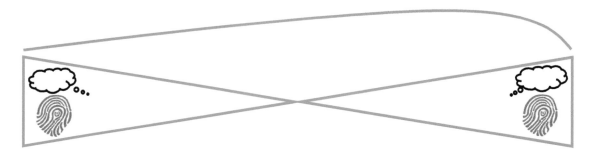

Profitability can derive from strategic risk taking, but it can also cause serious financial deficits.

Crop yield was high due to above average rainfall, but better pesticide use may also be a factor.

b) *Preferential evaluation/the art of concession*

For preferential evaluation and concession, use the template below to briefly summarise, empathise with, highlight and concede the strengths of the opposing ideas/evidence before outlining your position/evidence, again moving from the specific point of detail/divergence/principal objection out to the 'big picture'. This demonstrates that you have anticipated possible objections/counterarguments on the part of the reader/marker but can still forge an argument. As can be seen in the examples below, one of the best ways of doing this is to put your concessions in a subordinate clause, thereby putting the most crucial, new parts of the argument at the end:

Although CO_2 has increased, it would appear that levels of NO_2 give far greater cause for concern.

Despite Wu's suggestions, it is the authoritarian nature of patriarchy itself that needs addressing.

TIPS

 Note that, unlike concession, preferential evaluation is somewhat muted. It is not as forceful/argumentative as concession, and certainly not as forceful as refutation. Indeed, note the use of hedging ('appear') in the example above.

 As indicated on the templates above, in both sections of the sentence, the key point can be made by referencing either ideas or evidence. Remember, always be as specific and clear as possible and paint a picture for your reader by avoiding abstractions.

4) *Refutation*

Refutation is used when you want to explicitly disagree with the views or ideas of someone/a piece of evidence. Unlike concession/evaluation, you do not credit or assess the validity of the opposing view. Instead, you briefly refer to the main 'big picture' idea/evidence you are refuting and then state your specific, detailed objection based on what your research/knowledge has shown to be more compelling. It is for this reason that, unlike above, the template is shaped so as to encourage you to move from the 'big picture' to detail of the idea you want to refute, to your alternative/the specifics (which repeat the 'big picture' to detail sequence but in greater depth):

Yu's data, however, is unconvincing since genetics do play a pivotal in child development.

Social buffering is inaccurate; upper echelons theory is considerably better at explaining success.

TIPS

 Note the use of boosting ('do' and 'considerably') in the examples above. This can strengthen your refutation, but be careful not to overdo it. The evidence/point itself ought to convince the reader more than the rhetoric.

 To make your refutations and concessions more persuasive and credible, make the sentence that follows a persuasive sentence (see below). This will allow you to develop your objections by introducing the optimum number of counter-ideas/pieces of evidence (which you will then explore further in your analytical sentences).

5) Persuasive sentences

Persuasive sentences aim to convince your reader of the validity of your ideas, and can be particularly useful either before you present your evidence (as a topic sentence), for introducing your analysis, or afterwards as a means of summary/recapitulation. One of the most effective ways of being persuasive is to use what's known as 'the rule of three'. In rhetoric, it is thought that using three pieces of evidence is the optimum number to be convincing (one simply not being enough, two looks a little weak, and four seems to be trying too hard), so incorporating three key ideas/points into your sentences is the ideal number for being persuasive. Depending on where you want the focus to be, the three ideas can come anywhere within the sentence. However, the order in which you place the three ideas ought to mirror either their importance or their specificity. In other words, start with the least compelling idea or 'big picture' and end with that which is the most detailed and persuasive (as can be seen in the relative sizes of the light bulb icons in the templates below):

Rule of three at the beginning:

Drought, pestilence and fire are disasters that can all be overcome if we embrace genetic modification.

Emphasis, persuasiveness and confidence are all evident if you use the rule of three when writing essays.

Rule of three in the middle:

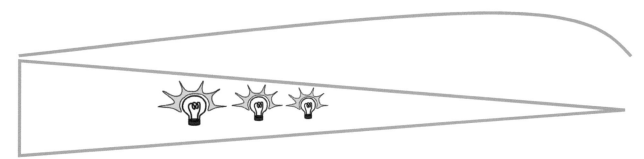

In the field of accounting, integrity, honesty and perseverance are the most essential traits in employees.

Increased levels of deforestation, mainly in China, Japan and Malaysia, is causing global warming.

Rule of three at end:

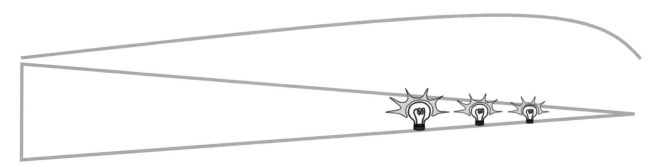

The study of history should be compulsory as it allows pupils to understand facts, fictions and values.

Genetic modification ought to play a vital role in overcoming disasters like drought, pestilence and fire.

6) *Argumentative/analytical sentences*

Argumentative/analytical sentences are probably the most important as they directly show the marker that you are answering the question/assignment task, critiquing or evaluating ideas and proving your point. These sentences often follow descriptive, narrative, evaluative, concessional, refutational and persuasive sentences and justify/provide depth to the views expressed therein. These sentences are likely to be significantly longer than those we have seen so far, simply because analysis requires a layering of depth and the consideration of multiple issues. There are likely to be numerous issues you want to interrogate, and it can be challenging to know how to sequence them (or even if a sequence is needed). The best way to present your analysis in a compelling, confident and clear manner is to either again move from the 'big picture' to specific detail, or present things chronologically. Some examples/extracts from argumentative sentences can be mapped onto the template as follows:

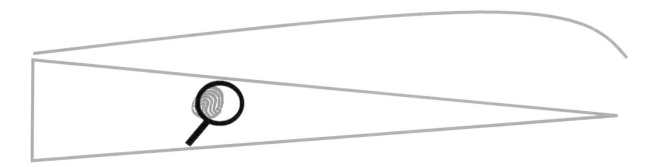

State liability is too arbitrary to have any effect domestically, let alone internationally and as such...

The limitation of synthesising these hypotheses is the failure to implement a mediating variable, since...

The term 'common assault' cannot accurately reflect the severity of domestic violence because...

TIPS

 Variety is the spice of life. Although you'll probably use mostly reporting sentences near the beginning of your paragraphs (to introduce the evidence) and evaluative, persuasive and argumentative/analytical sentences towards the end, use combinations of the above sentences to make your writing interesting, readable and thought-provoking. Although you need to adhere to the point (topic sentence), evidence/analysis and link paragraph structure mapped onto the Christmas Cracker template, you can use the above sentences in various places. Indeed, it's often a good idea to do so, particularly with reporting/descriptive/persuasive sentences, to hit your reader with new, confident insights.

 Vary the sentence length. Although argumentative/analytical sentences are likely to be the longest and most complex, and although it has been suggested that the 'overwhelming majority' of academic sentences are 'at least 12 words long' (Sowton, 2012, p.113), experiment with different lengths. Short, emphatic sentences (as used at the beginning of these tips) can be a useful way of drawing the marker's attention to important information, and they can inspire confidence. However, don't overdo this. Lots of short sentences, particularly when close to each other, can sound awkward and simplistic.

Putting it all together

Obviously, over the course of an essay, you will use combinations of the above sentence types to express your argument. Together they form your analysis and they are the building blocks of your paragraphs. Let's have look at the law extract from Chapter 1 to see how the sentences are combined to provide rich and insightful analysis while driving the argument forwards from the given to the new:

Law and domestic violence

Sentence	Sentence type/template
Legal responses to the issue of domestic violence are far from satisfactory.	Topic sentence:
Although CPS reports suggest that 'highest volumes ever' of domestic violence referrals were charged last year (over 70,000 [CPS 2014b]), there are numerous significant counterarguments which point out inadequacies in the legal framework and its ambiguous definitions.	Preferential evaluation/concession:
Despite repeated, valid attempts to create a definition of domestic violence which encompasses a wide array of actions (Smith, 1999 and Jones, 2001), the notion of domestic violence as meaning physical beating, remains the 'dominant view' (Stark, 2007, p.84).	Preferential evaluation/concession:
As Stark (2007) has testified, victims are reluctant to acknowledge their situation absent of physical violence (p.111).	Reporting sentence:
Furthermore, no specific 'domestic violence' offence exists, with instances being artificially categorised as regular offences instead.	Argumentative/analytical:
Indeed, they are mostly categorised as 'common assault' which does not accurately reflect the severity of domestic violence (Hester, 2006, p.85).	Argumentative/analytical:

| Additionally, state liability for failing to prevent domestic violence, though welcome, is set to a very high threshold (Osman v UK), and as such may not be robust enough to have much effect domestically save in exceptional circumstances (Burton, 2010, p.134). | Argumentative/analytical: 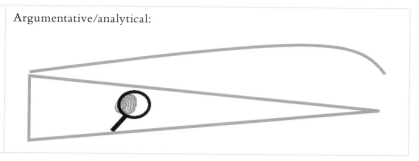 |

Note how the student has moved from preferential evaluation/concession sentences and reporting, to more detailed argumentative/analytical sentences, thus adhering to the template of the main body of paragraphs demonstrated in Chapter 4 (i.e. moving from a topic sentence and evidence though to analysis). Furthermore, notice also how frequently we see signposting (usually at the beginning of the sentences) to indicate that arguments build upon each other and intersect. As such, this piece of writing is very compelling.

Sentence construction

Now that we have considered the overall/'big picture' aims of academic sentences and mapped them onto templates, we need to dig a little deeper and consider some of the most common sentence structures (syntax). This is not intended to be a comprehensive account of grammar, and doesn't consider all the possible sentences you may come across or write, but seeing the overall 'big picture' aims of sentence construction will help you organise your thoughts and express them clearly and logically.

Syntax refers to the overarching rules or principles that govern sentence construction, particularly regarding word order. The main principle you need to keep in mind here (and which maps nicely onto Bruce's wave model of 'communicative dynamism'), is the transition from subject → verb → object or, much less frequently, subject → object → verb. Although other structures exist, these two sentence structures form the basis of over 87% of world languages (Tomlin, 1986, p.22). The subject → verb → object sequence is predominant in English, so we will focus on this basic structure for the remainder of the chapter.

For people with dyslexia, all this talk of subjects, verbs and objects might seem confusing and too abstract to be properly understood. It can be made much clearer if we:

1) Hone in on the fact that most sentences have three essential components, and

2) Rename the core components so that their labels more accurately describe what they do.

Instead of thinking of sentence structure in terms of subject, verb, object (SVO), it's more easily understood (and memorable) if we think of it as TOPIC, ACTION, DETAIL, or 'TAD'. Fortunately, 'TAD' can be made even more accessible and understandable if we map it visually onto the Christmas Cracker template, as we shall see below.

• Subject > TOPIC

The subject position tells us what the sentence is about, so a less abstract way of putting this might be to think of it as the **TOPIC.** The best way to make your sentences clear and emphatic is to ensure that the topic is not only mentioned as near to the beginning of the sentence as practicable, but to make your topics as concrete, tangible and 'real' as possible. If you bury your topics in abstractions or vague/fuzzy language (providing your topic isn't actually an abstract idea), your writing will lack the precision required of academic style. For example, wherever possible, avoid abstractions (such as 'society', 'media', 'internationalisation' or 'evolution') in favour of being specific:

Topic as an abstraction	Topic specific or clarified
Society	Working-class culture in… Society has become a meaningless term in the last ten years.
Media	Television adverts… The media, in particular television commercials…

Internationalisation	The 30% increase in students from China... Internationalisation has resulted in a disproportionate number of Chinese students.
Evolution	The genome sequence has doubled in size since... Evolution, especially in relation to slimes and moulds in southern Africa....

The need to be specific from the outset, or at least clarify/specify as quickly as possible, is why the topic section of the Christmas Cracker sentence template below narrows in focus, much in the same way we saw in respect of topic sentences and introductions. The apple is used to symbolise the topic because of its association with knowledge and the pursuit of ideas/wisdom (Eve famously picked and ate an apple from the tree of knowledge in the Garden of Eden, and of course Newton came up with his theory of gravity, apparently because an apple fell on his head):

• Verb > ACTION

Verbs are 'doing words' and often explain what is happening to the subject (topic). If the verb is aligned with an adjective (e.g. old, new, large, small, economic, political) or an adverb (e.g. quickly, slowly, usually, precisely, eventually), they indicate processes, change and types of movement. There may be other verbs in the sentence (e.g. auxiliary verbs, phrasal verbs and modal verbs), but what we are interested in here is the main verb/action in the sentence, the focal point around which the meaning and action of the sentence revolve. Consequently, it is easier to think of the verb section of the sentence as the **ACTION** section. This section is a crucial part of communicating a clear and compelling argument. Again, it needs to be as precise as possible (avoid nominalisations — see below) and have action at its core. For this reason we can visualise the action section as like a moving wheel, and its location at the centre of the Christmas Cracker template highlights its significance as a driver of the argument (passive voice is denoted by a wheel which is not moving [see pp.162–163]):

• Object > DETAIL

The object of the sentence is the thing that is 'acted upon' by the topic and the verb. It provides explicit new detail regarding what the sentence is about. It is the main point of the sentence and adds new information, so a better label for this section is **DETAIL.** The detail section drives forward and clarifies the argument, and since it contains the new information, 'communicative dynamism' peaks in this part of the sentence. The best way of visualising this part of the sentence, then, is as a set of consecutively smaller cogs (this an especially relevant image to think about given that this part of the sentence not only provides new detail but key explanations):

Again, ensure that you don't deprive your sentences of clarity, detail, emphasis and argument by burying detail in abstractions.

TIPS FOR THE ENDS OF SENTENCES

 Place the emphasis of your argument at the end of your sentences.

 Put the new, complex detail of the topics at the end of your sentences.

 Use the very last word of sentences carefully – this is where you should place your greatest emphasis and most insightful new ideas. In the case of using the rule of three at the end of the sentence, end with the most important/significant idea/detail.

 You can also think of the last words of sentences as a little like signallers and discourse markers. The last words often indicate what the next sentence will be about or what the next sentence will build upon, so ensure that the final words of your sentences express clear, concrete ideas and thoughts.

Common sentence structures

The English language contains four main sentence structures which comprise of clauses. These structures are differentiated from the six types of academic sentence already discussed. Earlier we were concerned with overall **function** and **purpose**. Here we are concerned with structure. Let's examine each main sentence structure in turn and map them onto the Christmas Cracker templates:

1) Simple sentences

These express a complete thought (independent clause) that can stand on its own without the assistance of other sentences or clauses. For example, let's take the descriptive sentence: 'Freud had a huge impact on psychoanalysis.' Here we have a TOPIC (Freud), ACTION in the form of a verb (impact), and a new piece of information or DETAIL (psychoanalysis). This type of sentence can be visualised thus:

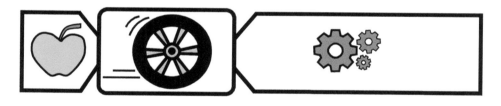

Freud   **had a huge impact**   **on psychoanalysis.**

2) Compound sentences

These sentences express two independent, but related, complete thoughts/clauses which are joined using a conjunction. For example, let's take the argumentative sentence: 'Freud had a huge impact on the field and his theory of dreams remains the cornerstone of psychoanalysis.' Both parts of the sentence, either side of the conjunction 'and', can stand alone and still make sense as complete thoughts. This type of sentence can be visualised like this:

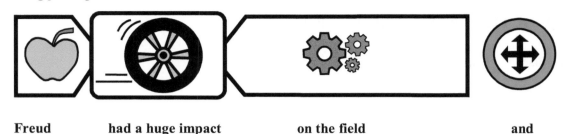

Freud   **had a huge impact**   **on the field**   **and**

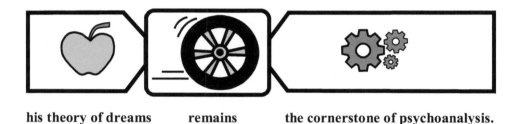

his theory of dreams   **remains**   **the cornerstone of psychoanalysis.**

3) Complex sentences

This type of sentence expresses an independent, complete thought/clause and a dependent, incomplete thought/subordinate or relative clause. Subordinate/relative clauses cannot stand on their own as they do not express a complete thought. Often they contain only a topic and a verb, and will be connected to the main clause via a conjunction (subordinate clauses) or a relative pronoun/adverb (relative clauses). Subordinate/relative clauses add supplementary and possibly non-essential detail to the main clause and qualify ideas. As such, they act as additional thoughts and can thus be represented as a thought bubble. Complex sentences, then, can be visualised in the same way as the simple sentence, but with the addition of a 'floating', dependent thought (thought bubble), which can appear anywhere within the sentence. Here are some examples of argumentative/analytical sentences:

Example a)

Freud's conception of dreams,   **despite being superseded,**   **is**   **still a valid psychoanalytical tool.**

Example b)

Despite being superseded, Freud's conception of dreams   **is**   **still valid psychoanalytical tool.**

Note: the subordinate/relative clause can appear anywhere within the sentence, and you must ensure that commas surround them to mark them off from the main clause.

4) Compound-complex sentences

These sentences express two independent, complete thoughts and one dependent, incomplete thought/ subordinate/relative clause. For example, let's take the argumentative/analytical sentence: 'Freud had a huge impact on the field and his theory of dreams remains the cornerstone of psychoanalysis, despite persistent controversies.' The dependent clause can again appear (or 'float') anywhere, but in this version, it can be visualised thus:

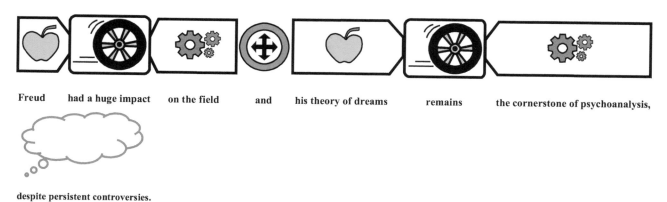

Freud   had a huge impact   on the field   and   his theory of dreams   remains   the cornerstone of psychoanalysis,

despite persistent controversies.

TIP

Use a subordinate/relative clause as a summative modifier. As you can see in the example above, the second main clause ends with detail (psychoanalysis). It can end there, but the final three words clarify the situation by adding the caveat that there were controversies. In other words, it sums up the situation and modifies/clarifies it by adding an additional level of detail. As such, the given to new, 'big picture' to detail sequence is maintained, and if anything, enhanced. This can be a valuable strategy for demonstrating that you know more than you are really saying, but in only a few words.

Putting it all together

Let's take a look at the academic sentences from the domestic violence example from earlier and see how we can map them onto these Christmas Cracker templates:

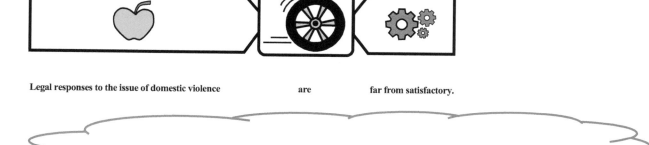

Legal responses to the issue of domestic violence   are   far from satisfactory.

Although CPS reports suggest that 'highest volumes ever' of domestic violence referrals were charged last year (over 70,000 [CPS 2014b]),

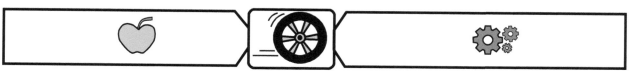

there are numerous significant counterarguments which   point out   inadequacies in the legal framework and its ambiguous definitions.

Despite repeated, valid attempts to create a definition of domestic violence which encompasses a wide array of actions (Smith, 1999 and Jones, 2001),

the notion of domestic violence as meaning physical beating,   remains   the 'dominant view' (Stark, 2007, p.84).

As Stark (2007) has testified,   victims   are   reluctant to acknowledge their situation absent of physical violence (p.111).

Furthermore, no specific 'domestic violence' offence   exists   with instances being artificially categorised as regular offences instead.

Indeed,   they   are mostly classified   as 'common assault',   which does not accurately reflect the severity of domestic violence.

Now it's your turn

Use the templates covered in this chapter to map out the remainder of the extract:

Additionally, state liability for failing to prevent domestic violence, though welcome, is set to a

very high threshold (Osman v UK), and as such may not be robust enough to have much effect

domestically save in exceptional circumstances (Burton, 2010, p.134).

TIP

Be careful with long sentences. Given that individuals with dyslexia have lots of ideas, sentences can become very long as you either a) try to pack all your thoughts into each sentence, or b) forget to punctuate and split up sentences because you're focused on just getting your thoughts out. Bear in mind that long sentences can confuse your reader. Indeed, the longer the sentence, the greater the risk of 1) incorrect punctuation/grammar, and 2) reader confusion.

Summary

- For students with dyslexia, sentences and grammar are one of the most challenging aspects of writing. This is partly because it involves sequencing, but also because the rules of grammar are so abstract. Use the templates as a starting point to help you understand the 'bigger picture' function/structure of sentences. Understanding the overarching purpose of sentences and why sentences are structured in the way they are will help you to write and structure them more confidently.

- Practice makes perfect. Use the templates and keep practising by writing random academic sentences. Try writing with the templates initially (these can be downloaded from the companion website), and then put them to one side as you become more skilful and confident.

- Initially, don't get bogged down trying to make every sentence perfect. Depending on how you work best, just write down your thoughts as fast as possible (this is known as 'free writing') and then re-organise them later using the templates. Try different techniques and ways of working to see what's most effective for you.

- Ensure your grammar and style is correct, formal, clear and precise. Academic writing is not a blog post or a piece of journalism – it's a formal, professional style of writing. Mastering it will serve you well for employability as you may need to write reports, proposals and studies as part of your career.

Bibliography

Aristotle, (2004) *Rhetoric*. Translated by W. Rhys Roberts. Mineola, NY: Dover Publications.

Bakhtin, Mikhail, (1981) *The Dialogic Imagination*. Edited and translated by Michael Holquist and Caryl Emerson. Austin: University of Texas Press.

Bruce, Nigel J., (1988) 'Communicative Dynamism in Expository Academic English: Some Strategies in Teaching the Pragmatics of Writing', *Working Papers in Linguistics and Language Teaching*, 11, pp.42–53.

Cooper, Sheila, and Patton, Rosemary, (2004) *Writing Logically, Thinking Critically*. London: Pearson Longman.

Eide, Brock L., and Eide, Fernette, F., (2011) *The Dyslexic Advantage: Unlocking the Hidden Potential of the Dyslexic Brain*. London: Hay House.

Hyland, Ken, (2000) *Disciplinary Discourses: Social Interactions in Academic Writing*. London: Longman.

_____ (2002) 'Activity and Evaluation: Reporting Practices in Academic Writing', in Flowerdew, John (ed.) *Academic Discourse*. Harlow: Pearson Education, pp.115–130.

Pinker, Steven, (2015) *The Sense of Style: The Thinking Person's Guide to Writing in the 21st Century*. London: Penguin Books.

Sowton, Chris, (2012) 50 *Steps to Improving your Academic Writing*. Reading: Garnet Education.

Strunk, William, and White, E. B., (2000) *The Elements of Style*. 4th edn. Boston, MA: Allyn & Bacon.

Thompson, G., and Ye, Y., (1991) 'Evaluation of the Reporting Verbs used in Academic Paper', *Applied Linguistics*, 12, pp.365–382.

Tomlin, Russell, (1986) *Basic Word Order: Functional Principles*. London: Croom Helm.

7 Academic Writing Style

Clarity and Precision

'Having dyslexia can make you creative. If you want to construct a sentence and can't find the word you are searching for, you have to think of a way to write round it. This requires being creative and so your "creativity muscle" gets bigger'.

(Benjamin Zephaniah: dyslexic poet, playwright and author)

The sentences contained within academic writing are never going to compete with a thrilling novel or be as elegant as a finely crafted poem, but style is something you need to be aware of and get right. You may have already come across this in your reading. Have you found that some writers are extremely difficult to understand (even if they are expressing relatively simple ideas), whereas others seem capture your attention and aid your understanding very effectively, even if the topic is complex? Why is this? Well, a lot of it comes down to the writer's style. Here we consider some style issues and common problems you need to consider in academic writing. This is especially important because, despite your best efforts, and despite using the templates recommended here, you might find that your sentences still wander a little, become grammatically incorrect or stylistically awkward. Remedying these problems will require practice, perseverance and extensive editing (perhaps with the help of your dyslexia tutor or Learning Support Advisor), but this is something that every writer, irrespective of dyslexia, encounters. Indeed, as the writer Ernest Hemingway once observed, when it comes to writing, 'we are all apprentices in a craft where no one ever becomes a master' (1962, p.42).

Writing with images and realities

Whatever your assignment title or genre may be, clarity is all. One way of making your writing clear and readable is to minimise abstractions and incorporate concrete, tangible facts, examples, images and references to reality. To demonstrate the difference, let's examine two pieces of writing. The first is a piece of journalism by the late A. A. Gill, here writing about his experiences with dyslexia and how people might be amused if they saw what his writing was like before an editor and scribe polished it:

> It was suggested that we should print this the way I write it, just so you could see, get some idea of the mess, the infantilely random alphabetti muesli of my 55-year-old writing. You'd get a kick out of it. No, it would really amuse you. People still laugh at me on paper: 'Oh my god, is that real? Is that how you write? You've got to be joking.' I'm not immune, but I've grown thick-skinned, if a little defensive. After all the awards, the pats on the back, the gimpy words that put the kids through school and put a chicken in the pot, you can scoff all you like. You can scoff for free. I get paid for these words, and I gave up caring when I discovered the rest of you spell phonetic with a 'ph' (Gill, 2010).

Now compare this extract with the following from a well-known book about Romantic-period women writers. The author, Professor Anne Janowitz, is writing here with the aim of 'introduc[ing] readers to the lives and works of Anna Letitia Barbauld and Mary Robinson' (2004, p.1). As such, we must assume that the book is intended to be fairly introductory and accessible. But take a look at the writing style. Is it clear and accessible? How does it compare with the A. A. Gill extract above?

> In this atmosphere of political retrenchment, Barbauld began a new phase of her intellectual life, codifying a tradition of literary value, and reinforcing the ethical codes she had believed in all her life. Barbauld developed her role as literary arbiter, using her power as an editor to produce editions of Collins' poems, a collection of essays from the *Spectator* and *Tatler*, and Richardson's *Letters*. Her great contribution to formulating both a tradition and contemporary taste was her edition of the *British Novelists*, for which she wrote long prefaces, and which she accomplished in less than two years, the full set completed in 1810 (Janowitz, 2004, p.99).

DOI: 10.4324/9781003190189-7

Both of these passages express very simple ideas. In the case of Gill, he is simply talking about his experiences of writing with dyslexia, and Janowitz is simply telling us that Barbauld started editing the works of others. But the way these ideas are expressed and their subsequent clarity are vastly different. Gill uses images and tangible realities (with which the reader is likely to be familiar) to paint a visual picture as to what it is like to write with dyslexia. In contrast, Janowitz, particularly in the first and last sentences, resorts to abstractions and nominalisations which the reader simply cannot visualise. For example, when reading these passages, we are likely to find ourselves imagining or visualising the following:

Passage	Images
A. A. Gill:	Print, some sort of mess, an infant, alphabet muesli, a 55-year-old, people laughing, someone speaking, thick skin, awards, pats on back, 'gimpy words', children, a school, a chicken cooking, someone scoffing, and money/words (all of which are mediated via various references to 'you' – the reader).
Anne Janowitz:	Barbauld, an editor, some books, and 'long prefaces' (what these might look like or how long they are is unclear).

As you can see, Gill's writing is full of things we can visualise – real things that we can see, hear, hold, smell, or may even have experienced ourselves. As such, the writing is clear, emphatic and persuasive. Janowitz's passage, on the other hand, is decidedly lacking in these traits. We, the reader, cannot see/visualise 'political retrenchment', Barbauld's 'intellectual life' (which lacks specificity), her 'codifying a tradition of literary value' (which is again unspecific) or her 'ethical codes' and 'role as literary arbiter'. Even when things get a little more specific, we are still unable to visualise, for instance, how 'long' her 'long prefaces' actually were. Admittedly the extracts are very different and have very different purposes (journalism vs. academic writing), but the message should be clear – if you want to make your ideas compelling, paint them in pictures, give your sentences some basis in reality; give them meaning which is clear. This is not the same thing as making them immature and childlike – they will still be academic. Indeed, academic writing can be just as stimulating, visual and tangible as that illustrated in the A. A. Gill extract. For example, let's have a brief look at the following passage by John Barrell. Here we have an excerpt from a huge 754-page history monograph about 'imagining the King's death' (in other words, there's not even a real execution of a monarch to get our teeth into). You can hear the yawns developing already, yet take a look at the writing style below. What images and tangible realities can you see?

> The notion that the political conflict of the period was to be regarded as a conflict...about the meanings of words, was a theme of numerous liberal or radical texts of the 1790s, from Elizabeth Inchbald's novel *Nature and Art*, for example, to a report of the committee of constitution of the London Corresponding Society, which proposed fixing the meanings of the words 'Republican', 'Democrat', 'Aristocrat', 'Royalist', 'Loyalist', 'Citizen', and 'Subject' as they were to be used in the society's debates and discussions. This last is one of several publications concerned to reappropriate the words in the vocabulary of reformers, which, they claim, have been deliberately distorted by the supporters of the Government, have become 'scare-crow words' in what Coleridge described as 'the Dictionary of Aristocratic Prejudice' – by which, added John Thelwall, 'the English turned inside out' (2000, p.2).

Although not as eclectic as the A. A. Gill passage, here we can see how a debate about the 'meanings of words' has been enriched and rendered convincing/engaging by referencing the core ideas to concrete examples and images such as:

• 'Liberal or radical texts of the 1790s', Inchbald's novel, a report by the London Corresponding Society, various labels which conjure up images of character types/political positions, society debates, reformers, the Government, 'scare-crow words', Coleridge, a dictionary, Thelwall, and an illustrative quotation.

Not only do we have conflict, prejudice and government censorship (one could imagine these being the core ingredients of a gripping novel!), but the passage is packed with detail and examples – no stone is left unturned or unrelated to specifics. This makes the writing extremely compelling, engaging and persuasive. Try to adopt a similar approach. As this passage surely proves, academic writing doesn't have to be dry or dull.

TIPS

As Steven Pinker (an authority on stylish writing) points out, 'a third of our brains [are] dedicated to vision...Many experiments have shown that readers understand and remember material far better when it is expressed in concrete language that allows them to form visual images' (2015, p.72). Having dyslexia, you already have the edge here (just as A. A. Gill did); harness your visual strengths to produce memorable, accessible and compelling writing by ensuring that your sentences contain 'concrete', real things you and your reader/marker can visualise.

 When reading, find an academic writer from your discipline who uses many examples, images and tangible realities to illustrate and prove their points. Then spend some time looking at how they organise their thoughts and present their case – use it as inspiration for your own writing.

Clarity

One of the key elements of good academic writing style is clarity. As the celebrated poet and cultural critic Matthew Arnold advised back in 1898, 'have something to say, and say it as clearly as you can. That is the only secret of style' (quoted in Williams, 2007, p.1). In academic writing, this amounts to two key principles:

1) Have something to say – construct an argument that includes evidence, analysis and evaluation.

2) Write clearly.

The rest of this chapter is devoted to this second principle.

Thoughts on clarity from the experts

Nearly all famous (and thus by definition, successful) writers, academic or otherwise, have commented on the importance of clarity. Here's a few words of wisdom that can be applied to academic writing:

Common problems which impede clarity

Clarity can be seriously undermined if your writing contains any of the following problems:

Problem 1): taking too long to get to the topic

To render your ideas clear, readers need to get to the topic of the sentence and see what it is about as soon as possible. If you take too long to get to the topic, the reader will become disorientated or bored, and your sentence will lack clarity and confidence (the argument will also be more obscure). Take a look at the following examples:

Problematic sentence	Commentary
Notwithstanding multiple controversies, disputes and the existence of denialism, it can be argued that <u>global warming</u> is responsible for increased rainfall.	Here, the topic is <u>global warming</u>, but the writer takes us on a circuitous and somewhat awkward journey through various details and no fewer than 14 words (including a passive verb – see pp.162–163 for more details) before even mentioning it. This is a classic example of unnecessary 'throat clearing'. Note how this looks when represented visually below. The writer needed to have been far more explicit, upfront and confident in getting to the topic.

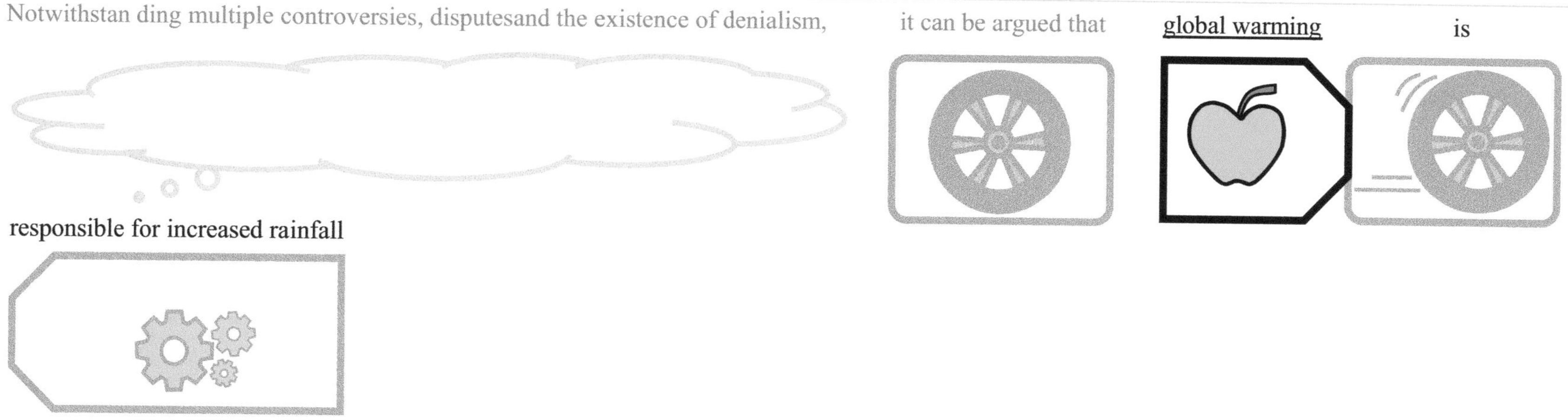

Notwithstanding multiple controversies, disputesand the existence of denialism,   it can be argued that   <u>global warming</u>   is   responsible for increased rainfall

Amended sentence	
<u>Global warming</u> is clearly responsible for increased rainfall, despite arguments to the contrary.	This version not only eliminates the needless repetition and awkwardness, but gets to the topic immediately. This makes the sentence clearer and shorter, and it also sounds far more confident and emphatic. Note also how the sentence now maps onto the Christmas Cracker template below:

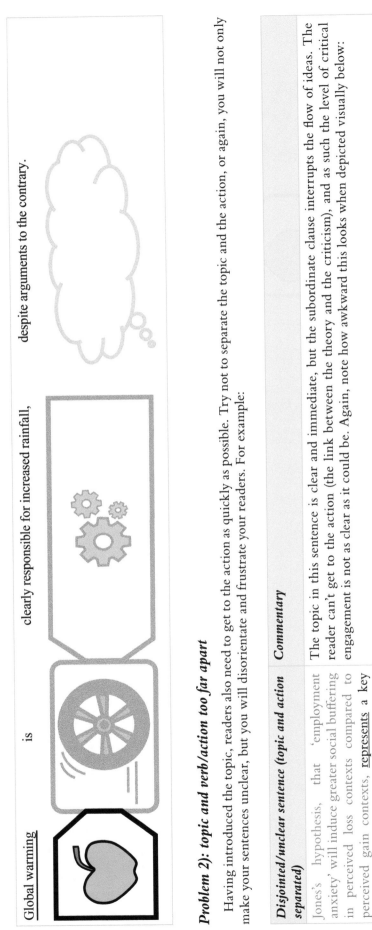

Global warming   is   clearly responsible for increased rainfall,   despite arguments to the contrary.

Problem 2): topic and verb/action too far apart

Having introduced the topic, readers also need to get to the action as quickly as possible. Try not to separate the topic and the action, or again, you will not only make your sentences unclear, but you will disorientate and frustrate your readers. For example:

Disjointed/unclear sentence (topic and action separated)	Commentary
Jones's hypothesis, that 'employment anxiety' will induce greater social buffering in perceived loss contexts compared to perceived gain contexts, <u>represents</u> a key oversimplification of the issue.	The topic in this sentence is clear and immediate, but the subordinate clause interrupts the flow of ideas. The reader can't get to the action (the link between the theory and the criticism), and as such the level of critical engagement is not as clear as it could be. Again, note how awkward this looks when depicted visually below:

Jones's hypothesis,   that 'employment anxiety' will induce greater social buffering in perceived loss contexts compared to perceived gain contexts,

<u>represents</u>   a key oversimplification of the issue.

Amended version	Commentary
Jones's 'employment anxiety' hypothesis <u>oversimplifies</u> the issue because of his presumption that it induces greater social buffering in perceived loss contexts compared to perceived gain contexts.	In this version, the student has grouped the topic at the start, and for the sake of being concise, the definite verb 'represents' has been replaced with 'oversimplifies', thus getting to the action more swiftly, eliminating the nominalisation and making the sentence sounds more emphatic and confident. The transition from given/subject to new information is also far more explicit. Crucially, though, note that despite the sentence comprising the same number of words as the previous version, the use of the words 'because' and 'presumption' raises the level of critical engagement and evaluation considerably, and would thus achieve higher marks.

Jones's 'employment anxiety' hypothesis   <u>oversimplifies</u>   the issue

because of his presumption that it induces greater social buffering in perceived loss contexts compared to perceived gain contexts.

TIP

Avoid slow build-ups – you're not a creative writer trying to build suspense! Get to the topic and the action as quickly as possible. Don't labour the obvious and avoid excessive 'throat-clearing' words such as 'actually', 'basically', 'generally', 'practically', 'really' and 'certain'.

Problem 3): using nominalisations rather than verbs

Nominalisations, or 'zombie nouns' as Helen Sword calls them, obscure clarity and weaken 'communicative dynamism' by turning action into abstract ideas and things (nouns). While some academics might like them as a way of sounding impenetrably intelligent, and while they can be useful for expressing complex ideas, it is best to use them sparingly. You can often spot nominalisations because they are words which typically end in 'tion', 'ance', 'ence', 'ment', 'ness' or 'ity'. Try to strike a balance between using nominalisations to show sophistication, depth and concision (as I have just done here!) and using plenty of verbs (action) to drive your argument forward, articulate your voice and give your writing clarity. Remember, readers expect actions to be in verbs. For example:

Action buried in nominalisations	*Commentary*
The assumption within this model that all RNAs are inherently problematic is an oversimplification of the transcription process.	The nominalisations here are highlighted in red but also notice that because of the nominalisations, the main action (oversimplification) is some distance away from its topic (this model). Notice that the nominalisation, 'transcription', is not highlighted. This is because it accurately describes a technical/scientific, complex process, and as such it should remain.
Amended sentence (action in verbs):	
This model oversimplifies the transcription process, because it assumes that all RNAs are inherently problematic.	In this version, the nominalisations have been turned into verbs, thus rendering the action of the sentence much more emphatic. The whole sentence is thus clearer, more confident and has more energy. Note also that the sequence of ideas has been altered to eliminate the gap between the topic and the action, which again improves readability and directness.

TIP

Be careful to keep nominalisations which condense complex meaning and encompass big issues (e.g. acculturation, fermentation, interdisciplinarity, clarity, decision, argument). In some cases, condensing meaning into a nominalisation can save on words and help you get to the point swiftly when dealing with complex arguments and theory. In these cases, consider making the nominalisation the topic or detail of your sentence rather than the action.

Try to avoid nominalisations when action is paramount. Remember, the conversion of verbs into nominalisations removes agency from a statement and thus renders your academic 'voice' and argument less clear.

For everything you could want to know about nominalisations and 'zombie nouns', see Helen Sword's fantastic video, which will give you an excellent insight into how they work and how they rob your sentences of action: https://www.youtube.com/watch?v=dNlkHtMgcPQ

Problem 4): action and detail too far apart

This advice is similar to that above regarding long build-ups and long distances between the topic and the action. Once you have given the sentence action, don't waste time getting to the detail by adding unnecessary or distracting material (such as non-essential subordinate/relative clauses or excessive wordiness). For example:

Distance between action and detail too great	Commentary
This model of the RNA transcription process is oversimplified, which may or may not have relatively little bearing on defunct models, because RNAs are inherently problematic.	The subordinate clause here (12 words) splits the action (oversimplified – which is clearly a critical part of the argument) from the main part of the detail (RNAs are inherently problematic). It distracts the reader with largely unnecessary detail and awkwardness, as can be seen in the visual representation below:

This model of the RNA transcription process   is oversimplified,   which may or may not have relatively little bearing on defunct models,

because RNAs are inherently problematic.

Amended version

This model of the RNA transcription process is oversimplified because RNAs are inherently problematic.	Here the writer wastes no time getting from the action to the detail (they are barely separated at all). As such, it again sounds far more compelling, emphatic, confident and clear and can be mapped far more readily onto the Christmas Cracker template, as we can see below. If necessary, the omitted detail can be added onto the end, either in brackets, as a new sentence or as a summative clause.

This model of the RNA transcription process   is oversimplified   because RNAs are inherently problematic.

Problem 5): sentence fragments

Each sentence/main clause should be grammatically complete and capable of standing alone as a self-contained thought (usually containing a topic, action, detail, main clause/subordinate clause). However, if you start trying to turn subordinate clauses into complete sentences/independent clauses, it becomes a sentence fragment because something will be missing (e.g. the topic, action or detail). For example:

Disjointed/unclear sentence (sentence fragment)	*Commentary*
Tests on the subject's DNA profile have produced some unusual findings. Traces of genome strands from Latin America and Sri Lanka.	The first sentence is perfectly acceptable, as it contains a topic (tests on the subject's DNA profile), action (produced) and detail (unusual findings). However, the second sentence lacks both a topic and a verb (action) and contains only detail pertaining to the previous sentence. The topic is clearly the same as the previous sentence, but having ended that sentence and started a new one, the student has broken the bond between them, and the second sentence cannot stand alone as a complete idea. It needs a discourse marker to add more detail.

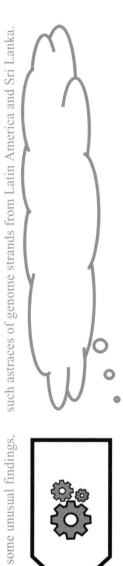

Tests on the subject's DNA profile   have produced   some unusual findings.   Traces of genome strands from Latin America and Sri Lanka.

Amended version

Tests on the subject's DNA profile have produced some unusual findings, such as traces of genome strands from Latin America and Sri Lanka.	In this version, the sentences are connected via the discourse marker 'such as', and the second part of the sentence adds more detail and an example. The sentence has become a complex sentence and can be mapped onto the Christmas Cracker template thus:

Tests on the subject's DNA profile   have produced   some unusual findings,   such astraces of genome strands from Latin America and Sri Lanka.

THE DYSLEXIC EXPERIENCE:

One key problem with sentence fragments is the dyslexic brain's strength in 'gist' thinking. Often the brain is making connections via 'gist' which don't get written down or are forgotten. This leads to incomplete/unfinished or fragmented sentences. You might think that what you have written are complete units of thought (grammatically), but they're not! Many dyslexic individuals then either forget to go back and add punctuation or struggle to know where it should go. Use the Christmas Cracker templates to ensure the core ingredients of each sentence are present between the full stops (and insert full stops where you have a complete set of ingredients).

Problem 6): sentence sprawls

With sentence sprawls, students can go in the opposite direction to that of sentence fragments and have too many equally weighted/important phrases joined with commas. For example:

Disjointed/unclear sentence (sentence sprawl)	Commentary
The exhibition of Blake's engravings was to be held at the Bodleian Library in January, but not all the keynote speakers could attend, so it was rescheduled for February at the Ashmolean instead.	There are simply too many independent clauses bolted together here, and the poor reader hardly has a chance to catch a breath or collect their thoughts. The sentence needs breaking up so that the topics, actions and details are clearly separated, and the appropriate structure (simple, compound, complex or compound-complex) is followed.
Amended version	
The exhibition of Blake's engravings was to be held at the Bodleian Library in January. Not all the keynote speakers could attend, so it was rescheduled for February at the Ashmolean instead.	This is much clearer as the ideas have been broken up into a simple sentence and a complex sentence. It is easier for the reader to decipher what is going on and the sentences sound more emphatic.

TIPS

Ensure all your sentences express complete ideas. Follow one of the main sentence structures (simple, compound, complex, compound-complex) and make sure that you incorporate all the core ingredients (topic, action and detail). If you can't see these, check/amend your sentence structure. Use the templates outlined above to help you. Remember, a Christmas Cracker doesn't work and won't go 'bang' if one of the handles or the main body is missing. The same applies to your sentences!

Focus on punctuation (especially full stops). When proofreading, highlight all the full stops and commas you find and then check that they mark out the ends of clauses and that commas indicate subordinate clauses, not new sentences.

Problem 7): misplaced or dangling modifiers

Your marker might well write the word 'dangling' next to some of your sentences, which can be very puzzling. A dangling modifier is a phrase or word which modifies or pertains to something which is not clearly expressed within the sentence. In other words, the subject of the sentence is either missing or unclear, and it's not clear how/why it's being modified. This leaves the reader confused. Dangling modifiers usually take the form of adjectives/adjectival phrases and adverbs/adverbial phrases. Let's take the following as an example:

Misplaced/dangling modifier	*Commentary*
Upon conducting the research, genetic modification seemed confusing.	The opening phrase here modifies something which is not stated in the sentence – namely the student researching genetic modification. As we can see on the visual representation below, the main 'doer' of the action (the subject/topic) is absent. As such, it almost sounds as though it is genetic modification that is confused, not the student! One of the best ways around the problem of writing dangling modifiers is to ensure that: a) The sentence has a clear 'doer'/subject of the action, and b) The 'doer'/subject is placed in the opening of the sentence so that it becomes the topic.

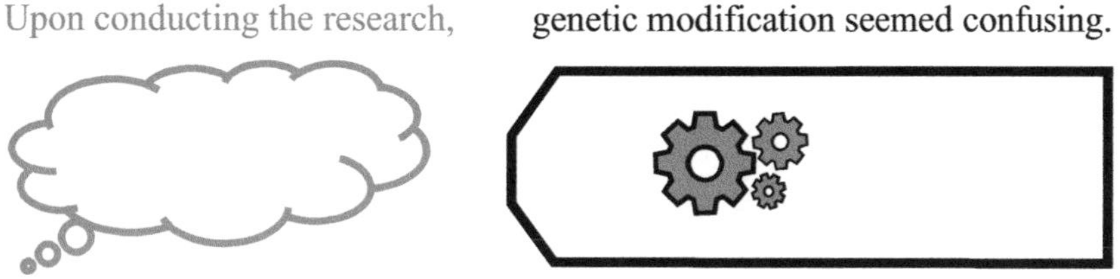

Upon conducting the research,   genetic modification seemed confusing.

Amended version:

Here we have the subordinate clause at the end of the sentence to provide detail and context, but crucially we now have a subject (the student) in the topic position. All in all, this makes the sentence clearer and more focused, and it no longer sounds as though it is genetic modification that is confused!

The student found genetic modification confusing, even after having conducted the research.

The student   found   genetic modification confusing,   even after having conducted the research

OR

After having conducted the research,   the student   found   genetic modification confusing.

Problem 8): *vagueness*

Your marker might well complain that your writing is vague or you use vague words. To be clear, academic writing needs precision. Clarity and precision are also more persuasive. You can't hide any lack of knowledge/ research behind vagueness, and you can't write in the same way that you talk (which is too casual). Vagueness can appear either at the level of word choice, pronoun use or in the sentence structure itself. For example:

Vagueness	Commentary
The scandal created by He Jiankui generated significant controversy. It exposed how a researcher could get away with operating a study that violated Chinese regulations on editing embryos.	The words 'significant controversy' is an example of boosting, but in this context it is not only vague (how do you define 'significant'?), but it is unnecessary because the incident has already been established as a scandal (a scandal, is by definition, significant). The phrase 'researcher' is too vague (it could be any type of researcher from any discipline), the phrase 'get away with' is not only colloquial/casual, but vague in the sense that it's not clear in what way He Jiankui managed to evade prosecution/ punishment, escape, or perhaps wasn't even noticed. Furthermore, the phrase 'operating a study' is vague in the sense that a study could be of literally anything, and 'operating' isn't clear – was he the leader, inventor, or merely a technician? The phrase 'Chinese regulations' is a little less vague as it narrows the sphere down to a geographical location, but what regulations apply? All of this needed to be clear and precise.

Problem 9): *wordiness, waffle and repetition*

One of the most important things to consider in academic writing is the need to get to the point. Avoid all unnecessarily long build-ups, 'throat clearing', padding, waffle, wordiness and repetition. This will not only help you adhere to the word count, but also increases the clarity and persuasiveness of your writing. Indeed, as Demetrius, the Greek rhetorician, stated, 'conciseness gives a certain amount of polish' (1963, p.10), thus making your writing appear more 'finished', complete and competent. Don't use 20 words when 10 will do. Here's an example of an unnecessarily wordy, repetitive, 'padded' passage and a more direct, concise version:

Wordiness, waffle, padding	Concise version
In this section I will cover three areas that I think have contributed to the continued existence of racism, these being culture, the economy and politics, all of which have meant that racism is an integral and internalised part of our society. However, I will not be looking at individual or specific cases of racism, rather exploring a broader explanation as to why it continues to the present day. (69 words)	Culture, the economy and politics are key areas that contribute to and perpetuate racism in society. (16 words) Note – what has been eliminated here is the excessive 'throat clearing' and signposting, the personal pronouns and the excessive/unnecessary justification of focusing on broad issues. What's also been eliminated is the unnecessary repetition (e.g. 'integral and internalised' and 'individual or specific cases').

TIPS

 Try a technique called '50%ing'. This is where you aim to reduce what you have written by 50% whilst retaining all the vital information. This is brutal and hard, but it will help you to practice being concise. It'll really help you think hard about what words are needed and where meanings/messages are unnecessarily similar or duplicate ideas.

 Try to remember that the triangle sections of the Christmas Cracker templates (introductions, main bodies, paragraphs, topic sentences and sentences) narrow from the 'big picture'/broad topic to detail for a very good reason. They not only indicate structure, but encourage you to keep moving forwards and get to the point. Always have the templates to hand when writing to help you keep on track.

 The ability to write concisely is not only good for academic writing and gives your work 'polish' – it's an essential skill to learn for employment. Most job application forms require a personal statement in which you'll need to state, concisely and with polish, how you meet the person specification (and in only a few pages or crammed into an online text box with limited characters). Once in the job, irrespective of what line of work you go into, you'll have to write emails, letters, reports, proposals, plans, strategies and the like. Most managers dislike lengthy, wordy reports, proposals or emails – they don't have time to wade through lots of detail. They need the key facts and take-away messages in a quick and accessible format to enable them to make informed decisions.

THE DYSLEXIC EXPERIENCE:

1) Given that individuals with dyslexia need to see and understand the 'big picture'/context, they often feel the need to explain the importance of context to whoever they are talking to. How many times have you found that people say to you 'just get to the point', or you have forgotten what the point was by the time you've explained the context?!

2) In academic writing, individuals with dyslexia tend to think that everything is relevant and needs to be outlined/discussed to establish the platform for their own argument, even though all that context/detail isn't necessarily needed, and the reader/marker just wants to get to the main message/argument as quickly as possible.

3) Lack of confidence can also be a reason why individuals with dyslexia labour context and don't get to the point. Often, people with dyslexia can be extremely stressed by criticism, usually as a result of being told off at school or bullied by unsympathetic peers because of poor recall skills, poor sequencing, difficulty remembering details, being disorderly and forgetful, or even being incoherent in conversation because of their ability to think and make connections quickly. The net result of this can be overcompensation in terms of being a perfectionist. You can become so fearful of criticism that you want to cover your back, but by doing so you don't get to the point.

Common style blunders:

Informality:

Academic writing is a formal genre, and as such, the style needs to be professional and objective. However, a lot of students make their writing not only vague, but too casual and colloquial. Unlike natural speech, conversation or informal emailing/messaging, you need to eliminate anything which is informal. Consider the following passage, which is inappropriately casual:

Casual language	Commentary
As the world braces for an eye-popping autumn wave of swine flu (H1N1), the relatively new, exciting technique of agent-based computational modelling I'm talking about here is playing a really good part in mapping the disease's possible spread, and designing things for its mitigation. Classical epidemic modelling, like which began in the 1920s, was built on differential equations etc. These things can't assume that the folks are perfectly mixed, with people moving about from the susceptible pool, to the infected one, to the recovered (or dead) one.	The words and phrases 'exciting' and 'really good' are too emotive and personal/informal, whilst words and phrases such as 'things' and 'like which', 'talking about' and 'the infected one' are far too vague/casual. Furthermore, words/contractions such as 'etc.' and 'can't' are again too casual and informal. The term 'folks' instead of 'individuals' is also far too casual, and, whilst not exactly a slang word (as in the case of 'eye-popping'), it's not far off it and is too informal for use in academic writing.

Lack of precision, insufficiently academic/journalistic style

Many students, especially those who have not written many academic essays before starting university, tend to adopt a journalistic style similar to that of a magazine article, blogpost, op-ed or newspaper. As well as often being informal, this style lacks the precision of academic writing and sometimes adopts a 'chatty' style of writing, addresses the reader or adopts rhetorical techniques intended to influence opinions, draw readers in, inflame the passions or act as a call to action. Such writing will lack the rigour needed in academic writing. Let's have a look at an example:

Lack of precision/journalistic style	Commentary
In these modern times in which we live, the nature of disease has changed **due to** our new rapid lifestyle changes. **Whereas** diseases that three generations ago would be fatal are now a manageable annoyance. This brings new issues that we have yet to face in our history. Modern medicine has put a stop to some pathogens **through** vaccinations. **However,** this will not be the case for all pathogens as they avoid extinction by mutating rapidly to the extent that new vaccines will be needed, as seen in the flu vaccine many of us receive each winter. Did you ever wonder why you need a new shot each year? Well, it's because of this mutation.	There are too many loose ends and unanswered questions here. For instance: How does the writer define 'modern times'? What is the 'nature' of disease? Surely lifestyles have always changed? How rapid are our lifestyle changes, and in what areas? Why choose to reference (unspecified) diseases from 'three generations ago'? There are many other examples, but did you also spot the appeals the writer makes to the audience? The passage also uses journalistic expressions such as 'modern times', 'manageable annoyance' and 'new shot', which lack the precision required of academic writing.

This example is undoubtedly readable and engaging, but it sounds like a blog post or newspaper article. Note that the writer not only talks about the issues in GENERAL terms, but forges a connection with the reader by using words such as 'our', 'you' and 'we', and rhetorical flourishes such as 'well', 'many of us', and asking the reader a question. This is perfect for a journalistic/op-ed style but not so for academic writing. Always try to ensure that everything you say is precise and rooted in concrete, specific, verifiable detail and evidence without appealing to the reader. Compare the above extract with the one below about Alzheimer's disease:

Precision	Commentary
Alzheimer's disease is the most common form of Dementia, accounting for up to 60% of all cases (Alzheimer's disease International). Dementia is a degenerative disorder of the brain, which can be defined as 'global impairment of memory and other cognitive functions in the absence of clouding of consciousness' (Lishman 1987, p.3). Characteristic features are confusion and loss of memory in the early stages, followed by personality disintegration in the later stages (Rinomhota & Marshall 2000). Statistics show that the incidence of Alzheimer's disease is increasing; currently, one person in 100 will develop it between 40 and 65, rising to 1 in 50 at 65–70 and 1 in 5 at 80 and above (Hunt 1996). The majority of useful research into Alzheimer's disease has only been conducted during the last ten years due to the new technology that has become available; this has led to the development of new drugs and a better understanding of the disease pathology.	Clear definition/clarification of subdivisions with data and academic definition. Summary of key symptoms with academic reference. Data on increasing prevalence with reference. Considered summary of the state/value of research with specific time frame and reasons (new technology) with clear, precise consequences (new drugs and better understanding). No rhetorical questions, appeals to the reader or vague, informal language.

Yes, this example is perhaps less engaging, but it is precise and leaves no stone unturned in demonstrating knowledge. As such, it will undoubtedly get a higher mark, and stylistically it's far more precise and academic.

TIPS

 A good way of making sure your writing is precise and formal (as opposed to journalistic) is to imagine yourself in a court of law. You are a barrister, defending your argument. To win over the jury, you need precision in your language, evidence and concrete facts/provable/plausible arguments – things which the barrister on the other side of the case (your marker) can't pick holes in, undermine or refute.

 Avoid colloquialisms, contractions, clichés and phrasal verbs (these are descriptions of action that could be condensed into one, often more formal/academic word). For example:

Instead of...	Try...
A lot of/lots of	Many
Big	Large/sizeable
Look at	Examine
More or less	Approximately
Things	Name specific objects/phenomenon
Talk about	Discuss/examine
Brought up	Proposed/raised
Step in	Intervene
Put forward	Raised/proposed
Go up and down	Fluctuate
Cut down	Reduced

Desperate to impress

I often show my students three essays when they first start at university and ask them to choose which they think is the best example of academic writing. One of the pieces is too informal, the other is an excellent piece of student writing, and the third is overly complex, full of jargon and too obviously desperate to impress. Curiously, the majority of the students pick this example as the best, presumably thinking that because it *sounds* clever, it must *be* clever and is therefore a good example of university writing. In reality, academic writing should not be filled with overly long words and sentences, or stodgy, unclear, pompous language which is sometimes clearly padded out to sound better or perhaps even meet the word count. No amount of padding or pompous, overly academic-sounding words will compensate for lack of research or detail. Many of the signs of being desperate to impress can be found in nominalisations, but they can also be found in overly complex boosting, academic, jargon-filled redundancies and excessively long sentences. Take a look at the following as an example:

Desperate to impress	Commentary/key
This essay expounds on the findings of an exhaustive literature survey pertaining to the risks, impacts, and <u>mitigation</u> of pandemics as well as knowledge gaps of pandemics within the scientific and medical community and the academy. Pandemics – defined as large-scale outbreaks of infectious disease that can greatly increase morbidity and mortality over a wide geographic area and cause significant economic, social, and political disruption – have proliferated exponentially over the past century because of the <u>amplification</u> of global travel and <u>integration</u>, urbanisation, changes in land use, and greater exploitation of the natural environment. These trends will likely continue and intensify. Significant policy attention and <u>deliberations</u> has focused on the requirement to identify and limit <u>proliferating</u> outbreaks that might <u>exacerbate</u> or cause causational leads into pandemics and to expand and sustain investment to build preparedness and health capacity.	Unnecessary/pompous words Unnecessary boosting Redundancies/repetition <u>Unnecessary nominalisations</u> (note that some nominalisations are acceptable as they are technical terms and/or compress meaning) Padding/waffle

The writer is clearly trying too hard to impress here with formal, academic-sounding words, but as a result, meaning is not always clear, there's more waffle than substance, and the writer uses two or three words (often nominalisations or jargon) when one will do.

Scientific style

The golden rule of all academic writing is clarity and precision, but nowhere is this more important than in scientific writing. The key to success in scientific writing is to make what you write CLEAR, ACCESSIBLE, CONCISE and COMPELLING/PERSUASIVE through the effective presentation of:

- Evidence

- Facts

- Arguments

- Reasoning/justifications

All of the above need to be presented through the clear, effective use of:

1) Description (to display technical knowledge)

2) Discussion (to display skills in evaluating, analysis and critical thinking)

3) Argumentation (to display that you can propose a hypothesis and solutions)

As we saw in Chapter 6, these can be achieved through a combination of:

1) Descriptive paragraphs

2) Descriptive-analytical paragraphs

3) Analytical paragraphs

We covered how to structure these paragraphs earlier, so let's now examine some exemplar student writing in each of these categories so we can see what stylistic features each type of paragraph uses.

1) Descriptive paragraph	Commentary
The diode is one of the most important components in electrical circuits as they allow us to control the direction in which current flows within a circuit. They have been widely used in many applications, such as rectification and regulating voltage. The changing of the behaviour of a diode is done through a process called "doping". Within a diode is a PN junction, which is the point at which "p-type" materials and "n-type" materials join. "P-type" (positive) materials, such as aluminium and gallium, have only 3 electrons in their outer shells. This absence of electrons will result in an overall positively charged material. "N-type" (negative) materials, such as phosphorous and arsenic, typically have 5 electrons in their outer shells, resulting in an excess of electrons. As a result, this abundance of electrons will make the material negatively charged. The addition of electron holes or excess electrons (also known as impurities) is called doping and is what affects the behaviour of a diode.	Definition and use. Importance outlined in an effective topic sentence. Implications/relevance of subject – demonstrates knowledge beyond the basics. Process and results. Explanation/demonstrating knowledge. Stylistic features/rhetoric which enables clear communication with reader. Note the use of: 1) Highlighting importance and relevance through careful, judicious signalling and boosting. 2) Evoking the relevance to 'us' as readers in respect of control and what it 'allows' us to do. 3) Examples and clear signposting ('such as' and 'typically') and wider applications – makes it seem important whilst highlighting broad knowledge and implications. 4) Examples of how things are 'done' and what this 'will result in' – makes it easy to understand whilst demonstrating knowledge. 5) Use of the pronoun 'this' to refer back and signpost relationships. 6) Description – knowledge explicitly demonstrated and described in a clear way ('is called', 'also known as').

2) Descriptive–analytical paragraph	Commentary
The results for the red LED were problematic. Figure 3a shows VT ≈ 1.60V, which is supported by the typical turn-on voltage of a gallium arsenide diode being approximately 1.30V (Storey, 2017). The graph depicted in Appendix [P] closely resembles the graph plotted in Figure 3a, with the turn-on voltage at approximately VT ≈ 1.6V. This suggests that the LED used in the experiment is a typical LED produced by manufacturers and behaved as expected. If the VT was closer to 0.7 than 1.6, then we could assume that the diode used was faulty [P]. We can presume from Figure 3a that the LED used was not an ideal LED, as there is a slight gradient. We can calculate that the internal resistance of the LED in the experiment is approximately 24.11Ω. [Appendix G]. However, the calculated internal resistance of an LED from a datasheet for manufactured red LEDs is 11Ω. [Appendix O]. This difference in resistance could be a result of the inaccuracy of the gradient in Figure 3a.	Clear, concise topic sentence highlighting unexpected/problematic results. Clear description referring to Figure 3a and Appendix P. Analysis of results and what they mean. Stylistic features/rhetoric which enables clear communication with reader. Note the use of: - Making connections ('shows', 'which is supported by', 'closely resembles'). - Clear signposting and integration of Figure 3a and Appendices. - Interpretation/analysis well signposted ('this suggests', 'however'). - Clear relationship invoked between reader and writer ('we'). - Limitations and logical reasoning established through hedging ('we can presume' and 'could be a result of').

3) Analytical paragraph	Commentary
<u>We can see</u> from Figure 2b (the behaviour of the diode when in reverse bias), that the current of the diode did not increase (in reverse direction) <u>even when</u> voltage was at -15V, <u>suggesting that</u> the diode had a reverse breakdown voltage, VB, of greater than 15V. **The current values when the reverse voltage, VR > VB, <u>was very close to</u> 0A.** This small amount of leakage current is expected as the diode was not ideal. **The ideal resistance of the diode is 0Ω when forward-biased and ∞Ω when reverse-biased (Bumm, 2020).** When calculating the resistance, <u>we see</u> that the behaviour of the diode <u>follows the trend</u> of the internal resistance <u>being very low when</u> in forward-bias (10.791Ω) and <u>very high in</u> reverse-bias (8.811MΩ). [C], [D]. <u>Although not exactly 0Ω and ∞Ω, it shows that the 1N4148 diode behaved almost ideally</u>.	Topic sentence immediately interprets the data and articulates what it means. Analysis of results and evaluation. Description. <u>Stylistic features/rhetoric which enables clear communication with reader.</u> Note the use of: 1) Evoking the relevance/importance of the results to the reader through signalling ('we can see', 'we see'). 2) Use of hedging ('this small amount', 'almost'). 3) Use of concession ('the ideal' and final sentence). 4) Signalling the conformity of results ('is expected', 'follows the trend'). 5) Use of boosting ('even when', 'very high').

All three of the above examples get to the point, do not waste words, integrate and signpost data, graphs and appendices effectively, and highlight logical relationships between concepts, ideas and data through clear signposting. In scientific writing, the evidence and facts are vital in persuading the reader, and as such the style should clearly highlight/establish relationships and signpost/signal implications and results. Furthermore, the style should remain precise throughout. Here's some top tips for success in scientific writing:

TIPS

 Avoid repetitive phrases or words. For example:

'The samples were stored in acid-washed bottles… The samples were transported to the laboratory within 12 hours… The samples were analysed for salinity and pH.' Mix up your words and phrases. A better version might be: 'The samples were stored in acid-washed bottles for transport… At the laboratory, the water was analysed for salinity and pH.'

 Focus on incorporating data, evidence and examples. Persuade and convince through evidence/research rather than generalisations or unsubstantiated claims.

 Use lists with caution. Lists can look desperate and too rhetorical, but with care can be persuasive. Don't make them too long and avoid repeated list structures – this impedes clarity and can appear repetitive and awkward.

 Use the rule of three. Remember, three ideas/pieces of evidence are the optimum number for persuasive purposes. The rule of three can be used effectively to list (briefly) examples and implications, and to signpost and introduce evidence etc.

 Signpost the way (but in a way that indicates evaluation/criticality/argumentation). Remember, signposting words/phrases such as 'however', 'by contrast', 'although', 'on the other hand' and 'additionally' all link ideas together BUT ALSO indicate/signpost critical engagement AND stance.

 Use subheadings to structure the writing and orientate the reader. Subheadings are very common in scientific writing (but are much less common in the humanities).

 ALWAYS integrate/introduce diagrams/visuals/figures etc. Don't just drop them in and assume the reader knows how/when to use/read them in relation to what you are saying. Avoid 'parachuting' quotes without introducing them/providing context.

Style considerations for reflective writing

In reflective writing, YOU are the main subject. As such, you can:

- Make extensive use of the personal pronoun

- Describe what happened and what you did

- Refer constantly to feelings, emotions and reactions, no matter how unscientific (although your analysis of them needs to be rigorous and academic)

However, the golden rule of all academic writing, the need for clarity, precision and academic rigour, still applies. With this in mind, take a look at the flowing example. Do you think this is a good, precise, academically rigorous piece of reflective writing?

> Our final hurdle was to compile sufficient information against a tight deadline in a group with a somewhat fractious nature, and after many days spent working together and helping each other out we finally got it finished. Interestingly, it was very apparent that two members of the group had done easily twice that of the other two, with the third member having contributed nothing whatsoever to the final Business Plan. One issue our group faced was a lack of leadership and a lack of respect. We had a nominal group leader but he wasn't always on time and often hadn't done the work, and could be easily distracted during meetings and let the conversation wander. I feel that I am quite a natural leader and I find myself directing most group activities I become involved with, through having quite a forceful and professional outlook, and acquiring both attention to detail and a wider scope of the task in hand, so inevitably I soon became the unofficial group leader. However, I felt that I was not entirely treated with respect by all of the group, and I suspect this was because I was the only female and also the only proactive one and the male members didn't like me being so forceful and controlling, whether consciously or not. I think this is an issue that must arise often in the workplace, particularly in the male-dominated world of engineering, but I found it very interesting to observe and work around, and in the end my clear organisation and forward thinking earned me their respect, at least in the manner in which they spoke to me.

This sample is undoubtedly reflective, but many of the reflections are entirely speculative and lack evidence and a grounding in the literature/theory. It also lacks a clear argument, structure and focus, and it uses some casual language. Furthermore, thinking back to the reflective writing structures we discussed on pp.94–95, it is unclear which part of the essay this extract comes from, as it appears to be a mixture of the 'what happened' and 'so what?' sections.

Here's a better example with commentary:

Sample reflective writing on teamwork	*Commentary*
During the week 3 writing task, I was worried that the friction of the previous week would continue, but was pleased to find that we began to 'gel' a bit better. This development aligns with Tuckman's concept of 'norming'. During this stage, group 'norms' are established, and members accept the diversity and idiosyncrasies of others allowing the development of a cohesive unit. Team roles begin to form, and new-found harmony and openness allows efforts to be directed to working out how the task can be achieved (Tuckman, 1965). **Prior to the meeting, Jane had posted a request that we brainstorm our ideas so that we could be sure our work was not overlapping or going off the point.** After doing this and seeing that we were all focusing on complementary areas I found her much easier to work with. **Will had a better understanding of the laws and policies we needed for our study and very kindly produced a handout for us all explaining some key points.** I was very grateful to him for this and felt it was more than was required of him. Cottrell (2003) explains that groups are enhanced if members are supportive, encouraging and sharing and I felt that Will displayed all these qualities with this one act. **We further discussed and refined our focus and agreed on how we would split the work. Each of us took a different topic with the exception of Lucy and Jane, who chose to work together. Lucy and Jane were first to post their work;** however, most of us felt it wasn't what we needed. After some deliberation, **I posted a message pointing out what I felt was good and what needed improving.** I tried to be diplomatic and constructive but was very worried I would offend them, or that they would feel I was trying to take over. I was aware that any criticism I made needed to be phrased in a positive way and suggest improvements rather than pick fault (Cottrell, 2003), however, I still found it a stressful task. I was pleasantly surprised that when Jane replied she was okay with what I said and had written a new piece on her own that I and the others thought was exactly what was needed.	– This is clearly an extract from the 'what happened' section and signposts a specific incident via an effective topic sentence (which indicates the incident and the student's reflections) – Clear evidence from the key literature/theory – Clear description of events and what happened – Clear reflections which are grounded in BOTH the literature/theory and feelings/emotions arising from what happened. HOWEVER – the extract is a little wordy and occasionally informal. Can you see where it could be made more concise? What phrases need making more formal?

Notice here that whilst the reflections are personal, the student works through them in an analytical manner. In other words, in reflective writing, you should subject yourself (your emotions and reactions) to critical analysis. Whilst the subject may be personal, you need to be careful to retain the dispassionate, unbiased, rational, clear, detailed, evidence-based academic tone/style required of academic writing.

Passive vs active voice

Your markers (or perhaps, as is more likely, spelling- and grammar-checkers such as Grammarly) may well have commented on your use of the passive voice. What is it, and why does it matter? Let's start with some definitions:

Active voice = this is where the subject (or topic) comes before the verb (action). The object (or detail) appears after the verb (or action). As such, the main emphasis and focus of the sentence revolves around the subject (or topic). This is the standard type of sentence we looked at in the previous chapter, and is aligned below with Bruce's 'communicative dynamism' wave:

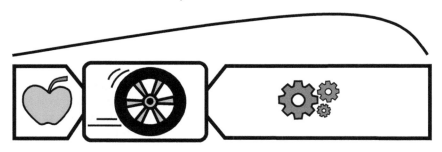

Freud   had a huge impact   on psychoanalysis.

Passive voice = in this type of sentence, the object (or detail) comes before the verb (or action). As such, the subject (or topic) is not the main focus – the main focus is on the object (detail). This type of sentence (again aligned with Bruce's 'communicative dynamism' wave), would look like this:

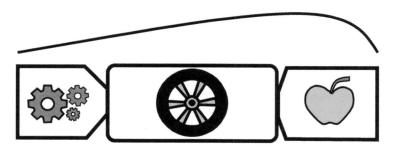

Psychoanalysis   was heavily impacted upon by   Freud.

The same information is conveyed here, but the sentence is less 'active' because although we still move from the given to the new, the action (verb) part of the sentence is less direct. It is for this reason that the wheel icon no longer has movement indicated. Additionally, whilst in the 'active voice' the subject (or topic) has a starring role and is the centre of attention, in the case of the passive voice, it is the object (or detail) that is centre stage. Put simply, rather than $2 + 2 = 4$, in passive sentences, we put that 4 is achieved by $2 + 2$. It is a less direct way of communicating ideas, and it is less clear who is responsible for what or what x did in relation to y.

In academic writing, the active voice (especially in the sciences) used to be avoided because it often places the writer at the centre of attention (e.g. 'we/I performed the experiment using' instead of 'the experiment was performed'). This was deemed to be insufficiently impartial and objective. However, today, the active voice is much more in favour. The benefits of the active voice are that it is:

- More direct

- More confident

- More compelling

The passive voice, by contrast, can come across as

- Indirect

- Lacking in confidence

- Lacking action

- Weak

- Uncertain

- Bureaucratic

A further pitfall of the passive voice is that writers can hide behind it to a certain extent. If you use active, plain, straightforward sentences, you'll soon be forced to confront any lack of knowledge or clarity.

So which should you use – active or passive?

Whilst you may see the use of passive voice in some publications and academic writing (I have used it in places throughout this book when I've wanted to be more nuanced or less direct), try to use the active voice in your essays as much as possible. You should always be clear and specific. The passive voice sometimes obscures key detail or impedes clarity, so if in doubt, always use the active voice.

There is, however, one occasion when you might want to use the passive voice. Sometimes it is worth being a little more indirect to avoid sounding too judgemental or accusatory. It may be that you want to make the tone of your writing sound less 'political'. Compare and contrast the following examples:

Passive voice	Active voice
In management, the lack of women in pivotal roles has <u>been attributed</u> to patriarchal attitudes – biological and emotional differences have <u>been invoked</u> to legitimise existing hierarchies and male dominance in such lines of work. <u>Women's roles in management have been subject to a 'glass ceiling' and a lack of access to the boardroom.</u>	In management, patriarchal attitudes lead to a lack of women in pivotal roles – senior management have used biological and emotional differences to legitimise existing hierarchies and male dominance in such lines of work. Senior management have confined women's roles, imposed a 'glass ceiling' and excluded them from the boardroom.

Note that whilst the text in red is undoubtedly more confident, assertive and in some respects clear, it is a little too accusatory in its tone. Indeed, if you're not careful, you can sound aggressive in such circumstances. Sometimes you need to be more guarded, and this is where the passive voice can be helpful. In the underlined words/phrases above, you can see that the student-writer is less involved, more distant, and thus more balanced. This gives the writing an objectivity and critical distance that the marker will appreciate.

Using acronyms

Most students will come across and use acronyms, but they are often used extensively in the sciences and social sciences. They are a valuable way of reducing your word count, reducing the awkwardness of repetition, and will help you get to the point more swiftly. However, there are some key points you need to remember when using acronyms to enhance readability and conform to academic style/conventions:

- Do not use acronyms in your title, and do not attempt to define them in the title. The only acronyms that should appear in titles are those that are well known, commonly used, and not subject to different versions or uses. For example, the acronym CD is most often associated with data storage, but unhelpfully it is also an acronym for Critical Dimension (in semiconductors), Circular Dimension (in optics) and Certificate of Deposit (in economics), so can easily lead to confusion. However, USA is normally associated with the United States of America, so it is safe to use in a title and without definition.

- Always spell out the full acronym the first time you use it (and put the acronym in brackets). Subsequent appearances can just use the acronym. Do not repeat the full version later in the essay.

- Never invent acronyms as a way of reducing the word count.

Final thoughts on style and sentence structure: mix it up

Vary your sentence length. This not only ensures variety and avoids monotony (by providing and varying rhythm and pace), but can be useful depending upon what sort of message you want to convey and what impact you want to have on your reader/marker. As Demetrius suggested, 'a great idea comprised in a small compass is more forceful and vigorous…A command is concise and brief, and every master uses few words to a slave; but supplication and lamentation are lengthy' (1963, p.65). In other words, short sentences are generally suited to bold claims and come across as sure, confident, vigorous and authoritative. More reflective, less certain ideas are best dealt with in longer sentences. By combining the two, you enhance the style and variety of your writing and can convey different messages (along with other techniques such as boosting and hedging).

Summary and checklist for writing in an academic style

Academic writing ✓	Personal/informal writing ✗
Logical and impersonal	Emotional or personal
Objective	Subjective
Formal English	Uses contractions, abbreviations, colloquial language, phrasal verbs and is often 'chatty'
Based on research	Based on opinions or non-peer-reviewed material (e.g. Wikipedia)
Is precise and concise	Can be rhetorical, make generalisations, and can be vague – effect is more important than precision and evidence
The 'I'/self is not the core focus (except in reflective writing)	The 'I'/self is often central
References sources	Usually few sources

Bibliography

Barrell, John, (2000) *Imagining the King's Death: Figurative Treason, Fantasies of Regicide, 1793–1796*. Oxford: Oxford University Press.

Demetrius, (1963) 'On Style', in Warrington, John (ed.) *Aristotle's Poetics, Demetrius on Style, Longinus on the Sublime*. London: Everyman's Library, pp.61–132.

Gill, A. A., (2010) *A Pioneering New Way to Face up to Dyslexia*. Available at: https://samedifference1.com/2010/03/22/a-pioneering-new-way-to-face-up-to-dyslexia/ (Accessed: 30th March, 2017).

Hemingway, Ernest, (1962) *The Wild Years*. New York: Dell Publishing Company.

Janowitz, Anne, (2004) *Women Romantic Poets: Anna Barbauld and Mary Robinson*. Tavistock: Northcote House Publishers Ltd.

Pinker, Steven, (2015) *The Sense of Style: The Thinking Person's Guide to Writing in the 21st Century*. London: Penguin Books.

Sword, Helen, (2012) *Beware of Nominalizations (AKA – Zombie Nouns)*. Available at: https://www.youtube.com/watch?v=-dNlkHtMgcPQ (Accessed: 12th October, 2016).

Williams, Joseph M., (2007) *Style: Lessons in Clarity and Grace*. 9th edn. New York: Pearson Education, Inc.

8   Proofreading and Editing

'Dyslexia, for me, is rather like being a six-fingered typist on LSD'.
(Stephen Richards: prolific author, director and owner of Mirage Publishing)

If you've had a dyslexia assessment, it's likely that when your work is marked, allowances will be made for spelling and grammatical errors. Students are often given stickers to attach to their assignment, requesting that the assessor mark sympathetically and focus on content and argument/ideas rather than the surface errors students with dyslexia typically make. However, this is not to say that you shouldn't make every effort to get your work right and to eliminate as many errors as possible. This is not only important because funding for proofreading through the Disabled Students' Allowance is increasingly rare – practising proofreading and editing for yourself will set you up well for future employability and will help you avoid any slip-ups that may impact upon your chosen career, irrespective of what 'reasonable adjustments' employers are legally obliged to make.

Famous proofreading and editing gaffs

There have been numerous instances of even non-dyslexic writers failing to proofread or edit their work. This can cause immense problems and embarrassment and highlights why proofreading and editing are so important. Some well-known examples include:

1) In 1988 the University of Wisconsin handed out more than four thousand graduate diplomas with the incorrect spelling 'Wisconson' typed at the top of every certificate! The error was finally spotted six months later. Officials denied that the university had failed to proofread, claiming that they had checked all the certificates, but only to verify the spelling of the students' names and degree subjects!

2) In 1631, a printer in London produced one thousand copies of the Bible with a crucial mistake in the Ten Commandments. King Charles I fined the printers and demanded that all one thousand copies be burnt, although seven copies survived!

13. Thou shalt not kill.

14. Thou shalt commit adultery.

15. Thou shalt not steal.

DOI: 10.4324/9781003190189-8

3) Early in 2010, Gregorio Iniguez, director of the Chilean mint, was fired after he authorised the production of 1.5 million 50-peso coins that incorrectly spelt the country's name as 'Chlle'. Unfortunately, by this point, it was too late, and the coins are still in circulation! (Vappingo, 2017)

Grammar and spell-checkers – help or hindrance?

One of the problems today's students face is an overreliance on technology. There is often an assumption that word processors, voice-recognition software and grammar-checkers will eliminate all of your mistakes and 'typos' for you. They DO NOT! Indeed, they can often be the cause of them. The following sentence is typical:

The effects of depression can be very decapitating.

The writer meant that depression can be very 'debilitating', but the word processor autocorrected it to 'decapitating', which obviously means something very different.

Similar problems blighted the life of the dyslexic writer A. A. Gill. For this reason he rarely communicated to his editors and publishers via email or computer. In an interview on the BBC Radio 4 Today programme on 12th December, 2016, Helen Hawkins, Gill's editor at the *Sunday Times*, revealed how she had found a rare email from him in which he had typed 'intestine' instead of 'interesting' (BBC, 2016). This is undoubtedly an example of the autocorrect function or the spell-checker in action. Indeed, because individuals with dyslexia often mix up the ordering of letters, it's easy to see why an automated computer predict function should confuse 'intestine' with 'interesting', as many of the letters are the same. But as we have already seen, even non-dyslexic, professional writers, editors and publishers can be caught out. For example, the website www.bookerrata.com (which reviews and rates published typos and errors) brands the novel *Under the Volcano* by Malcolm Lowry (as published by Perennial Classics in 2000) 'horrendous' as it contains no fewer than 39 errors, of which the following is merely a sample:

Page number	Error	Correction
ix	'not **jut** of himself but of a phase of history'	just
16	'he lit a new cigarette **form** the one he'd been smoking'	from
22	'but **he** waiter…refused to serve them'	the
54	'his feet **barley** touching the ground'	barely
72	'She was sitting on the parapet gazing over the valley with **ever** semblance of interested enjoyment'	every
157	'Better **too** let them have their way'	to
158	'how could he expect to **see** anything so revolutionary as a hot dog **in** Oxford Street? He might as well try ice cream at the South Pole'	sell and on

According to Bookerrata, the 're-proofed' version is only marginally better, and still only gets a rating of 'sloppy' (Bookerrata, 2017).

Students often ask why they need to bother editing and proofreading when software such as Grammarly or the autocorrect in Google Docs can do it for you. After all, Grammarly can be used as an easily accessible plug-in on most web browsers, email and Microsoft Word, and Google autocorrect is usually automated and predictive. They are both undoubtedly useful tools, but there are two reasons why you shouldn't rely upon them:

1) Grammarly isn't perfect. It's got better over the years, and if you pay for the 'Premium' version, it can also advise on style, clarity, delivery, tone, consistency, fluency and plagiarism. However, it is prone to the following mistakes:

    • It has a tendency to confuse subject/verb agreements in complex sentences (e.g. 'lines were printed out using PRF to allow determination of exactly which pieces of code were being executed'. Grammarly will suggest changing 'were' to 'was', here, but because there are 'pieces' of code [i.e. more than one – plural], 'were' is correct. Notice also the inconsistency – Grammarly picks up on the second use of 'were' in the sentence but not the first [which it has down as correct]).

- It can get itself confused over the use of prepositions (e.g. 'the rotation through 180° was accomplished by moving in a sweeping motion in the opposite direction'. Grammarly wants the writer to delete the 'in' here, but the preposition is essential in telling the reader that it is the movement that needs to be in a sweeping motion [and not something else]. It is, therefore, correct. Again, note that Grammarly is inconsistent because it has an issue with the first 'in' but not the second).

- It can get very confused regarding article/determiner use (e.g. 'two basic functions were required: movement and detection. Movement covers motion in all required directions (i.e. forwards, left, right and backwards)'. Grammarly will suggest adding an article/determiner before movement, but because movement in this context is a proper noun, no article/determiner is required).

- It often can't tell what a name is and what isn't (resulting in incorrect capitalisation).

- It often gets confused regarding context. For instance, a sentence on the previous page reads 'individuals with dyslexia often mix up the ordering of letters'. Grammarly would like to change this to 'individuals with dyslexia often mix up ordering letters', which changes the meaning from spelling to ordering mail!

- Google Docs and Gmail predictive autocorrect is often better, but you can end up accepting or missing suggestions and edits that are entirely different from what you wanted to say. The algorithm is not necessarily infallible or trustworthy.

If you use the free version of Grammarly, an additional issue is that it is designed to tempt you into buying the 'Premium' version by flagging hundreds of additional issues, which you can only access once you've handed over your hard-earned cash. Often, these stylistic issues are not as severe as you might think, so they aren't necessarily worth the upgrade.

2) Using Grammarly and Google autocorrect can be a valuable tool for learning, but only if you use them as a bridge to writing independently. If you rely upon them, you are not developing your writing, editing and proofreading skills. If you encounter a scenario whereby Grammarly or Google isn't available (e.g. a writing task in an interview scenario, in the workplace or in the field), you have nothing to fall back on. As such, developing your writing skills in a way that you can use them independently of the software is a good skill for employability and the wider world.

Editing and proofreading strategies

So, what exactly is editing and proofreading and how do you do it? Most students adopt one of the following approaches:

Quite a few of these clearly rely upon others, but there are many things you can do yourself to iron out 'typos', spelling errors and grammatical problems, as we shall see throughout this chapter. It's not easy, particularly if you have dyslexia, but here are some ideas and techniques to help draw upon your visual strengths and get your dyslexia working for you, rather than against you.

Editing

According to Susan Bell, editing occurs at two levels:

1) The ongoing edit. This is where you edit as you write. In fact, editing is often writing. It consists of the ongoing deleting, re-phrasing, copying, pasting and re-reading that occurs as you are actually composing.

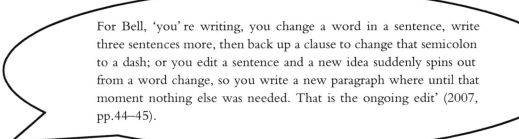

For Bell, 'you're writing, you change a word in a sentence, write three sentences more, then back up a clause to change that semicolon to a dash; or you edit a sentence and a new idea suddenly spins out from a word change, so you write a new paragraph where until that moment nothing else was needed. That is the ongoing edit' (2007, pp.44–45).

2) The draft edit. This is where you have largely completed the assignment (or perhaps a section of it), and you stop writing, take a step back and revise what you have done, taking in the sense of the whole and the 'big picture'.

Whichever type of editing you do, the point is that writing involves lots of revision and 'tinkering'. As William Zinsser has advised:

'Rewriting is the essence of writing well: it's where the game is won or lost…Most writers don't initially say what they want to say, or say it as well as they could. The newly hatched sentence almost always has something wrong with it. It's not clear. It's not logical. It's verbose. It's clunky. It's pretentious. It's boring. It's full of clutter. It's full of clichés. It lacks <u>rhythm</u>. It can be read in several different ways. It doesn't lead out of the previous sentence…The point is that clear writing is the result of a lot of tinkering' (2006, p.83).

In other words, writing is not something that can or should be left until the last minute, so time management is essential here. Forget the all-nighters dosed up on caffeine, writing frantically before a 9 am deadline. If you have dyslexia, you need to start writing early, get yourself organised and start writing little bits at a time, making gradual inroads into the word count to give yourself enough time for extensive revisions and checking.

TIP

Don't think of writing and editing separately. Writing is recursive and involves many revisions, reconsiderations, and even new positions, even at the editing and proofreading stages. Think of the 'writing process itself', of which editing and proofreading is a part, as 'a process of discovery' (Rectenwald and Carl, 2016, p.38).

What sort of things need checking when you edit your work?

Unlike proofreading, editing involves looking at the 'big picture'. Rather than getting bogged down with spelling and punctuation errors, stick to the 'macro' level, making sure to check:

Structure and coherence – does the flow of ideas make sense? Can you map your ideas and arguments onto the Christmas Cracker templates?	✓ / ✗
Signposting and linking of ideas.	✓ / ✗
Appropriate register and vocabulary – no casual language.	✓ / ✗
Adherence to the question/assignment task.	✓ / ✗
Argument – ensure you have one, that it is well signposted and has a logical structure.	✓ / ✗
Concision – are you using too many words? Could you say the same thing more directly or quickly? According to Elizabeth Lyon, 'some of the most effective editing involves tightening…Shorten a work and it becomes better' (2000, p.237).	✓ / ✗
Clarity – is what you are saying clear and understandable?	✓ / ✗
Content – is it in the correct place and under the correct headings/subheadings?	✓ / ✗
Academic rigour – will it stand up to the marker's scrutiny?	✓ / ✗

What sort of things need checking when you proofread your work?

Proofreading, as already indicated, looks at the micro detail and involves very careful reading and re-reading to eliminate spelling, punctuation, grammatical or mechanical errors. Typical issues you may want to keep an eye out for include:

Spelling errors – pay particular attention to key terms and names (I once had a batch of essays on the poet Percy Shelley, but only a couple of students managed to spell Shelley correctly throughout their essays, despite spell-checking and despite having the poet's name in front of them on their books!).	✓ / ✗
Use of contractions or faulty abbreviations – eliminate abbreviations such as 'isn't' for 'is not' (the former is too casual) and double-check acronyms for accuracy and consistency.	✓ / ✗
Duplication of words – don't use the same words too frequently across the same sentence or nearby sentences. Use your thesaurus to show a broad vocabulary range.	✓ / ✗
Formatting – ensure the mechanics are correct (if the marker wants it double-spaced, make sure it is).	✓ / ✗
References – check their accuracy and that you are using the correct style/conventions.	✓ / ✗
Inaccurate cross-referencing (especially of page numbers) – ensure that during editing, if you move text or ideas around, you check whenever you refer backwards or forwards that these signallers are correct.	✓ / ✗

Singular/plural mix-ups – ensure that you are consistent (e.g. 'are' is plural and 'is' is singular – double-check what they refer to is correct).	✓ / ✗
Tenses – ensure consistency and make sure the past remains the past and doesn't suddenly become the present.	✓ / ✗
Punctuation – check your apostrophes are in the correct places and that full stops indicate the end of a sentence (check for comma splices and run-on sentences).	✓ / ✗

Techniques for effective editing and proofreading

The problem all of us face when editing and proofreading is that we are familiar with our own work. As such, rather than re-reading the text and being able to spot the errors, what often happens is that our brain and eyes read what ought to be there rather than what's actually on the page. In other words, our eyes and our brain play tricks on us. As the famous American author Mark Twain wrote in 1898:

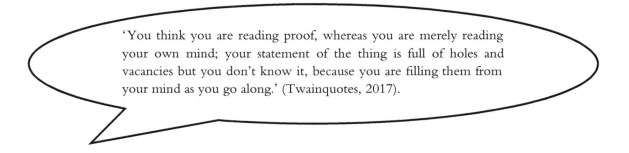

'You think you are reading proof, whereas you are merely reading your own mind; your statement of the thing is full of holes and vacancies but you don't know it, because you are filling them from your mind as you go along.' (Twainquotes, 2017).

This is doubly problematic for students with dyslexia, however, as one of the problems is that dyslexia causes you to have trouble knowing that you are making mistakes in the first place, without the additional tricks the mind can play on us all. But additionally, the brain also tends to skip chunks of text, even if you are not 'reading your own mind'. Research has shown that the mind can skip over letters, incorrectly placed letters and even words without losing any sense of meaning. There is little scientific explanation as to why this happens, but the brain seems to prefer seeing larger units of meaning rather than small errors. As such, the brain can be inefficient at recognising words, possibly as a result of prediction (Rayner et al., 2006, Davis, 2012). Indeed, we all tend to predict text as we read (I even encouraged this in the reading chapter earlier), even if there are mistakes. This is exactly

why your Barin can Raed this

despite the obvious errors and incorrect capitalisation! Your brain simply fills in the gaps and automatically predicts what is there and what is meant. Indeed, this represents a further problem you may face if you have dyslexia. As mentioned in Chapter 2, individuals with dyslexia can often lapse into a sort of semi-daydream state of 'autopilot' while reading, so you end up not taking anything in, whether this is the meaning or the mistakes.

For you to be able to edit and proofread effectively, then, you need to be able to de-familiarise the familiar. You need to make what you have written look different, or approach it from a different angle, to trick the brain and your eyes into thinking that you are reading it for the first time. Some ways in which you can do this are as follows:

1) Distance yourself and take a break

By not looking at your script for a day, or even an hour or so, you can come to it with a fresh pair of eyes and a more considered perspective. Individuals with dyslexia get tired easily, so by taking regular breaks, you can renew your energy and see things differently. Don't leave it too long between writing and editing/proofreading though – the short-term memory associated with dyslexia will mean that you might forget too much of the material, which can often result in you being so fresh that you can't remember what you were supposed to be arguing. The trick is to refresh the brain and the eyes without falling out of the 'groove'.

2) Break the task into manageable chunks

The dyslexic brain only likes short, intense bursts of activity, so only look at short blocks of text at a time to avoid losing concentration and reading on 'autopilot'. Indeed, this approach can be extended to editing and proofreading for specific errors. Try reading for one type of problem at a time rather than attempting to identify every single error as you read. One way of doing this is to read the script (or perhaps even sections of the script) multiple times. For example:

- First reading: check for clarity and appropriate style/register.

- Second reading: check for academic rigour.

- Third reading: check for consistency and appropriate structure (hold the Christmas Cracker templates against the paragraphs/overall essay to see if the flow of ideas aligns).

- Forth reading: check for adequate signposting.

- Fifth reading: check references.

- Sixth reading: check for and eliminate repetition and redundancies – tighten/shorten the essay.

- Seventh reading: check punctuation and spellings/grammar (hold Christmas Cracker templates against your sentences and see if the sequence/flow of ideas aligns).

Try various approaches, see which works best for you, and mix and match as you see fit.

3) Look for and check the action

Much of the action of your essay and its argument takes place in the topic sentences, verbs and evaluative/critical language, which are primarily found in the evaluation, persuasive, analytical and argumentative sentences. Go through the script highlighting these (perhaps in different colours) to check the logic, structure and forwards momentum of your argument. This will also allow you to cross-reference key sentences and phrases with the assignment task/question to see if you are answering it and giving the marker what they want.

4) Focus on punctuation

Circle or highlight all punctuation marks. This will encourage you to see the structure of your sentences. Perhaps highlight commas in orange (to indicate a pause) and full stops in red. This way, the colours match those of traffic lights and indicate similar functions. Then check that each punctuation mark is used correctly and that you have enough to render your ideas clear and readable.

5) Read slowly, word by word

This will enable you to concentrate on looking for errors and 'typos' rather than taking in content. This is an intense form of reading for anyone, let alone if you have dyslexia, so be prepared to take very regular breaks to 'reset' your concentration.

6) Change the look

You need to try and trick your brain into thinking that you are reading the script as a stranger would, so an effective way of defamiliarising the familiar is to change the appearance. This can be done in numerous ways:

- Most people write directly onto a computer (either typing or using voice recognition software), so print it out. The very fact that it is on paper rather than the computer screen makes it look different and can really help you identify surprisingly obvious errors and 'typos'. Your dyslexia/DSA advisor should be able to advise on whether there is funds available to help with the printing costs associated with this.

- Print the script out on different coloured paper (anything that suits other than white). Perhaps use coloured overlays. Some individuals with dyslexia find overlays very useful, particularly for reducing visual stress.

- Print out in a different font. If you typed the essay in Times New Roman, change it to Calibri or Rockwell (anything that takes your fancy, providing it is readable). This can again trick your brain and eyes into seeing the script afresh, especially in respect of spotting spelling errors or 'typos'. Converting a document to PDF format can also help. PDFs tend to look much more professional, and can again con your brain into thinking you are reading something new.

- Lay the text out differently by creating a text scroll. One of the biggest problems with working on a computer screen, as is illustrated in the image below, is the inability to see the 'big picture'. If you scroll up or down to check something, the passage you were just working on disappears off the screen and is 'lost'. Using two screens can certainly help, especially if working with different documents, but the most effective way of seeing the structure, coherence and argument is to see it all at the same time. As indicated below, print out the script on single-sided paper and lay it out either horizontally or vertically. This will enable you to skim and scan both backwards and forwards for structural errors, logic and inconsistencies.

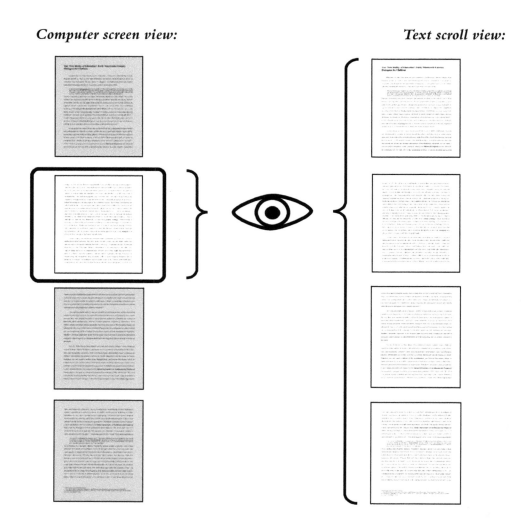

Computer screen view: *Text scroll view:*

Experiment to see whether you prefer reading vertically or horizontally, and lay the papers out accordingly (you may find that because you read vertically on the computer screen, reading horizontally, as in the example below, provides an additional level of defamiliarisation). You can even print out the Christmas Cracker templates and place them onto the papers to check the logic, consistency, cohesion and structure. Text scrolls can work particularly well if you highlight the topic sentences, action (verbs), evaluative/critical language, and even the evidence (although you might find this disorientating if you highlight too many things at once). Below I have highlighted the following:

Red = topic sentences

Green = evidence

Blue = argument and analysis

As you can see, the topic sentences here are fine, but there is possibly too much evidence. More specifically, you can see that the fourth paragraph contains some good analysis/evaluation but no evidence, and the final paragraph ends with evidence and no sense of final evaluation/analysis, which may need attention and modification. If necessary, literally cut the pages, paragraphs or even sections up and try them in different places. Then amend the version on the computer, re-print and try again until you are satisfied.

7) *Change the sound*

 Instead of reading silently, read aloud. As Steven Pinker has noted, 'the rhythm of speech' will help you identify problems because 'if you stumble as you recite a sentence, it may mean you're tripping on your own treacherous syntax. Reading a draft, even in a mumble, also forces you to anticipate what your readers will be doing as they understand your prose' (2015, p.115). So, if you find yourself running out of breath, your sentences are probably too long, but also listen to the sounds and the rhythm. Obviously, your writing is not intended to be sung or rival the melodious sounds of a lullaby, but listen for awkwardness and lack of cohesion, flow and rhythm.

8) *Try dual editing/proofreading*

 As with dual reading/dual assistive reading, if you find your mind wandering and you are working on two (or perhaps even more) essays at the same time, try swapping between them to sustain interest and trick your mind out of the familiar.

9) *Cut the waste*

 As already mentioned, since 'some of the most effective editing involves tightening', try reducing your word count by eliminating unnecessary words. Sometimes this can be difficult (not least because it is somewhat soul-destroying pressing the delete button after spending so many hours carefully crafting your sentences). Indeed, it is often difficult to identify what is unnecessary. There is a function in Microsoft Word that highlights certain words and recommends that you 'consider using concise language', but here again this can be unreliable/inaccurate. The 'Paramedic Method' devised by Richard Lanham (2006) is more dependable and can help you identify unnecessary words. The Paramedic Method involves:

a)   Identifying and then eliminating too many prepositions (e.g. of, in, about, for, onto, into) and 'throat-clearing' words. Get to the point as quickly as possible. For example, instead of

- In Jones's theory, income from land ownership ought to be in the region of about 12% per annum (17 words), try

- Jones argues that land ownership revenues should be roughly 12% per annum (11 words).

(Note how the second example is not only more concise but more emphatic and confident).

b)   Identifying and eliminating 'is' verb forms. For example, instead of writing

- This essay is an analysis of John Keats's poem 'Ode to Psyche' (12 words), try

- This essay analyses John Keats's poem 'Ode to Psyche' (9 words).

(Again, note how the second example is not only more concise but more emphatic and confident).

c)   Check to ensure that the 'action' of the sentence is expressed in a simple verb and that it has a clear, close connection with the subject. Additionally, check for unclear or unnecessary nominalisations. As we saw earlier in Chapter 7, one way of making your sentences have more action (which makes them more readable) is to ensure that you don't turn verbs into nominalisations or abstractions. Take a look at these examples:

Verb buried in a nominalisation/abstraction	*Simpler verb – more action*
Demonstration	Demonstrates
Suggestion	Suggests
Expansion	Expands
Proliferation	Proliferates

During editing and proofreading, check that you haven't relied too heavily on abstractions and nominalisations and make your sentences have explicit action which is close to the doer/subject of that action.

d)   Make sure you are getting to the point as quickly as possible. Check to ensure that 'build-ups'/'throat clearing' (introductory/contextual comments) and 'wind-ups' (closing, concluding remarks) are as short as possible. Even question whether they are necessary at all. Take a look at the following example:

- In terms of the research methods the authors basically used primary source data, collecting the data themselves in physics laboratories (17 words).

The 'build-up' here is not strictly necessary (also note that the subject of the sentence is a little unclear), and the adverb 'basically' adds nothing of any value to the meaning/argument. The sentence would be far more concise, confident and readable if both the build-up and unnecessary 'throat clearing' were eliminated and the 'doer' of the sentence were moved into the subject/topic position within the sentence. For example:

- The authors used their own primary source data collected from physics laboratories (12 words).

TIPS

 Avoid 'there are' sentences. Although you might think the build-up 'there are' demonstrates knowledge (which is good of course), you can do this far more quickly by eliminating it and just getting to the point. So instead of:

- There are two ways in which we can make non-executable specifications executable (13 words),

Try

- Non-executable specifications can be made executable in two ways (9 words).

Try reducing wordy build-ups with one word. Take a look at the following examples and see if you can reduce them to ONE word. The first four have been done for you:

Wordy build-up	*Corrected version*
At this point in time	*Now*
Has the ability to	*Can*
In light of the fact that	*Because*
In the vicinity of	*Near*
Has the potential to	
The question as to whether	
Made the arrangement for	
Performed the development of	
Is used to detect	

e) Eliminate redundancies (pairs of words that basically say the same thing). Redundancies often occur either because they creep into the writing from outside influences in popular culture (television, advertising, journalism etc.) or as a way of trying to mask an underlying lack of confidence through unnecessary boosting. For instance,

- 'absolutely essential' sounds more convincing than 'essential'
- 'completely eliminate' sounds better than 'eliminate'

Redundancies can be an effective way of boosting in oral presentations, but in writing, they are completely unnecessary (or should I have just written unnecessary?). Take a look at the following sentences and see if you can eliminate the redundancies – the first four have been done for you:

Redundancy	*Corrected version*
At the present time the law is vague	*At present the law is vague*
European poetry continues to remain the focus	*European poetry remains the focus*
A review is currently underway	*A review is underway*
The lecture theatre was an empty space	*The lecture theatre was empty*
The draft essay is currently being written	
This interpretation offers alternative choices	
The legislation introduced a new precedent	
The visitor will be a famous celebrity	
The village is absolutely full of wealthy millionaires	

As you will see here, eliminating redundancies, particularly in respect of investigating the precise meaning of words, can take some thought. For example, in the case of 'present time' the word 'time' does not refer to any particular time (and certainly not the present), but 'present' is by definition a period of time, but defines the times as being right now. In this case, then, you would keep 'present', as this is more specific, gives the reader more information and already indicates time without pointing it out a second time. In essence, then, you need to think very carefully about the words and choose the one which contains the most meaning, detail and clarity and reduces unnecessary repetition or labouring of the point.

f)   Eliminate needless repetition. Some repetition can reinforce your point (as in recapitulation, see p.126), but elsewhere it can eat into your word count without you gaining any extra marks. It can also make your writing look laboured or clumsy. Take the following as an example:

The poem illustrates a remarkable absence of feeling. For example, in line 2 of the poem there is virtually no feeling, as is illustrated by the <u>bleak</u> description of the colours. The use of colour in the poem is <u>bland</u> and contains <u>no detail</u> to <u>enliven</u> it or <u>imagery</u> to make the poem come <u>alive</u> for the reader (58 words).

There are two problems here:

1)   Needless repetition of the same words owing to a lack of synonyms – this makes the passage stylistically awkward and inelegant (as highlighted in corresponding colours), and

2)   Needless repetition of similar points/words (as is emphasised in corresponding colours and underlined).

By eliminating needless repetition, the passage could be made shorter (thereby increasing room for more words dedicated to generating new points, analysis and marks), and it would sound more confident/emphatic. For example, a better version might look like this:

The poem illustrates a remarkable absence of feeling. For example, in line 2 there is virtually none, owing to the bleak description of colours and the lack of imagery. This fails to make the text come alive for the reader (40 words).

Through careful editing we have saved 18 words here – 18 words which could now be used to compose an additional short analytical, evaluative or argumentative sentence or introduce concession or refutation – any of which would help to increase the mark. This really highlights the extent to which 'tightening' through editing can make a difference to the quality of your work, providing you devote some time to it before submission.

TIPS

An invaluable tool to help you with synonyms is a good thesaurus. This will help you find words that you can deploy to avoid repetition, but it will also help you increase your vocabulary. This will help you to write better, and you'll become more fluent and confident because you'll have a greater range of linguistic tools at your disposal.

Be careful when using pronouns (e.g. 'they', 'their', 'we', 'who', 'which', 'these' and 'this'). They can help you avoid repetition, but make sure it's clear what they refer to (the first of our common errors below).

Common errors

As you can probably see, there are numerous things to look out for when editing and proofreading your work, and different individuals are likely to have different recurring errors needing attention. However, some of the most common mistakes that occur in student writing are as follows, so it's worth keeping a particular eye out for them:

 1) Unclear pronoun references/agreements

Ensure your pronouns refer to their referents (nouns). Words such as 'this' and 'they', 'he' and 'she', for instance, need to link back to their subjects/topics clearly.

For example, how clear is this sentence?

> In the experiment, the presence of particles was not demonstrated, but Jones (1999) and Smith (2000) have argued otherwise. Indeed, he claims that their presence was self-evident, and he provided evidence to prove the matter.

The problems here are the references to 'he'. Does 'he' refer to Jones or Smith? Does the first 'he' refer to Jones and the second to Smith, or do they both refer to Jones? Or Smith? A better, clearer version of the sentence might look like this:

> In the experiment, the presence of particles was not demonstrated, but Jones (1999) and Smith (2000) have argued otherwise. Indeed, Jones claims that their presence was self-evident, and he provided evidence to prove the matter.

Note that the 'he' now clearly refers back to Jones, and there is no room for ambiguity.

TIP

As a final check, try looking for words such as 'he', 'she', 'this' and 'they' in the search facility of your word processor. Then check that what they refer to is clear.

 2) Easily confused words

Ensure that easily confused words are correct – common errors revolve around words such as affect/effect, advice/advise, their/there and practice/practise. For example, can you spot the errors in this sentence?

> Lecturers, it is claimed, enjoy the opportunity to effect student achievement positively, although there actual affect on students' learning and future professional practise is hotly disputed.

The correct version of this sentence should look like this:

> Lecturers, it is claimed, enjoy the opportunity to affect student achievement positively, although their actual effect on students' learning and future professional practice is hotly disputed.

A spell-checker/grammar-checker might not identify these, so you need to pay particular attention to them. Check your dictionary if you are unsure which version of the word to use as they often have subtle differences in meaning.

 3) Apostrophe errors

Apostrophes indicate either possession or contractions. Be careful of words such as 'will not', 'cannot', 'your', 'it is' and 'there' (no contraction) and 'won't', 'can't', 'you're', 'it's' and 'they're' (contractions). Contractions are too casual for academic writing, so make sure you check for them and convert them into their more formal version. With apostrophes indicating possession, ensure that:

- The apostrophe is placed before the 's' when the noun is singular (e.g. Anna's essay, Joe's party, Smith's theory, Jones's matrix).

- The apostrophe is placed after the 's' when the noun is plural (e.g. the conference starts in two weeks' time, the researchers' results, the students' housing).

There are some exceptions to these rules (such as if there are more than one Jones, possession becomes Joneses'), so if you're unsure it's always best to check a good resource such as:

http://www.apostrophe.org.uk/page2.html
http://www.grammarbook.com/punctuation/apostro.asp

4) Misplaced commas/comma splices

Commas indicate relationships between parts and signal the commencement of a new clause, a subordinate clause and the beginning of non-essential information. They are especially handy when making lists or using the rule of three. Without them, you can accidentally end up sounding like a psychopath. Compare the following well-known examples of comma usage:

a)   Some people enjoy cooking, their families, and their dogs.

b)   Some people enjoy cooking their families and their dogs.

In a) we have a relationship between parts and a clear list, whereas in b) no such relationship exists. As such, it sounds as though some people actually cook and eat their families and their pets…!

Comma splices

Comma splices are very common in student writing, and it happens when you try to join two independent clauses with a comma rather than a conjunction or a semi-colon. As we saw in Chapter 6, conjunctions bolt independent clauses together seamlessly and often explain the relationship between the ideas expressed in each clause. Compare these examples:

a)   At the commencement of World War One the British army consisted of 400,000 soldiers, by the end of 1918 it had totalled over 4,000,000.

b)   At the commencement of World War One the British army consisted of 400,000 soldiers, but by the end of 1918 it had totalled over 4,000,000.

Notice how the conjunction 'but' not only welds the two independent clauses together but clearly signposts the relationship between them (it indicates the contrast/increase and its immensity).

Run-on sentences

Run-on sentences occur when you combine two sentences WITHOUT using proper punctuation or a conjunction. For example:

Incorrect:

> Monte Carlo methods are techniques that use large amounts of random sampling to achieve results these have many applications in physics and mathematics.

Correct:

> Monte Carlo methods are techniques that use large amounts of random sampling to achieve results. These have many applications in physics and mathematics.

Or

> Monte Carlo methods are techniques that use large amounts of random sampling to achieve results, and have many applications in physics and mathematics.

 5) Plural/singular mix-ups

Double-check that your words are singular when they need to be and plural when referring to more than one object/issue. It is very easy for spell-checkers, grammar-checkers and auto-predictive functions to use or recommend the incorrect version. For example, despite talking about technology and its recommendations in general (plural rather than singular), my spelling and grammar-checker can identify absolutely nothing wrong with the following version of the previous sentence and my clarifying comment at the end:

Incorrect version: It is very easy for spell-checkers, grammar-checkers and auto-predictive function to use or recommends the incorrect versions, yet obviously, there are more than one function mentioned here.

Correct version: It is very easy for spell-checkers, grammar-checkers and auto-predictive functions to use or recommend the incorrect version, yet obviously, there is more than one function mentioned here.

Even Grammarly only identifies the 'are/is' mistake in this sentence.

 6) Topic (subject) – action (verb) disagreements

This is a problem very much related to the one above and occurs when the verb or action part of the sentence is plural and the topic or subject/noun is singular, OR when the topic/subject/noun is plural, and the action/verb is singular. For example:

The genome mutate very quickly (**singular topic, plural action**)

The genomes mutate very quickly (**plural topic, plural action**)

Deforestation are exceptionally detrimental to air quality (**singular topic, plural action**)

Deforestation is exceptionally detrimental to air quality (**singular topic, singular action**)

 7) Casual, informal or imprecise language

As discussed in the previous chapter, avoid the type of language you'd use in emails, text messages or Facebook/Twitter posts. This includes not only contractions but also:

- **Slang:** (e.g. 'kids' instead of 'children', 'nowadays' instead of 'currently', 'gutted' instead of 'disappointed').

- **Clichés:** (e.g. 'over the moon', 'this day and age', 'a level playing field', 'when all is said and done').

- **Imprecision:** (e.g. 'stuff', 'a bit of', 'really', 'quite'). Imprecision is also closely associated with hedging language, which needs to be used very carefully.

 8) Over-hedging/compound hedging

As we saw earlier, hedging can have useful applications, but run through your text to ensure that you haven't overdone it or used hedging where you can be certain of the facts/arguments. Always see if you can fill in any hedging with certainties in the form of examples, facts, data or references, as hedging can often mask a lack of reading, knowledge or understanding. Be particularly aware of the following common mistakes:

- **Compound hedging:** (using two or more hedging or qualifying words in the same sentence – this will make your sentences sound very unconfident, and it will undermine your argument). For example:

Overly hedged: The reduction in the number of Jellyfish in some UK waters may be due to global warming.

Amended version: The 20% reduction in the number of Jellyfish around Scotland (Jones, 2016), may be due to global warming.

(Note that 'some UK waters' has been replaced by a specific location and the 'reduction' has now been specified. The hedging regarding global warming is retained owing to lack of scientific understanding in this area).

- **Contradictory hedging:** (boosting in one part of the sentence but hedging in another). This will make your writing sound as if you can't make up your mind! For example:

Contradiction: The 20% reduction in the number of Jellyfish around Scotland (Jones, 2016), it would seem, is undoubtedly due to global warming.

Ensure that you are consistent. For example:

- **Amended version 1 (boosting):** It is clear that the 20% reduction in the number of Jellyfish around Scotland (Jones, 2016), is definitely due to global warming.

    OR

    Amended version 2 (hedging): It is suggested that the 20% reduction in the number of Jellyfish around Scotland (Jones, 2016), may be due to global warming.

The above examples are far from being a comprehensive list of possible mistakes in your writing, but they are certainly the most common, and thus you'd be wise to keep an eye out for them. Look at feedback from your markers and previous essays. You may find that you have particular proofreading and editing errors that repeatedly appear, so hone in on those mistakes and practise identifying and correcting them.

Summary

- Don't leave editing and proofreading to the last minute – making time to re-draft, polish and check your work will reap dividends. You will need to proofread and edit several times to iron out all the mistakes.

- While it is true that if you have a dyslexia assessment, markers will be sympathetic towards spelling, grammar, sequencing and punctuation errors, try to present a piece of work which is as polished as possible. Aim high.

- Proofreading and editing your writing are vital skills to learn for when you face the world of work. Employers are unlikely to be as sympathetic as university lecturers towards your dyslexia, despite their legal requirement to make 'reasonable adjustments'.

- DON'T rely upon your spell-checker/grammar-checker/auto-predict function – they can sometimes help, but sometimes get you into real trouble. Always use a 'human eye' for checking your work.

- Ensure your spell-checker/grammar-checker is set to the appropriate language/country! In the UK, for example, lots of students find themselves making basic spelling errors simply because the default setting of their spell-checker is US English, not UK English, thus resulting in mistakes such as 'color' instead of 'colour' and 'behavior' instead of 'behaviour'.

- Always check the essay's overall structure (effective introduction, strong thesis statement and topic sentences, evidence is relevant and embedded effectively, and analysis and argumentation is incorporated which answers the question/assignment task).

Bibliography

BBC, (2016) *Today*. Monday, 12th December. Available at: http://www.bbc.co.uk/programmes/b084thdy (Accessed: 12th December 2016).

Bell, Susan, (2007) *The Artful Edit: On the Practice of Editing Yourself*. London: W.W. Norton & Company.

Bookerrata, (2017) *Under the Volcano by Malcolm Lowry*. Available at: http://www.bookerrata.com/books/undervolcano.html (Accessed: 30th March, 2017).

Davis, Matt, (2012) 'Aoccdrnig to a rscheearch at Cmabrigde Uinervtisy, it deosn't mttaer in waht oredr the ltteers in a wrod are, the olny iprmoetnt tihng is taht the frist and lsat ltteer be at the rghit pclae. The rset can be a toatl mses and you can sitll raed it wouthit porbelm. Tihs is bcuseae the huamn mnid deos not raed ervey lteter by istlef, but the wrod as a wlohe'. Available at: https://www.mrc-cbu.cam.ac.uk/people/matt.davis/cmabridge/ (Accessed: 22nd October, 2021).

Lanham, Richard A., (2006) *Revising Prose*. 5th edn. London: Pearson.

Lyon, Elizabeth, (2002) *Nonfiction Book Proposals Anybody Can Write*. New York: The Berkeley Publishing Group.

Pinker, Steven, (2015) *The Sense of Style: The Thinking Person's Guide to Writing in the 21st Century*. London: Penguin Books.

Rayner, Keith, White, Sarah J., Johnson, Rebecca L., and Liversedge, Simon P., (2006) 'Raeding Wrods With Jubmled Lettres There Is a Cost', *Psychological Science*, 17(3), pp.192–193.

Rectenwald, Michael, and Carl, Lisa, (2016) *Academic Writing, Real World Topics*. Peterborough, ON: Broadview Press.

Twainquotes, (2017) 'Letter to Sir Walter Bessant, 22nd February, 1898'. *Directory of Mark Twain's Maxims, Quotations, and Various Opinions*. Available at: http://www.twainquotes.com/Proofreaders.html (Accessed: 30th March, 2017).

Vappingo, (2017) *10 of the Biggest Proofreading Screwups of all Time*. Available at: https://www.vappingo.com/word-blog/10-of-the-biggest-proofreading-screwups-of-all-time/ (Accessed: 30th March, 2017).

Zinsser, William, (2006) *On Writing Well. The Classic Guide to Writing Nonfiction*. 7th edn. New York: HarperCollins Publishers.

Quick Reference Guide

Reading skills and finding evidence

Name	Icon	Page number
Evaluation:		pp.10, 98, 114, 115, 122
Evidence:		pp.13, 98, 105, 106, 108, 114, 115, 122
Data and statistics:		pp.13, 105, 107
Formulae:	$E = MC^2$	p.13
Skimming:		pp.21–34
Scanning:		pp.34–37
Reading for the 'gist':		pp.36–37

Dual reading:		p.38
Dual assistive reading:		p.38
Detailed reading:		pp.39, 40

Critical thinking skills

Name	*Icon*	*Page number*
Analysis:		pp.98, 114, 115, 122
What's the problem?		pp.46–48
What's the motive?		pp.48–49
What's the context?		pp.49–50

Are there problems with the methodology?		pp.50–53
How good's the evidence?		pp.53–55
Are there rival causes?		pp.55–57
Is there ambiguity?		pp.57–58
Are there any assumptions?		p.58
Are there appeals to popular opinion, beliefs or emotion?		p.58
Are there false causes or dilemmas?		p.59

Is the author biased?		pp.59–60
Are the conclusions valid?		pp.60–61

Writing skills

Name	Icon/template	Page number
Introductions:		pp.75–79, 89, 95
Main body of essay:		pp.75, 79–86, 89, 91–93, 95
Conclusions:		pp.75, 86–89, 95
Topic sentences:		pp.98, 99–101, 114, 115, 120–121, 122, 136
Main body of paragraph:		pp.98, 114, 115, 120–121
Paragraph links:		pp.98, 121–122

Parachuting:		pp. 105–106, 152
Quotation:		pp.13, 102, 105, 106, 108, 109, 114
Summarising:		pp.14, 102, 104, 105, 108–109, 115
Paraphrasing:		pp.14, 103–104, 105
Communicative dynamism:	Sentence Given New	pp.114, 115, 116, 129–131

Signallers and discourse markers

Sequences, enumeration and time:		p.125
Relation:		pp.125, 142
Recapitulation/reformulation:		p.126

Examples:		p.126
Reporting:		p.127
Advance labelling:		p.127
Boosting:		pp.128, 142
Hedges and qualifiers:		p.128

Sentences

Descriptive, narrative and explanatory:		p.131
Reporting:		pp.132, 136
Even-handed evaluation:		p.132
Preferential evaluation/the art of concession:		pp.133, 136
Refutation:		p.133

Rule of three at the beginning:		p.134
Rule of three in the middle:		p.134
Rule of three at the end:		p.134
Argumentative/analytical:		pp.135, 136–137
Topic:		pp.138–144, 147–149, 151, 154, 162
Action:	Active	pp.138–144, 147–149, 151, 154, 162
	Passive	pp.147, 151, 162
Detail:		pp.138–144, 147–149, 151, 154, 162
Subordinate clause:		pp.141–142, 147–149, 151, 154

Overcoming writer's block

Name	*Icon/template*	*Page number*
Semi-productive breaks:		p.72

Draw pictures:		p.72
Eliminate distractions:		p.72
Breaks:		p.72
Free writing:		p.72
Talking:		p.73
Building blocks:		p.73
Three-tier model of intensity:		p.73

Editing and proofreading

Name	*Icon/template*	*Page number*
Distance yourself/take a break:		p.170

Break task into manageable chunks:		p.171
Look for and check the action:		p.171
Focus on punctuation:		p.171
Read slowly:		p.171
Change the look:		p.171–173
Change the sound:		p.173
Dual editing/proofreading:		p.173
Cut the waste:		pp.173–176

Index

For Product Safety Concerns and Information please contact our EU
representative GPSR@taylorandfrancis.com
Taylor & Francis Verlag GmbH, Kaufingerstraße 24, 80331 München, Germany

www.ingramcontent.com/pod-product-compliance
Ingram Content Group UK Ltd.
Pitfield, Milton Keynes, MK11 3LW, UK
UKHW050831080625
459435UK00009B/72